HARD-HATTED WOMEN

STORIES OF STRUGGLE AND SUCCESS IN THE TRADES

EDITED BY MOLLY MARTIN

Photographs by Sandy Thacker

THE SEAL PRESS

Copyright © 1988 by Molly Martin.

All rights reserved. No part of this book may be reproduced in any form without prior permission from the publisher, except for the quotation of brief passages in reviews.

The following stories were originally published, in slightly different form, in the magazine *Tradeswomen:* Beth Szillagyi, Mary Ruggiero, Rose Melendez, Fran Krauss, Naomi Friedman, and Gigi Marino. Vicki Smith's story first appeared in *Lesbian Contradiction*. We gratefully acknowledge the editors of these magazines for permission to use the works.

Library of Congress Cataloging-in-Publication Data
Hard-hatted women : stories of struggle and success in the trades / edited by Molly Martin. -- 1st ed.
    p. cm.
  Bibliography: p.
  ISBN 0-931188-66-0 : $10.95
    1. Women--Employment--United States--Biography.
  2. Working class women--United States--Biography.   3. Women--United States--Biography.   I. Martin, Molly.
HD6095.H34 1988
331.4'0973--dc19
[B]   88-23850
                                                      CIP

All photographs copyright © 1988 by Sandy Thacker, with the exception of the photo of Molly Martin on page 265, which was taken by Janet Delaney.

Cover photo by Sandy Thacker.
Cover design by Clare Conrad.

Printed in the United States of America.
10 9 8 7 6 5 4 3 2

Seal Press
P.O. Box 13
Seattle, Washington 98111

Acknowledgments

Thanks to all the women who helped to make this book, who answered questions, read parts of the manuscript, and provided support. I'd especially like to thank:

Barbara Wilson of Seal Press for suggesting this project, and then helping me to believe I could pull it off.

Faith Conlon, my editor at Seal Press, who has been a joy to work with and has confirmed the importance of the editor's role in the publishing process.

Pat Cull, whose skill as a typist as well as a carpenter is highly valued in the tradeswomen community, for help with manuscripts, and for her inspiration as a pioneer.

Ronnie Sandler for help with historical research.

Rita Mandoli for her editorial comments on the manuscript.

Madeline Mixer, a long-term advocate for women in trades, for providing U.S. Department of Labor statistics.

CONTENTS

Introduction by Molly Martin	3
Beth Szillagyi: SHEET METAL WORKER	17
Mary Ruggiero: WELDER	33
Jessica Hopkins: STATIONARY ENGINEER	37
Pat Cull: CARPENTER	45
Trudy Pax Farr: STEELWORKER	55
Fai Coffin: DRYWALL ROCKER AND TAPER	63
Rose Melendez: POLICE OFFICER	71
Mari Lochhaas: FISHER	81
Gloria Nelson: OPERATING ENGINEER	88
Fran Krauss: IRONWORKER	102
Polly Jerome: RURAL BUILDER	109
Johnnie James: MINER	118
Nina Saltman: CARPENTER FOREMAN	122
Vicki Smith: SPRINKLER FITTER	143
Lucy Lim: UTILITY SWITCH OPERATOR	150
Terese M. Floren: FIREFIGHTER	156
Naomi Friedman: PLUMBING CONTRACTOR	171
Gigi Marino: MERCHANT SAILOR	176
Juanita Sanchez: MACHINIST	187
Marian Swerdlow: SUBWAY CONDUCTOR	193
Laura Deane Mason: RURAL CONTRACTOR	202
Cassandra Miller: ELECTRONICS INSPECTOR	212
Susan Eisenberg: ELECTRICIAN	216
Judith Foster: TRUCKER	225
Mary Baird: PHONE REPAIR TECHNICIAN	235
Sue Doro: MACHINIST	254
Notes on the Interviewers	263
Resources	264
About the Editor	265

This book is dedicated to all the pioneer women who pave the way for us in non-traditional work. Their struggles become our success stories.

Introduction

I know how to type because in high school my mother fervently insisted that I take typing and shorthand, the skills that insured her own independence as a working woman. After some resistance, I complied. Even then, in the sixties, few other career options existed for women. I can't fault my mother's vision. She knew the importance of possessing marketable skills. How was she to know I'd end up an electrician?

Twenty years ago I wondered why my male friends could work their way through college as construction laborers when I was relegated to lower paid "women's work." With the help of student loans, I managed to graduate from college with a degree in journalism only to leap naively into a job market bloated with other baby boomers. When I hit the big city of Seattle in 1974, Woodward and Bernstein had just exposed Watergate and newspaper reporter jobs had achieved sudden popularity. I never got past personnel at the two Seattle dailies, watching helplessly as a clerk shoved my application to the bottom of a huge stack.

More than a career, I needed a steady job. Printing had always interested me, so I looked into that apprenticeship program, but was discouraged because of my college degree. I should practice journalism, they said, and leave the printing to the less educated. Desperate for any paycheck, I even applied to do phone soliciting part-time for the classified section, thinking that perhaps I could work my way up in the newspaper business. I was overqualified, they assured me, and I would surely quit to take a better job.

I found part-time clerical work, though the agency explained it had to exclude me from fifty percent of the jobs unless I promised to wear dresses (I refused). I was a dynamite file clerk at a dollar-eighty an hour, but all it got me was more work, never a raise in pay. I worked at a variety of short-term, low-paid jobs, and continued to apply for every white-collar job I thought I could do. I even considered topless dancing when the rent came due. Finally I was hired as a parking lot attendant at two fifty-five an hour. The company hadn't wanted to hire me because the job had always been done by a man—the boss confessed later he didn't think a woman could handle it.

Discouraged after two years of job hunting, I joined a newly formed organization, Seattle Women In Trades, hoping to find work in the construction industry. I quit the car parking job and managed (by virtue of my low income) to qualify for a six-month electrical maintenance training program at Seattle Opportunities Industrialization Center, although I had to fight being channeled into the secretarial program. ("But you've already studied typing and shorthand. You'd be wasting good skills.") When I finished the program, I sought to enter the union apprenticeship program, only to learn that I didn't meet the qualifications. The age limit at that time was twenty-five. I had just turned twenty-six.

Determined by this time to work as an electrician, I joined a male friend in San Francisco who had decided to change careers. We started a contracting business remodeling the electrical systems in homes and small commercial buildings. A year later, I joined an all-female collective, Wonder Woman Electric, where I worked for three years. During those years as a contractor, I became intimate with countless crawl spaces and attics, drilled and fished wire through unnumbered walls, and sweated on extension ladders changing live services. I must admit there were times when I'd find myself in places disgusting or frightening enough to make me wish for a career as an office worker. But the days when the job was finished, when we stood back to admire our pipe work, when we flipped the switches and everything worked—those days made all the frustration and dirt worth it.

Then in 1980, I got a chance to join the Brotherhood. Construction in San Francisco's downtown was booming, and even with travelers (workers from other union locals), IBEW Local 6's hiring hall was nearly empty. In order to keep contractors supplied with skilled workers, the union began accepting electricians who had learned their skills outside the apprenticeship program. For two years I worked as an "inside wireman" dispatched through the hiring hall to construction jobs on commercial downtown highrises. In 1982 I was laid off and, because of a downturn in construction and my low seniority, never called by the union again.

During that period of unemployment, in the course of doing some tradeswomen organizing, I met the equal opportunity specialist whose job was to recruit women for trades jobs in the City of San Francisco. She urged me to fill out an application, and I was hired as a maintenance electrician for the San Francisco Water Department, a job that's afforded me the opportunity to learn about a whole new dimension of a complex and highly technical trade. For the past six years I have maintained all the electrical equipment at the department's pump stations, reservoirs, and corporation yard, from one-thousand horsepower motors and accompanying switchgear down to electronic controls. My mother would be proud (though perhaps a bit jealous) that I take home more than twice the pay she might be making as a skilled secretary.

My story and the stories of the women in this book reflect the most recent wave of activism in a long struggle by American women for equality in employment. Women have labored in skilled crafts alongside men since pre-revolutionary times when they worked as sawyers, loggers, grist mill operators, carpenters and printers. The first signed copies of the Declaration of Independence were printed by a woman, Mary Goddard. The circular saw was invented by a Shaker woman in a community near Boston. Its invention revolutionized the building industry because until then lumber had been sawed and hewn by hand.

The exclusion of women workers from the skilled crafts also has a long history. Women were allowed to learn skills when industry needed labor, but were viewed as a threat to male workers when the economy contracted. Instead of helping women to gain skills, unions (with a few notable exceptions) historically acted to exclude women as well as ethnic minorities from particular crafts. Women made up a large percentage of printers until the early 1800s when the trade was unionized, and female typesetters also were driven out of their craft when a union was organized for the benefit of men.

In the early part of the twentieth century, most of the unions in the American Federation of Labor disallowed women members. One international leader voiced their position: "Keep women out of the trade, and if not, out of the union." When, after World War I, women were expected to quietly relinquish jobs they had acquired when men entered the armed forces, they organized to protest layoffs. Among them were female streetcar conductors, who fought to protect their jobs in several U.S. cities, but eventually were forced out of the transportation industry. Jobs in industrial crafts were opened to women during World War II only to be closed when the war ended, and women were again effectively excluded from the trades until the early 1970s.

Title VII of the 1964 Civil Rights Act made race and sex discrimination by employers and labor unions illegal, but not because of Congress's sympathy for the plight of women workers. Sex discrimination had been added by segregationist Southern Congressmen only as a strategy to keep the bill from passing. Society still didn't view women as equal participants in the workforce, but at least the law was on our side, and the concept of affirmative action began to gain popularity.

In the sixties, black and Hispanic men started to use the

laws to sue construction trade unions, contractors, and police and fire departments for discrimination. By the early seventies, women also began to demand access to blue-collar jobs. We formed organizations to pressure lawmakers to include women in civil rights legislation and to enforce affirmative action laws. We sat in at contractors' offices and stood in line at union halls. We picketed, petitioned and wrote letters, and we pounded the pavement looking for construction jobs.

Women's struggle to enter skilled trades also was helped by two federal regulations which took effect in 1978. First, Executive Order 11246 amended the 1964 Civil Rights Act, setting up specific goals and timetables for women in the construction industry, and requiring employers to commit themselves to affirmative action programs to assure equal opportunity. It also made the contractor responsible for a harassment-free workplace, and for combating isolation of female employees. Second, U.S. Department of Labor apprenticeship regulations set numerical goals for women apprentices based on participation of women in the local labor market, and specified recruitment techniques.

Today, in 1988, the barriers have not been completely broken, but women at least have a foot in the door. Despite our gains, however, occupational segregation still is firmly entrenched. The federal goal for women construction workers has not been met or increased since it was set at 6.9 percent in 1981. Only about 1.1 percent of construction workers in the U.S. are women. Women represent only about eight percent of all precision production, craft and repair workers. No contractor has ever been debarred, lost a contract, or lost money because of failure to hire women. Federal law only asks them to make a "good faith effort" to meet affirmative action goals.

The apprenticeship regulations require that women make up about twenty percent of each class of new apprentices, but statistics show that women constitute only three to four percent of apprentices nationwide, although our dropout rate is no worse than that of male apprentices. Our organizing efforts continue to focus on union apprenticeship programs because they offer the best training and most secure future in the skilled crafts.

Apprenticeship programs are based on the medieval guild system in which an apprentice was indentured to a master craftsman for a specified number of years. The journeyman was then free to travel around and practice his craft. In the U.S., apprenticeship programs are administered by the federal government and the states through Joint Apprenticeship Committees which represent employers and unions. They include a combination of on-the-job training and classroom instruction. Typically, the programs are four years long, at which time the apprentice "turns out" as a journeyman.

As more and more women join the workforce and become single heads of households, access to training in the skilled trades becomes increasingly important. Trades jobs pay decent wages, typically two or three times what a woman can expect to earn in a traditional female job. Only a high school diploma or GED is required, and apprentices are well-paid during the training period. Also, current economic indicators show an increased need for skilled trades workers over the next two decades.

Women continue to constitute large proportions of workers in traditionally female occupations—eighty percent of all administrative support workers, sixty-nine percent of all retail and personal services sales workers. For many years, the wage of the average woman worker has hovered somewhere around sixty percent of that of the average man. But women have continued to grow poorer. In the last decade the number of families headed by women has risen dramatically. This trend, combined with occupational segregation and low wages, is resulting in a disproportionately high number of women and children in poverty.

The campaign against these economic injustices must be waged on a number of fronts, from local grassroots community organizing to federal class action litigation. Throughout my career as an electrician, I've participated in grassroots organizations that work to open up the skilled crafts to more women and to provide support for tradeswomen who are typically isolated and harassed on the job. Many of us who work in the trades also actively organize outside the job in such groups because we're tired of the isolation we endure in male-dominated occupations. We know that our working lives get easier in direct proportion to the number of women on the job, and that those numbers won't increase without our organizing efforts. One of our worst fears is that young women will not be allowed or encouraged to enter the trades, and those of us who remain will just move along as a little lump on the demographic chart until the end of our working careers.

Over the past decade, support and networking groups have sprung up all around the country. In 1979, Tradeswomen, Inc., a national membership organization, was founded. In 1981, a few volunteers started a quarterly magazine, *Tradeswomen*, to inform women about non-traditional careers and to counter the alienation we experience on the job. Since then, we've collected and published dozens of essays by women in blue-collar work.

When I began talking to the editors of Seal Press about publishing this book, our initial idea was to anthologize first-person narratives that had appeared in *Tradeswomen*, but they mostly featured San Francisco Bay Area residents, and we wanted a more representative cross-section. With a limited amount of time, I put out a call for submissions to the national Tradeswomen, Inc. membership and to feminist bookstores across the country. I asked tradeswomen I'd known and worked with over the years to do outreach in their particular geographical areas. I also called women whose writing had appeared in the magazine and asked them to write their own stories. A few of the narratives in this book are based on interviews, but most were written by the women themselves.

The most gratifying part of editing this book has been talking to tradeswomen all over the country, many of whose stories do not appear in this book simply because of lack of space. I hope the readers of these narratives are as inspired as I was talking to the authors, who widened my own vision and sense of the tradeswomen community. Many I know only by voice. I loved picking up the phone and reaching Lisa Parnell's Alabama drawl, which she thickened for my benefit. Lisa is a miner, and finding a good time to call her was not easy. She often works sixty-hour weeks, and even on Sunday mornings I'd interrupt her sleep after she'd worked the night shift on overtime. I had conversations with women whose children I heard calling for attention in the background, who had to drive two hours to a job the next day, who were working overtime, who didn't own a typewriter, and who still promised to meet my deadline. I wondered how they did it all.

Deciding which stories to include in the book was not an easy task. From the stories I received, I tried to feature some of the more common apprenticeable trades that employ women—carpenter, electrician, plumber, stationary engineer, machinist, operating engineer, sheet metal worker, welder, sprinkler fitter, ironworker. As it turned out, not all the women here wear hard hats. I decided to include a wide range of occupations, partly for diversity, but also to emphasize the affinity we share as workers in blue-collar, non-traditional jobs.

I wasn't surprised to see a few common themes emerge as I read the stories. Whenever tradeswomen gather together for meetings, conferences or potlucks, one topic of conversation is certain to be sexual harassment: the unwelcome touching and requests for sexual favors that almost all of us have experienced sometime during our careers. But we also face another pervasive and sinister kind of harassment which is gender-based, but may have nothing to do with sex. It is harassment aimed at us simply because we are women in a "man's" job, and its function is to discourage us from staying in our trades. Many of the contributors to this anthology give examples. Rose Melendez tells of a fellow police officer pointing a gun at her head and asking her to show him how fast women can run. Mary Ruggiero and Sue Doro were threatened with safety hazards when their work was sabotaged by male co-workers.

To combat harassment, each of us develops her own particular survival skills. Jessica Hopkins believes in actively "womanizing" the workplace by refusing to play by men's rules and develop a thick skin. Sometimes humor works best. When Marian Swerdlow began work as a subway conductor, she says she was propositioned so consistently that she finally joked about giving a civil service exam for the position, with a filing fee and a physical. Often, direct confrontation is necessary: Fai Coffin stepped on her harasser's hand. Beth Szillagyi made her limits clear when she got mad and yelled back.

Many women have quit the trades rather than endure such harassment. But those of us who have survived tend to remember our positive work experiences and downplay the negative; denial is one of our survival mechanisms. All of the women in the book use their real names, and most are still working at the jobs they describe, which may contribute to selective memory. And, in spite of harassment, we do experience genuine comradeship with some of our male co-workers.

The women represented here are survivors, which testifies to their great strength and endurance, but also to their love for their work. They explain the many benefits of work in the trades—the sense of satisfaction when a technical skill is mastered, the pleasure of seeing a real product at the end of their labor. One thing Nina Saltman loves about construction work is that she can take long vacations between jobs without damaging her career or seniority. Most jobs are union, a protection only about twenty percent of the American workforce enjoys. Wages are set by union contract, not the employer's whim, so women earn the same pay and benefits as men. When women are accepted into unions, we tend to make loyal members. One contributor is president of her union local and several others are active trade unionists.

The trials of learning a non-traditional craft are recounted by many of the authors in this anthology. Overcoming our childhood socialization to aspire to anything *but* a "man's" job, learning to use tools we had never seen, becoming competent in an alien and hostile world, gaining self-esteem with each new skill are some of the themes explored here.

Not all of us learned our trades through formal apprenticeship programs. Craft unions have been as reluctant as employers to accept women into their ranks. When Naomi Friedman was not accepted by the plumbers union, she persevered until she found a sympathetic contractor to train her while she worked for free. Judith Foster joined a women's trucking collective where skills were patiently and supportively shared.

In my outreach, I tried to include rural as well as urban women. Polly Jerome's experience is testimony to the need and ability of rural women to develop a multitude of skills. Laura Deane Mason, a rural contractor, details the difficulties of trying to make a decent living in an area where everybody is a seat-of-the-pants carpenter.

Our work can be as physically challenging as a strenuous sport. In her story, Mari Lochhaas takes us through an exhausting day of commercial fishing in which she barely has time to eat. Construction work, in particular, is hard labor, pushing one's physical as well as emotional strengths to their limits. In fact, tradeswomen draw on the same resources that competitive athletes do. Two of the contributors to this book have built their physical strength into a successful avocation. Fran Krauss and Terry Floren both are national powerlifting champions.

These occupations are also some of the most dangerous, and several women recount stories of on-the-job accidents and hazards. A number of Trudy Pax Farr's co-workers died while she worked at the steel mill, but it wasn't until someone was killed while doing her particular job that the danger really hit home. Female tradesworkers are often more conscious about workplace safety than their male counterparts, and generally are more aware of their own physical limitations, using brains and leverage instead of brawn to do the job.

Being both a mother and a hard-hatted worker sounds like a contradiction in terms. Yet more and more women are doing both and inventing novel ways of caring for children. Apprehensive about her co-workers' reactions, Susan Eisenberg concealed her first pregnancy for six months while working construction. Gloria Nelson, determined to continue nursing her baby, tells of surprising her co-workers by pumping her breasts during breaks on the site. She and her husband share parenting responsibilities, each working outside the home for six months, then doing childcare the other six.

Some women's families were surprised at their daughter's choice of career. Lucy Lim's parents, who had always emphasized the importance of education, could not understand her decision to leave a retail job to become a miner. Families could also be supportive, and even inspirational. Gigi Marino's fascination with her father's life as a seaman propelled her into the same career. Jessica Hopkins only realized exactly what her father did for a living when she found herself practicing his trade of stationary engineer.

Several women mention aging as a growing concern of both women and men in trades. Mary Baird and her fellow telephone installers worry about their ability to climb poles as they get older. Pat Cull didn't start the carpenters apprenticeship in construction until she was thirty-two. Now forty-six, she hopes as a maintenance carpenter to be the first woman to retire in her trade. Fai Coffin, who was forty when she decided to change careers, encourages middle-aged women to follow in her footsteps.

Racism is ever present in the American workplace, but we encounter a particularly virulent form in trades which are still considered to be the domain of white men. Any worker is subject to hazing, and women of color often can't tell whether they are objects of harassment because of race, gender, or status as apprentices. None of us are immune to racism. The invitation to participate in ethnic humor and put-downs is often how white women are welcomed into the club. Johnnie James, a black miner in Alabama, was surprised by the open hostility she encountered. Lucy Lim talks about how racial stereotypes affect women seeking non-traditional jobs. Still, many women credit affirmative action goals as a positive force in their search for work. Cassandra Miller was given a chance to enter her trade partly because she is black.

Several of the women in this book recount the experience of being mistaken for a man in their work clothes. When we perform our jobs with confidence and strength, we contradict the myth of feminine weakness. Our competence by itself can threaten men whose egos are tied up with their image of doing a macho job, and they sometimes take refuge in the belief that we are all lesbians. As with racism, all of us—straight and gay—encounter homophobia. Lesbian-baiting is one form of harassment often used to divide women on the job. In fact, some of us *are* lesbians, and many struggle with the question of whether to come out of the closet to our co-workers. Pat Cull claims her decision to be out as a lesbian on the job has given her power, and actually waylaid comments from male co-workers. Vicki Smith thinks she may never overcome the alienation she feels as a lesbian and never-married mother.

Economic and cultural factors have a strong influence over our ability as women to earn decent wages, as Mary Ruggiero's story illustrates. She offers a unique perspective as a woman who worked both during World War II and in the second wave of non-traditional hiring. Laid off after the war, she was allowed to return twenty years later when her skill as a welder was again in demand during the Vietnam war.

Many of us have chosen our trades out of economic necessity. Sue Doro wasn't thinking of feminism when she trained to be a machinist. She was desperate for income to support her five children after she was left by her husband with no child support. In a local economy based on weapons research and manufacture, Juanita Sanchez talks about making peace with her decision to gain a skilled trade in that industry.

The narratives in this book describe a world which is not often written about, a world where each woman's personal struggle translates into political change. These stories are both universal and unique, ordinary and revolutionary. While the feminist movement has advocated for women's economic empowerment, it has concentrated almost exclusively on promoting women into white-collar and management positions. Far too little attention has been given to the efforts of those women who are breaking into blue-collar trades—efforts which must succeed if we are to achieve real economic choice for *all* women.

Hard-Hatted Women is an attempt to give voice to these pioneering tradeswomen—who are paving the way for future generations of girls and women to aspire to "non-traditional" work.

Molly Martin
August 1988

Beth Szillagyi • Sheet Metal Worker

One of my Sunday morning rituals used to be making some coffee and poring over the classified section of the newspaper. I'd comb through every job listed therein, no matter how small the ad. Why? Plain and simple: I was fed up. I was angry. Fed up with working for starvation wages at a bank while they expected you to wear nice clothes (dresses and skirts only; no culottes, slacks or pantsuits allowed); angry at being treated like a "dumb secretary" by several of "God's gifts"; fed up with always having too much month left at the end of my money; fed up with trying to decide if I should buy some decent groceries or put gas in the truck. Not only was I fed up and angry, but stubborn too. So week after week I was faithful to the classifieds.

One Sunday in June my stubbornness paid off. It was already muggy, I burned the toast and spilled sugar, and the only milk we had was green. I stubbed my toe on the way out to the front porch and spilled my coffee. But I didn't give up. I limped to a lawn chair and began perusing the ads. And there it was, under "Trades, Industrial":

"The Sheet Metal Workers Local 84 Apprenticeship Committee is now taking applications for its annual test. Women and minorities welcome."

Something clicked in my head—I knew that was my job. So what if I had no idea what sheet metal workers did? So what if it was all men? All they could do to me was laugh. But as it turned out, they didn't have a chance.

I took note of the date and time for applications and decided to call in sick at my job Monday. The next day I drove by the union office several times trying to hang on to my disappearing courage. What was I, anyway, a woman or a mouse? When I finally entered the building, there was this tough-looking guy sitting behind the desk smoking a stinky cigar. He looked up and tried not to do a double-take; it was my guess not too many female types had walked through the door.

"I suppose you're here for an application?" he asked resignedly.

"Yes, sir, I am." He handed it over and I proceeded to fill out the strangest application I'd ever seen:

"Have you had any shop classes in high school?" (Hah, are you kidding? The only shop I had was in Home Ec—"Shopping for a Family.")

"Have you been to a vocational school?" (I don't even know where it is.)

"Do you consider yourself to be mechanically inclined?" (Well, considering I helped Mom rewire the vacuum cleaner plug, yes. No need to mention that we blew all the fuses in the house in the process...)

"Are you afraid of heights?" (I've been skydiving—is 3,000 feet high?)

By the time I'd finished writing, I was more than a little depressed. I didn't have a snowball's chance in hell with no shop classes or anything. I handed the business agent the paper and he informed me in a gravelly voice that I'd receive a postcard in ten days about where to take the test. I would need identification and my high school diploma.

The next ten days were a roller coaster. At times I felt very positive about my chances, and then I'd berate myself for even going to the union office in the first place. But sure enough, ten days later, a postcard arrived which began with "Dear Sir and Brother." Ignoring that temporarily, I read on and found that the testing would take place at my old alma mater August 6.

That was more than a month away and I knew I'd never last at the bank, so I quit and faked selling insurance for awhile. I hated lying to my new boss because he seemed like a nice guy, but I was a desperado by then, only without the spurs. So he assumed he had a lifelong agent, and I prayed daily and desperately about that test.

The big day finally arrived, and I was amazed to find two hundred men staring at four women. Immediately we women gathered together and were soon talking like we'd known each other for years. When I scanned the competition I saw several men I'd gone to school with. I bet they never thought they'd see me again. In high school I was in Future Secretaries and getting ready to get married.

Once in the classroom, I was immediately at ease. My "little voice" said everything was going to be all right, and the man distributing test booklets said this was a new test that wasn't gender specific. I took heart and dug in, and it was the easiest test I've taken in my life. It consisted of three parts: basic math, basic mechanics and spatial relations. The hardest part was the spatial relations. A typical question was a picture of a cube unfolded with dots on two sides. The answers were what this cube looked like folded up. That part was tough, but I looked around and saw everyone else screwing up their faces trying to imagine folded-up cubes, so I didn't feel so bad. The basic math was very easy: addition, subtraction, multiplication and division of whole numbers and fractions. There were also a few percentage questions. The mechanics part was not difficult either; all it took was a little common sense.

At the end of the session, the man got up and said it would take three weeks for the computer to grade the tests. I sang at the top of my lungs on the way home, not letting any doubt at all enter my good mood. However, three weeks went by with no word. I was going nuts, and when I couldn't stand it any more, I wrote the business agent a note. As it turned out, the computer had broken down, delaying test results for another week.

A few days later I got a bad case of cramps from being so

nervous. I was at my mom's when it happened, so I just stayed there overnight. The next day I woke up to the phone ringing. It was my roommate.

"Call the union office," she said.

"Oh, you're kidding?"

"No, I'm not kidding, dumbhead. This guy called and said he'd been calling all day."

I had to sit there awhile to calm my poor heart. Could it be? What if the call was just to say "Sorry, but..."? With heart in throat, I shakily dialed the office. Cigar answered the phone.

"Where in hell were you yesterday?" he demanded. "I tried calling this number you gave me all damn day." I made the snap decision not to tell Cigar I had cramps, so I said I was at work.

"Well, you got yourself a job, kid, so get your buns down here before noon and fill out some forms." He hung up without a good-bye. I sat there stupified. And bawling. My mind refused to grasp the conversation.

I went straight to the union office (the cramps were gone). Cigar was tight-lipped at first:

"I don't think women should work here," he stated bluntly.

"Why not?" The bottoms of my feet had begun to itch. I shuffled them on the floor to no avail.

"Well, we do heavy work," he said, puffing the omnipresent stogey.

"I lift weights." (shuffle, shuffle)

"We work up high." (puff, puff)

"I've been skydiving." (shuffle, shuffle)

"The men are crude." (puff, puff)

"I've been in the Army." (shuffle, shuffle)

"They swear every other word." (puff, puff)

"So do I." (shuffle, shuffle) "Dammit."

Cigar scratched his brow, clearly perplexed. He forgot to puff smoke.

"At least give me the chance," I said. "Everyone should get that, shouldn't they? But that's my Equal Opportunity Speech

Number 3063, which takes sixteen minutes and thirty-two seconds."

Cigar almost cracked a smile then; he had a hard time trying not to. He hid his quivering lips behind the stinky cigar and handed me a list of tools and his card. "If any of those turkeys give you any shit, you let me know."

"Thanks," I said, starting to get up.

"Oh, and by the way, you did very well on the test." He riffled through papers on the desk and pulled out a computer printout. "Third," he said, pointing to my name. "Ninety-seven percent. That's a score to be proud of, young lady."

I tried not to look flabbergasted on the way out and almost tripped over the threshold.

That was 1979. Time flies when you're having fun, and I've had fun. Plus an education and a half. I learned that sheet metal workers work with the movement and circulation of air in buildings (heating, air conditioning, ventilating and exhaust) and any equipment relating to that. I've worked on everything from air handling units that push tons of air and will literally knock you off your feet, down to the smallest bathroom exhaust fan. On the outside of a building we work with ways and means of keeping water from getting into the building (gutters, downspouts, caps, flashing, valleys, siding) and architectural sheet metal, which is sometimes rather ornate (copper-clad roofs, steeples, etc.). We need to be familiar with all kinds of tools and materials as well as what goes on in the other building trades.

I also learned about people (men, in particular), and their reactions to uppity women such as myself. For instance, I heard that my shop organized a cleaning and painting expedition before I arrived to clean up the place and paint over the graffiti on the bathroom walls. I had fun imagining a bunch of men, mops and brushes in hand, waiting for me to inspect. I'm not bothered by graffiti, but I got a good laugh out of it anyway.

The first day I was in the shop, so was everyone else, regardless of where they were working. They all tried to look like they were ordering supplies.

"We thought you'd be a fat-assed bull dyke," one roofer told me bluntly (roofers are not known for beating around the proverbial bush). Everyone also thought I'd be afraid of the roofers—they are an earthy bunch who tend to get loud and rowdy, but no more loud or rowdy than Friday night bowling with "the girls." We got along rather well; they somehow sensed I meant business.

Once, another apprentice and I were moving a large piece of duct to the back room. Harold came running back, saying, "Beth, you don't have to lift that!"

"Harold, just tell us where you want this, please, because I'm scientifically balanced and don't want to put it down." When we were finished, I asked Harold if I could talk to him.

"Feel this," I said, flexing my right arm. He was unsure what to do.

"Really, Harold, come on. I don't bite hard." Harold gingerly took my upper arm between his fingers.

"Squeeze," I said, grinning. He did, half-heartedly. "Come on, Harold, squeeze it!" He finally put a little elbow grease behind it and a look of shock dawned on his face.

"That's pretty good," he said.

"See, it didn't fall off, either," I laughed. "Thank you for your concern, but I know if something is too heavy." After that Harold would squeeze my arm a few times a week to "make sure it was still there."

For the most part, all the guys were considerate and answered all my questions. We joked back and forth—they about "a woman's work is never done," and I, "what do men *want*?" I tried my best and they knew it. They helped, but, of course, for every rule there's at least one exception. . . .

The first guy I had trouble with was twenty-seven years old, which surprised me, because the younger ones were usually more receptive and open to new things. For a few days everything went fine; then one afternoon while we were shearing metal he asked me to get him a square. I brought him a non-adjustable one, the first one I laid eyes on.

"Oh, you goddamn stupid broad," he said, rolling his eyes

to the heavens, "I wanted an adjustable square!"

That did it.

"Listen, you goddamn stupid man," I yelled, "if you wanted an adjustable square, then why the hell didn't you just say so? That's why the good Lord gave you vocal cords!" I was on a roll and unable to stop. "And furthermore, I may be ignorant, but I am not stupid! You will at least give me some credit for coming here in the first place and trying to learn something from *jerks like you*! Do you understand in your lousy pea brain what I'm saying, because if you don't I'll gladly go over it again!!" Without waiting for a reply, I turned and stomped out to the alley and puffed viciously on a cigarette. The rotten bastard! I could easily have wrung his slimy neck!

By then, the guilty party had arrived at the back door. "Beth?"

I didn't answer.

"Beth, I—uh, I'm sorry. I'm a stupid male chauvinist pig, I'm sorry."

"Why don't you just leave me alone?" I yelled.

He needed no further encouragement, but apologized again and went back inside. I looked at my watch and was grateful to see it was time to go. I would head straight home to the tub and drink some wine.

He was waiting at my truck. "Look, I can't leave until you know how sorry I am," he said. "I had no right to say what I did. It does take guts to put up with a bunch of idiots like me. I won't leave until you accept my apology." He stuck out his hand. "Friends?"

I still felt like sticking in the knife, but looking at his face tore me up; he looked half sick. "Okay," I said, shaking his hand, "friends."

Later this same journeyman and I worked together on a roof. On the way up, I started reading the graffiti on the elevator walls. It was the usual raunchy stuff until I got to the bottom.

"Wow, would you look at this!" I exclaimed.

"Guess who wrote it?" He was grinning.

"Well, it wasn't me, and I'm sure it wasn't you..."

"You're wrong, woman. It was I."

Amazing, isn't it, what a little screaming match can do? What was it this fellow wrote on the wall for everyone to see?

WOMEN ARE HERE TO STAY!

I also met Romeo in the form of an electrician. At first I thought this guy must be single or divorced by the way he acted, but that was a very naive assumption on my part. He was very friendly and interested in what it was like being a woman in the trades. I told him a few crazy stories and remained distant. One day out of the blue, he said, "You know, we could have a very nice time together if you get my meaning..."

"Uh, sorry, I'm not interested," I replied.

"Aw, come on, hon, don't be an old stick-in-the-mud," he said, flashing a sweet smile. "Why don't you give me your phone number and we can go out sometime?"

"Why don't you give me yours, so I can talk to your wife about what you'd like to do?" (I'd been warned about Romeo a few days earlier.)

He was momentarily surprised, but regained his composure in seconds. "My wife wouldn't have to know."

"Yes, Mr. Juan, but I'd have to know, so why don't you go pick on someone your own size?"

"Leave your number somewhere and I'll copy it down." It was like I'd just conversed with a coil of rope. After that he started doing things like blowing kisses at me when other people were around. It was embarrassing the hell out of me until I remembered a trick one of my friends told me. The next day I boldly approached Romeo and told him I'd changed my mind and that my number was written on a box of nails in the kitchen.

"Oh, baby, you won't regret this, I can assure you," he said.

"Yeah, neither will you," I replied, hoping my scheme would work.

Wednesday I was almost afraid to go to work. I hung close

to people all day long so Romeo wouldn't find me alone. He did, anyway, like a cat stalking a mouse.

"That wasn't very funny at all," he said. "Dial-a-Devotion!"

"Well, did I get the point across?"

"It made me mad!" he fumed.

"*You* make *me* mad!" I fumed back and stomped off. He didn't bother me after that, but at times I'd catch him looking at me and shaking his head like he couldn't understand how I could pass up such an offer.

My luck didn't get any better with electricians; they seemed to be my cross to bear for Woman Tinner 101. I met this one downtown while knocking a hole in the wall at Sangamon State University. There I was, innocently doing my job with my partner Gene watching from below. The electrician was at the first hole tearing out some wires. He glanced over at us and asked Gene, "Why you letting that boy do all the work?"

"Ya better look again, friend," Gene replied. The electrician took a good look and dropped his screwdriver.

"You goddamn women!" he bellowed. "They oughta draft you dykes!"

(Wow, was this really happening?)

"They can't draft me," I volunteered sweetly.

"Cuz you're a woman, right? Cuz you're exempt, aren't you?" He waved his hammer at me.

"No, buddy, they can't draft me because I'm in the National Guard!" This buzzard had begun to irritate me. "And if you don't like it, I have a few ideas just where you can stick it!" Gene gasped and I turned back to my wall and pounded on it for all I was worth. Windbag muttered to himself for awhile and finally left.

Thankfully these kinds of incidents are rare. Most of the men are more than willing to at least give me a chance. I decided from the beginning to try to keep things cool, but I also wanted it to be known that they could not push me into a corner. I had a pretty large bag of tricks that I wouldn't hesitate to use. I haven't had to yet, fortunately.

Sheet metal apprentices are required to attend classes for four years—shop and drafting. Welding is also required after the second year. For a long time, the classes were hard for me because I'd never had any practical experience. The men, for the most part, had at least taken shop classes in high school. I spent many a night hunched over the kitchen table reading and drawing. I got a drafting textbook and started from the beginning.

This all paid off during my second year. It is the custom every year for all apprentices to compete in a contest, the winners competing in the regional, state and nationals if they got that far. I won the local competition, much to my dismay. The regional competition was two weeks away, and by the end of that time, I was an emotional wreck. I crammed until the wee hours and wore out many a pencil lead from drawing. I even began to dream sheet metal.

The big weekend arrived and we all packed into cars and headed for Decatur. There I learned I'd won by default. The other second-year apprentice didn't show up. So, like it or not, I was going to the state competition. I went through the regional contest anyway, to get the feel of it, and if the other guy would have shown up, he would have won. I screwed up royally. In the drafting section I got a fitting I'd seen but never drawn. In the fitting contest I made the fitting right, but with the wrong seams—a definite "fail."

My shop teacher gave me the second-year books later that day. "C'mon, champ," he said, patting my shoulder. "You can do it." I didn't inform him that I was going home to have a nervous breakdown.

And so began an even bigger crash course in tinning. I had two and a half months to read two binders full of material and to learn thirty fittings. Every night with few exceptions I was back at the kitchen table reading furiously. Weekends were the same, only in eight-hour stretches. I was a lean, mean sheet metal machine, vowing I would not screw up like I did at the regional.

The state competition was in Rockford. There were other

women there, but I was the only apprentice. I brought my roommate along for moral support. I heard people whisper, "There's the woman tinner!" They came up to me and congratulated me on my guts. What guts? I was scared to death!

At 7:30 a.m. on the day of the competition we arrived at the apprentice school. First on the agenda was drafting. We had two hours for eight fittings. I had a feeling no one would get done, so I took my time and made sure all the measurements were accurate. I didn't finish, but neither were there any mistakes or erasures. The second part was a written test that I doubted a journeyman could pass. Again, I took my time and got ninety out of a hundred finished. The fitting part of the contest was next. The fitting required was a tee on a forty-five degree angle. Phew! One I knew how to do! I went slowly, and was just finished when they called time.

My shop teacher was waiting outside. "How'd it go?" he asked.

"So-so, not real well," I said. "What say we go find everyone else and hit the bar?" It felt good to sit in a squooshy chair in the bar and unwind with my friends. People I'd never seen before came up and wished me luck.

The banquet was at seven that night and the place was packed.

"How'd you do?" the drafting teacher asked.

"Okay, but not that great I think," I answered.

"None of that! You probably did better than you think!"

"We'll see," I said, ordering another Bloody Mary.

The tables were cleared and the crowd quieted as a speaker stood up in front. He started with the fourth-year people. Our apprentice won third place. Then third-year; again, our apprentice won third. My hands were sweating profusely as they started on second year.

The speaker announced first place, second, and when he came to third place he said, "And third goes to someone with a lot of guts—" There was that word "guts" again, and I knew— "Beth, will you come up here, please?"

Everyone was clapping, the wives hardest of all. Things got

blurry, but I somehow managed to walk up to the front; it was like a dream. I could hardly wait to call my mom.

Local 84 carried third place in all four years, and we went home one big happy family. I was extremely glad that only the first and second place people went to the nationals. I didn't think my nerves could stand another go of it. Maybe next year....

I've been on many jobs over the years, on a lot of roofs and on top of a lot of air handling units. The learning and challenge has been endless, but the high point of my career was during the summer of '82, working on the dome of the State Capitol in Springfield.

In mid-May, six men and I met on the grounds with tons of tools, scaffolding, lumber and metal. It was a long way up (409 feet at the tip of the dome's flag pole), and hoisting the equipment was estimated to take one to two weeks. While waiting for the crane, three men went to the top. They would be setting up boatswain chairs and ropes so they could begin to patch the dome. The boatswain (pronounced bosun) chair looks like a child's swing. It's rigged up with ropes and pulleys so one can raise or lower oneself if one is stupid enough to get in and go over the side of the building. The rest of us went up to the base of the dome to bolt two large cables together on which we'd hook our safety lines.

"Come on out here," Larry the foreman directed, after we climbed numerous stairs. "But be careful because there's nothing to hang onto until we get this cable set up." Once I was out in the gutter, Dean handed a coil of half-inch cable out to Larry and I grabbed one end and started around the dome with it. The gutter was wide, but I was shaking in my boots nonetheless. A bird flew out from somewhere and I almost jumped out of my skin.

"That's it," I screamed. A muffled "okay" floated around from the other side and Larry came around to measure how much more cable we needed. We bolted them both together with three U-bolts on each end, and I felt much better knowing there was now something to hook onto.

There was a slight problem with the safety belt, as they are all made to fit men. On the tightest adjustment it was still rather roomy, but Larry tugged on it hard to make sure it wouldn't go over my hips. "It's hard to find shoes, too," I said, grinning.

The first few days I spent patching the walls right above the gutter. Much to my amazement, there were bullet holes in the dome, in addition to the cracks and holes caused by weathering. It was easy work and I enjoyed myself. The original dome was sheet zinc. We were patching it with lead-coated copper. Since they were two dissimilar metals, we couldn't solder them, so we used pop rivets and caulking.

We got word that the crane had arrived, so everyone went back down. I never got used to the stairs—rickety, rusty spiral staircases straight out of Alfred Hitchcock movies. It was even eerier when you could hear voices drifting up from the rotunda below. There were dead pigeons everywhere, so there was always a dead-thing, musty odor assailing one's schnoz.

The crane could only lift up to the lower roof of the dome, about forty feet up. Once all our equipment was there, four men went back up to the balustrade level, and three of us stayed down to tie equipment off. The others were probably fifty feet above us, which is a long way to pull things by hand, so they hoisted the bare essentials—eight sections of scaffold, the hoist and plywood. That done, we went back up and put together the scaffold, half in and half out of the gutter, and put the hoist together. We hand-cranked the hoist motor up and were ready to hoist everything else, including a gang box for storing tools and materials and the four-foot brake (a tool used for bending metal).

The hoisting and lifting was the worst part of the job. Climbing the stairs several times a day was also almost painful. I felt like a first-year cub again, barely managing to stumble home and into the shower before the Sandwoman threw a bucket of the stuff at me. After about a week I got used to it somewhat and could stay up till ten o'clock.

An added attraction for me were all the ERA groups rallying

in the Capitol rotunda. Women from NOW were there every lunch hour, and so were the hunger strikers led by Sonia Johnson. The Grassroots Coalition of Second-Class Citizens chained themselves to the railing in front of the Senate chambers (and were later carried out bodily in the wee hours), held a sit-in in front of the Governor's office, and finally spurted animal blood all over, saying it represented women's blood. Anti-ERA groups were there, too, wearing gingham dresses and bonnets.

I went down on lunch hour to talk to the pro-ERA women as often as possible. They were thrilled to know there was a woman working on the dome. There was so much strength and unity there; I knew how the suffragists must have felt in the early 1900s.

The time finally arrived when I was to go "up top." Three hundred and forty-four steps and none of them empty-handed. Carl and Terry were my co-workers.

"Now if you don't want to go down the side, don't worry about it," Carl said.

"Yeah," Terry added. "If you never do it, don't worry."

"Oh, I'll do it," I replied. "It just may take a few days!"

For two days I "womanned" the ropes and sent Carl and Terry down the drill and metal as needed. I had no problem looking over the side or reaching over to hoist a tool or bucket, but I wasn't too sure of actually going out there. But then I'd think of the women downstairs fighting for the ERA, and I knew I'd do it.

At the end of the second day, I was ready to go "down the side" with Carl. You walk up to the top of the stairs through a scuttlehole (a small doorway) right at the top of the dome. You get your safety belt and chair and step gingerly outside and *immediately* (no shit!) hook your safety belt to the half-inch cable running around the base of the observation deck. You check all lines and bolts and hook your chair to the cable. You get into the chair, take off the safety belt and then, by use of the pulleys on the chair, lower yourself "down the side." I made it through the scuttlehole and had to stop. The sides of the dome went out a ways and then they dropped fast, looking like there was nothing there but air. I was scared and not afraid to admit it.

"Carl, I have to go back in."

"Okay, no problem."

The next day, June 8, I finally did it. Terry was handling the ropes and Carl was at my side playing coach.

"Lean back in the chair, woman!" Terry hollered. "If ya don't, you'll slide right out!"

"Thanks a lot!" I yelled back. What a comforting thought.

"Take your time," Carl said. "Pull that rope there up toward the block and tackle and down you go."

He demonstrated and I followed suit. It wasn't hard at all; it was just the idea of being up so gawdawful high! Planes flew lower than this! You are probably safer up there, however, than down on the street.

After I practiced with my "new feet" for awhile, it began to feel good. I loved being up there and seeing for miles. After a little more practice, Terry sent down a tool bucket and I started to work. He also made a little speech at the top of his lungs about how another male domain was dashed by an uppity broad. I laughed so hard I dropped my screwdriver and watched in horror as it bounced and slid out of sight. I prayed there was no one down there, for surely it would kill someone.

We were up there for two more weeks, and then there was patching up in the tower to do. We replaced all the metal on the observation deck, and Terry and I went all the way up to the flag pole to patch there. I also worked on my own on the balustrade levels, cutting off the old metal, measuring, and making up new metal. I plugged along, singing woman songs and getting one heck of a tan. We discovered there was a family of chicken hawks living somewhere on the roofs. They were beautiful to watch, but they didn't like us and finally flew away. I often wonder if they ever went back.

A lot of water has passed under the bridge since that job. I've been married and divorced, been a victim of marital abuse. I've had an abortion for the same reason. I couldn't bear the thought of my husband beating on a helpless child. I've made new friends and gotten along. Soon, I'll get my card, and that's when the real test begins. Admittedly, I'm more than a little nervous, but if things start to get too hairy, I'll remember the sounds of those women's voices floating up from the Capitol rotunda and one of my favorite quotes from Mother Jones:

"No matter what the fight don't be ladylike!"

Mary Ruggiero • Welder
Interview by Joanne Carlson

I'm from New Jersey originally. After high school, I worked as a tea taster's assistant at Lipton's tea and loved it! I made the first Lipton's soup, you know? But my boss couldn't keep his hands off me, so I quit and went to look for a new job.

This was right before World War II started in 1939. The unemployment office asked me if I wanted to do a male-oriented job like mechanics or something. I said I'd do whatever paid the most, and so they signed me up as a welder trainee, which paid a dollar-twenty-five an hour then. My parents thought I was crazy. I went to an eight-week training course at Dickenson High School where I practiced handling torches and tools. Fifty percent of my class were women and the rest were older men trying to get better jobs. We all got jobs and went to Eastern Aircraft where they were working on government contracts. Management treated us like VIPs. People were so patriotic! Nobody wondered whether you could do the job, because the need was there.

Most of our co-workers accepted us, but there were some men who were threatened. The women who were really good were more likely to be victims of sabotage. I remember one woman who was such a talented welder she put the men to shame. They moved her to another job and I never saw her again. Guys were scared of getting drafted. They didn't want the women to replace them, so they pulled stunts. Someone cut the chain holding up a big motor mount I was welding. It fell down on me and burned my arm to the bone.

The women weren't jealous of each other during those years like they sometimes are now. There was such cooperation. We got paid the same as men and got the same work and training. I was the first woman in New Jersey to be certified as an aircraft welder. I'd say half of the workers at Eastern during the war were women in all kinds of trades. We weren't trying to prove anything, just win the war. During lunch we'd sit and sing songs like "Don't Fence Me In." Sometimes us girls would rent a hotel room and stay in town to go out dancing to big band music. I was very peppery and had lots of dates.

We worked right up to the Hiroshima bomb and then they marched us out like cattle. We had been happy the war was over. They said I didn't want the war to end, but that wasn't true. I just wanted to keep my job. I was a damn good welder. But after the war nobody would hire us. Employers would look at me and say, "What are you, some kind of freak? A woman can't weld."

When I met my husband I was working on an assembly line for Western Electric as an electrical coil inspector. It was production line type work, all done by women. Only the foremen were men.

I quit my job to raise a family. We moved to California and I got a job as a secretary in my kids' parochial school. I was at the school one day when one of my girlfriends, who used to be a sheet metal worker during the war, said she'd been called back to work at the Alameda Naval Air Station. This was 1966, about the time of the Vietnam war. So I rushed down to see if they needed any welders.

The woman at the employment office said, "This is most unusual!" My husband was skeptical. After all, I was forty-six, no kid then! It had been twenty years since I'd handled a torch! I took all the tests, and the foreman couldn't believe I could handle a torch so well. They called me to work in two weeks. I had to start off as a welder's helper because my foreman wouldn't give me credit for time I had been certified. A lot of new techniques had been developed in twenty years. I had to certify as a heli-arc welder. I took evening courses at Chabot College to catch up. They gave me course credit for things I already knew. I knew more about gas welding than my instructor. Over a year later I was doing journeylevel work and they still wouldn't give me credit. I had to complain to the Civil Service Commission in order to get journeyman certification. There was a big difference in pay.

The guys at work had a real different attitude than during the war years. Most men didn't want a woman around. They made fun of me, they'd sabotage my work bench and my tools. One guy said, "I got a woman at home, who needs one on the job?" Management is responsible for a lot of the harassment. They support the fellows' hostility rather than stick up for us. They have a lot of old-fashioned macho ideas about what kind of work women should do. They think we belong in the kitchen.

Mostly I ignored all the insults and the dirty pictures. I didn't want to make trouble; I just wanted to work. But I didn't let them pick on me. I filed plenty of grievances, and then management would just transfer me rather than disciplining the men. I said, "Just because I can't pee against the wall don't mean I can't do my job." I stuck through it all and cried all the way to the bank. You know, when you're young and pretty, you can get away with a lot more. I didn't give up. I felt if I couldn't weld, I'd rather not be working.

I retired on disability at age sixty-three. I hurt my back on the job. When I had to go out on disability, I was so depressed because I didn't want to leave. I said to the woman in personnel who'd fought to get me hired, "All this fighting all these years, what good did it do?" She said, "You did so much for women by just being here." It was then that I realized my persistence had made a difference. There's a constant battle going on and women haven't won it yet. There still are no women in the welding shop; they're go-fers. I believe women deserve the same break in peacetime as when there's a war on.

I like to encourage young women to get into the trades, and

never to let anyone discourage them from accomplishing what they want in life. I've gone out and given speeches. There are so many girls left alone today to raise their families because of divorce. By having a trade, you can make your own choices. You have problems no matter where you work. You've got to sweat it out, rise above it all, and think about the meat and potatoes. Don't be afraid of challenge. No man lifts more than he can. Heck, if a war broke out today, they'd drag me out of a wheelchair to weld. You have to be needed to be appreciated. But the main thing is never give up!

I'm now sixty-eight and live in San Leandro, California, with my husband, a retired real estate broker. We have five kids and eight grandchildren. My mother was a dressmaker and union activist. She was a fighter. My daughter works on the line for General Motors and she's a union activist, too. She told her union, "We're all fighters in this family." And it's true.

Jessica Hopkins • Stationary Engineer

I went to an all-girls Catholic high school for "young women" from working-class families. We were given a good education there, though the focus of the schooling was on improving our lot in this world by enabling us to catch a husband (and for those few to continue on to college—enabling them to earn an MRS. degree). We were not turned loose however, without a few skills to survive till the day we wed. We were taught how to type and take shorthand. If there was anything that turned me off more than the idea of getting married and being supported by a man, it was the prospect of earning a living by typing and taking shorthand. Not a good start.

I graduated in 1968. As a product of parochial schools and a Latin home (we'd immigrated from Perú) I was as a lamb among the lions. I was naíve, broke and full of dreams. The nuns had fed my mind with literature, history and even the idea of professional success (as the woman behind the man), but they had delivered me as fodder to the corporate world. I was ready to serve coffee; dress, speak and act appropriately; turn out a legible business letter with no spelling or punctuation errors; and be grateful for my minuscule paycheck.

For the next fourteen years I struggled to break loose from this fate by supporting myself, on and off, through non-traditional occupations. Each time I started to savor my freedom something would swat me back into the hated role of office worker, my fall-back survival role. I tried a variety of occupations, each with its own reality adjustment: musician—you can't live on free beer and your friends' applause; private investigator—you start becoming suspicious of everybody; reporter for a news service—disillusionment with the concept of unbiased reporting; apprentice goldsmith—the boss moved a "casting couch" in; sound engineer—you can't live on free beer and a portion of the band's take; go-fer in the recording industry—egomania; researcher for a socially responsible, antipsychiatric abuse, activist organization—sixteen-hour days, six-day weeks, food stamps, burnout; apartment manager—I couldn't take one more Sunday morning call to come kill a roach!

Somewhere along the way I decided if you can't beat 'em, join 'em. I took courses in personnel management, organizational troubleshooting, statistics, conflict resolution, program administration, policy formulation and implementation. My responsibilities tripled, someone else typed my letters, my salary got a bit better and still I was asked to make the coffee. By this time the writing was on the wall, but I was too frazzled to see it.

Then, one day in 1982, I hired two female carpenters to come build cabinets in the office. They were skilled, strong, happy, well paid and independent. Through them I learned about an upcoming Tradeswomen, Inc. conference at Laney College in Oakland. I went to a workshop at the conference for women interested in getting into the trades. When asked how to gain basic skills to become employable in the trades, the workshop leader replied, "Beg, borrow or steal a job."

I begged a job with a contractor doing roofing through the summer at a dollar an hour less than his male teenaged helper. And, I started showing up at worksites and union halls in three counties, applying for apprentice openings in the carpentry, electrical and sheet metal trades. One contractor kept promising they'd have work for me: "... Tomorrow. Just be here at 5:45." I was Charlie Brown trusting Lucy: I'd be there at 5:30, I'd stand around until all the guys had been sent out, and then someone would finally say, "Nothing today, come back tomorrow, we'll have work for you then." Then I'd go and roll out more tar paper and nail in cedar shakes in the ninety-five degree sun for four dollars an hour. If it hadn't been for my female carpenter friend urging me to hang in there, I might have given up and headed back to the office.

One day I got a notice from Women in Apprenticeship Program (WAP) that the stationary engineering trade was accepting applications for their next apprenticeship class. An added note said to be sure to study for this one, it was a tough test. I had no idea what the trade was, but the challenge appealed to me, so I decided to apply. By then I was working at a loading dock for four dollars an hour, plus tips, and I was ready for any job that paid well.

I missed an early opportunity to find out what this trade entailed. I had asked my father what the name of his trade was, since I thought he was some kind of engineer. He replied, "Well, I guess you'd call it industrial maintenance." Great, I thought to myself, at least I wouldn't have to weather charges of nepotism! Only later did I find out that industrial maintenance is another title for stationary engineering. I went to the WAP study sessions a few times. Too embarrassed to ask what I was studying for, I kept my ears open and tried to glean some clues from the study materials. I took the test with fifteen hundred other people and came in number fifteen—this assured me a job interview within the next year and a half. When my first interview came up I still didn't know what kind of work I was applying for. By this time I did know it was the same as my father's trade, but I hadn't been able to tell him, in his abounding pride that I'd chosen his field, that I didn't know what it was. There was also a credibility problem—as a woman daring to break into a male-dominated field I was supposed to be "hungry" for this particular trade. So, I asked my father what he thought I should say if I was asked in my interview about why I wanted to work in the trade. That's when I first found out about boilers and chillers and compressors.... At each subsequent interview I learned more about the trade and by the time I was hired I actually had a fairly good idea of what the job was all about. I also had a fairly good idea that women weren't welcome.

That was two-and-a-half-feels-like-five years ago and was my introduction to a whole new world—a new world of machinery and heating and cooling systems, and the world of the apprenticeship system, a male-dominated union and, of course, the sexual politics of the workplace.

Stationary engineers are responsible for the operation, maintenance and repair of heating, air conditioning and ventilation systems, fire and life-safety systems, pneumatic and electronic control systems, and all their auxiliary fixtures and machinery: fans, pumps, valves, motors, controllers, miles of pipes, couplings, bearings, gears.... We work in office buildings, hospitals, hotels, production plants and waste water treatment plants.

I was hired into a sixty-year-old, twenty-four-story office building in the financial district of San Francisco. I am the only woman in a crew of three engineers—the chief, the journey-level engineer and myself, an apprentice. The building lacks an air conditioning system, but compensates by having 1600 wooden sash windows that open and close. Though sash windows are not normally within the purview of a stationary engineer, I've changed or fixed close to two hundred of them.

I think what makes an old building like this such an interesting learning experience is the opportunity to problem-solve with no clues from a computer—though I'm eager to eventually learn about computer-controlled systems. I have to understand how each system works and how it interacts with the other systems. This means keeping your ears and eyes open to sounds that aren't quite right or to visual clues that might indicate a problem. One highlight of my time in this building was solving an eight-year-old mystery that had plagued two chiefs and a handful of journeylevel engineers. I did it by thinking the system through and looking for what I knew I must find—and I did.

The building had been losing water out of the fire system

for years. There were no sprinkler or fire hose leaks and we had replaced the old shut-off valves on the drains with new ones. Theories abounded about back-pressures and failed check valves. I dismissed each theory as improbable. The beauty of a plumbing system is that each part has an obvious logical and sequential function. Take it one step at a time and all mysteries are revealed. After considering all the theories and the elusiveness of the problem, I decided it had to be something basic and simple: there had to be a drain in the system that didn't appear in the blueprints. How to find it in miles of unlabeled pipes? First, I eliminated portions of the system where no one would ever put a drain. Next, I eliminated the areas that had been suspect for years—I knew they'd been gone over with a fine-toothed comb. I chose the least accessible part of the system—pipes disappearing into a concrete ceiling with no prints showing where they went. I knew that sprinkler pipes reduce in diameter as they go further out in the system in order to maintain pressure. I considered the pipes where they entered the concrete: not this pipe, it's too big, must feed the top of the building and that's been checked; not that pipe, it's too small, feeds this level and that's been checked. What about this pipe? Just big enough to go up about one floor. But the pipe that feeds that floor is over there! Up one floor I found a sprinkler line that fed a room with a defunct ventilation system. Squeezing myself over and under old ducts, I climbed way to the back of the room. In the furthest, darkest corner my flashlight found a hole in the brick wall. I stuck my hand through the hole and found a drain valve. Holding very still, I heard water flowing. I'd found it! We replaced the valve and once again have a tight fire system.

In my job, I can find myself being an electrician, a locksmith, a plumber/pipefitter and mechanic all in one day. I am not the strongest woman in this trade—far from it—but I've not had any problems. Occasionally I have to ask for help, but not out of proportion to the help I give. There are calm days when things happen at a sane pace, and days like the one I had some months ago: two fire alarms—one real, one false; people stuck in an elevator; an air quality inspector with questions; a major steam leak; one engineer out; a supply fan down; a false bomb threat; toilets overflowing—along with the usual daily maintenance problems. Sometimes it can feel like you're in a war zone. Mainly though, the work is a lot of fun. It's not often that a grown woman can play in grease all day, tear apart and rebuild a fan, love her occupation and get paid well. Of course, the payoffs go beyond the pocketbook. I'm learning marketable skills that will give me a certain independence once I have my journey card, and I've already gained a feeling of confidence I once lacked.

All of this does not come without a price, however. Though I have earned the respect of the men I work with and the other tradesmen in the complex, it has been a long, hard row to hoe. I'm still expected to prove myself and yet I must never expect full acceptance. I'm still considered a woman in a "man's" job. This attitude puts a lot of pressure on me (and other tradeswomen) that is completely unnecessary but will probably persist for at least one more generation of tradeswomen. Until then there are daily indignities that tell you you're not accepted: my boss saying the reason he hired me was to piss one of the guys off; our apprentice class representative to the Joint Apprenticeship Training Committee telling us that he'd prevented a rape that day—he'd changed his mind. The men also love to tell stories of how dumb the female tenants of the building are—the guys fiddle with dead thermostats and say the heating problem is fixed and the women believe them (the irony is that the guys actually believe that the women believe them!).

One time I was vying for a job in a new building with a modern air conditioning system. I was offered the job, but the apprentice coordinator at the union hall wanted them to hire a young man on the hiring list who had never worked a day in this trade. The coordinator told me that this kid was more qualified than I was (as a successful third-year apprentice) because his father was a chief engineer! Our union local business agent, in a newsletter to the entire membership, has referred to the female engineers as enginettes. It goes on every day in both subtle and blatant forms. Often the men will make some patronizing comment that is meant to show me how accepting of tradeswomen they are... and then they'll turn around in the next breath and laugh about some tradeswoman built like a "gorilla."

There is also the added pressure of having very little in common with the men I work around. My mental meanderings lean to the philosophical rather than the athletic; my spiritual leanings are perhaps best described as a new age/goddess/eastern mix, rather than traditional religious dogma; my politics are left-of-center/radical feminism rather than nationalistic Reaganism; my approach one of quiet optimism rather than aggressive cynicism. I don't fit in. I am a problem for these guys—I'm easy to get along with, I have a sense of humor, I do a good job, yet I don't allow racist/sexist/homophobic/anti-Semitic comments and "jokes" to go unprotested. Pornographic material goes in the garbage, and I insist that the female point of view is valid and one to be considered. Why add this stress to my job? Because if I don't speak up: a) things will never get better, b) they'll get worse, and c) I couldn't respect myself if I didn't.

The workplace will never be woman-ized merely by virtue of women working there. It has to be actively woman-ized by the women entering the trades who can say: "I am here, I'm going to do my job as myself, not as one of the boys, I am valid without your acceptance, get out of the way—I'm trying to get my job done." I remember after one particularly bad day in the lunch room when the woman-bashing ("jokes") had reached a particularly hateful pitch and I started to cry. One of the guys said they were just trying to toughen me up, that I needed a thick skin to make it in a man's trade. I reminded them that it was not a man's trade, merely a male-dominated trade. I told them that I didn't need a thick skin to solve a mechanical problem, I didn't need to be tough to take a pump apart and rebuild it, I didn't need their macho initiation rites to turn a wrench. I told them they'd have to look elsewhere for their cold, tough bitch. I was going to go on in my soft-hided way and continue being a good engineer. I think we've gotten along a lot better since then. No doubt about it, the work is a breeze, any woman who wanted to could do it, but the male environment adds a lot of stress to the job.

As an individual I could not manage to deal with this stress all alone—I'd end up having to divide my waking hours between work and stress reduction disciplines. So, I have a wonderful alternative—a support group. Goddess bless these women who are there to meet once a month—to listen and laugh and suggest and advise and commiserate and inject humor into the surreal working world we share, the world where we're not welcome, but where we nevertheless choose to be.

How long will I last in this trade? It's difficult to say. Sometimes I imagine becoming a chief engineer so I can show them how it is done right, sometimes I imagine forming a work co-op with other tradeswomen. And there are times when I just feel like saying, "Let the boys wallow in their own muck without me." Perhaps I'll be a teacher, or go build a simple cabin in the woods—with a full heating and air conditioning system, pneumatically controlled to maintain a comfortable environment....

Pat Cull • Carpenter

It's hard to believe that I'm forty-six years old and in my fifteenth year of doing carpentry for a living. Seeing the reactions I get from people on the street when I'm in my overalls, or from other carpenters who don't know me, I can tell that they don't believe it either. At this age, I should be comfortably settled in a long marriage being supported by my husband, have a couple of kids and probably a few precious grandchildren. Instead, here I am, hauling plywood for cabinets, three-by-twelves for picnic tables, two-by-fours to frame walls, sheet rock to cover them, four-by-fours and eight-by-eights for assorted work orders. And not just hauling them but cutting them to specifications and putting them together to make whatever it is that is required. It occurs to me that, with luck, I may be the first woman in California, perhaps in the United States, perhaps in the whole world (OK, I'm being a little grandiose) to *retire* as a carpenter.

Here I am, so old that I'm thinking about things like retiring and how much my pension will be. Old enough to worry about whether I'll have to eat dog food and where I'll live (I can *build* houses but can't afford to *buy* one). Old enough to worry about whether or not I'll be able to carry my share for the next twenty years. It would be intolerable for me not to be able to do that. I've seen how the younger carpenters (male) treat the older carpenters (male), how they denigrate their abilities and knowledge. How the old ones get by as best they can without letting on that they can't see well enough to read the tape, can't lift the concrete form without too much pain, can't bend and frame a building too long lest they lose too much time from work for back trouble. The young ones don't seem to realize that the old ones have forgotten more than they'll ever know, so they make cracks about "carrying" the old guy and doing his work, about how he's worth nothing and doesn't know anything. I see this and I think—what are they going to do to a sixty-plus-year-old *woman* carpenter? That's why I worry.

Age has been an issue for me ever since I got into the trade. I began getting gray hair when I was a freshman in high school and was totally gray before I was thirty. From ages thirty to thirty-three, I dyed my hair to its original very dark brown, almost black, but finally succumbed to curiosity and let it grow out to see just how gray it had become. After watching how older men were treated during my first year of apprenticeship, I was sure I'd have to dye my hair for the rest of my life. But once I saw this striking head of gray hair that I had missed, I knew I could never dye it again and have trusted Mother Nature's judgement about that ever since.

To go back a little further, I am a working-class woman of Italian/English descent who worked in factories to get a Master's degree in social work. I've worked hard at every job I've ever had. I was raised with a strong work ethic: any job worth doing was worth doing *well*. I believe I was a good social worker but the last job I had in that field, which lasted for three years, confronted me with many trying questions. I was responsible for "treatment" programs for delinquent children and in a position to play God—decisions I made affected these kids and their parents for a long time. It got harder and harder to know if what I was doing was "right" or "wrong." I gave some thought to getting into a non-traditional job, something that involved working with my hands rather than my head and psyche. That had had some appeal for me since I was nine years old. My parents had spent a year building their own house on weekends and I was occasionally given the opportunity to hammer some nails (where the hammer marks wouldn't show).

I checked out a few things like being a typewriter repair person for IBM, an installer for the phone company, and a repairperson for the local utilities company. It was hard to be serious about changing careers when I had such a well-paying job, though. I thought the answer might be to change jobs within my field, so I applied, was tested and promised a job as a psychiatric social worker for San Mateo County. On the strength of the promise, I moved to California only to find that the promised job was swept away because they "discovered" I was a lesbian (I was very out of the closet) and therefore inappropriate to deal with male clients who might need "maternal nurturing" and "appropriate female role models." I prudently decided that the time had come for me to follow through on my aspiration for non-traditional work.

I went to the Women in Apprenticeship Program (WAP) which in 1974 was under an umbrella organization called Advocates for Women, to inquire about apprenticeships. The book that I was given to look at had over three hundred apprenticeships, most of them with an age limit of thirty-two. When I met with the counselor for WAP, I told her that I was pretty discouraged because I was interested in carpentry and it was one of the programs with that age limit. I was about a month away from my thirty-second birthday and figured I was dead in the water. But she said that carpenters were only open for two weeks every two years for new apprenticeships and they happened to be open right then. The problem was that the carpenters were going on strike the next week and it promised to be a long strike, lasting beyond my thirty-second birthday. So my only chance was to get a job in the next two days *before* the strike.

After I went to the union hall and got my hunting licence (a piece of paper that a contractor would sign saying he'd hire you for three months), I went out looking. I'd never been on a construction site in my life and thought it might be an interesting way to spend the day. It was quite a trip because no one had ever seen a woman on these jobsites before. The men would stare at me and some would make cracks, thinking I would walk on by, but then I'd go up to them asking for the foreman. They'd all bust out laughing, as if this was the most ridiculous thing they'd ever seen. I went to these sites all day and found only one guy who didn't say no. I went back to him at the end of the day and told him that no one had hired me and that if he didn't give me a job, I'd never be a carpenter—I'd be over the age limit after the strike. Well, hey, I'd have to be a pretty dumb social worker not to recognize a Guilt Button when I saw one and even dumber not to push it! Before a strike, contractors are laying people off, not hiring, but I just knew this foreman was someone who probably told his buddies over a beer that he would hire a woman if he thought she could do the job. However, he wasn't all that enthusiastic when presented with reality in the form of my myself. He sighed and asked, "Have you dug any ditches?"

"No", I said, "I've been sitting at a desk as a social worker for years."

"Well, how about building a bookcase for yourself at home?" he asked, searching for some excuse to hire me.

"Bricks and boards." I couldn't honestly give him any help about my experience since I had none at all.

"Let me look at your hands." Though they certainly were callous-free, I do have big hands and they must have been what convinced him to take the chance. He hired me the Friday before the strike, so that when I went to work after the strike, my age still counted as being below the age limit.

That first week I worked as a carpenter, I thought I was going to die. I was down in Palo Alto and it was well over a hundred degrees the whole week. I showed up the first day after the strike with my brand new tools and tool belt, but I didn't have any idea what to do with them. The Sears salesman had picked them out for me from the apprenticeship tool list, but I hardly knew the names of them, much less how to fit them into my new tool belt or actually use them. The foreman who hired me set my tools up in my belt and assigned me to a partner.

The first thing my partner said to me was, "Go get some eight duplexes and some sixteen commons." I had no idea what he was talking about, but I thought it might have something to do with nails so I went over and read the labels on the nail boxes until I found what I needed. The other foreman on this job made it very clear that he didn't want me. He told me, "If there are any problems on the job because of a woman being here, you are the one that's going to be fired."

This foreman put me up on a twenty-five-foot wall. There were two-by-fours spaced about every three feet horizontally and I climbed up on them to fasten other two-by-fours vertically with sixteen-penny nails, which are three and a half inches long. So I had about fifty pounds of stuff in my tool belt, and there I was climbing this twenty-five-foot wall, fastening myself to it with a safety belt while I pounded these three and a half inch nails. My hands were bloody and the sun was beating down—I honestly don't know how I did it. And there was the additional stress of other guys of all trades taking long detours on the jobsite just to see what I was doing, while the foreman's admonition hung in my mind. He watched me all the time and if I stood still for a moment, I heard about it and was threatened all over again. But I grasped and loved the fact that you could tell if what you were doing was right or wrong. If it was wrong, you could take it apart and do it over. And best of all, at the end of the day I could actually look at what I had accomplished—a heady experience for an ex-social worker.

There is no longer an age limit in the carpenters union and they now have continuous open enrollment for the apprenticeship program. The California affirmative action regulations for women and minorities give minimal financial penalties for offenders, so you no longer hear things like I used to hear. The foremen no longer laugh out loud in your presence or ask what your husband thinks or tell you that they've already hired a woman. They've gotten smarter and now say, "Come back in two weeks" to avoid any lawsuits. They weren't so smart when I was an apprentice and managed to convince them to take a chance. Strangely enough, I think that being in my thirties was a factor in getting hired initially. I wasn't a kid trying something out for a lark; I was an older adult with serious intentions.

On my first jobs, they gave me the hardest tasks they could find and then sat back to watch me struggle. Once I was assigned to carry four-hundred-pound steel beams with a guy who was about six feet tall and weighed about three hundred pounds. I was five-foot-two and weighed about a hundred and twenty-five pounds. I felt like I was walking on my knees carrying the beams and after doing it twice, I said I wouldn't do it again. I've always felt that it was extremely important for me to do a good job because I would be a reference point for hiring women after me—but I didn't think that included getting seriously injured. I expected to be fired, but instead they gave me the *next* heaviest job, setting up steel scaffolding by myself. I was okay (though exhausted) and made a kind of breakthrough for myself—as well as for them—to know that a woman *could* do this job.

I believe my employers, and co-workers, eventually recognized how hard I worked and how hard I tried to learn the trade. I worked for a large company for more than five years until I got my present job with the city. At one point, the local public television station came out to the job I was on for a documentary on women in the trades. They roamed around the jobsite interviewing me and various men on the job. The day after the film was shown on TV, I went to work furious at the superintendent because, in his interview, he had likened hiring women to hiring fourteen-year-old boys. My foreman was furious with me for saying I wanted his job because all he had to do was read prints and tell people what to do—he didn't have to work at all! Neither the superintendent or the general foreman understood what I was offended about. Nor did I really grasp at the time what offense I had given. Later, on the same job, the superintendent told me that hiring women was more cost-efficient because, while they were slower, they did the job right the first time and therefore avoided costly corrections. Since I was the only woman he had ever employed, I was proud (and amused) to serve as the basis for this grand generalization.

I never worked with another woman on the jobsite until I was a ninety-five percent apprentice (just about finished). It wasn't until then that I recognized the differences in treatment of co-workers according to age also extended to women, but in a distinct way. Because I was older, I was rarely seen as a sex object in the way that the younger women were. They had to deal with the "come fuck me" kind of harassment while I had to deal with the "she can't do it" kind of harassment. They were subjected to sexual harassment while I was subjected to sex-*based* harassment. It was hard to tell how much the difference in treatment had to do with my being an "out" lesbian since the women I worked with were either straight or in the closet, but I'm inclined to think that their age was more of a factor.

I did face some problems being an out lesbian, but I thought them minor and very rare compared to the daily barrage my female co-workers had to deal with. I felt that being up front about my sexuality waylaid innuendos from the men. They couldn't sit around and speculate about my being a lesbian because I had already told them. That gave me some measure of power. By being out and being older, I avoided most of the come-ons—though a classic sticks in my mind. A young guy was making moves so I told him I was gay. Astonished, he said, "You mean, you've never slept with a man?" I didn't bother pointing out that being a lesbian didn't necessarily mean that you'd never slept with a man. Instead, I just nodded to acknowledge that that was true for me. Then he said, "You mean I'd be the *first*!" He just couldn't understand why I thought that was funny.

I loved carpentry immediately and still love it. I love the feel and smell of wood, love having something come out just the way I planned it, love knowing that my work helps to make people's lives better. I remember being on housing jobs that were being framed in wood; getting my tools and walking to my position on the site in the half-dark of daybreak when all was quiet, smelling the distinctive odor of wood and feeling joy in the brief moments before the noise of our work lacerated the peace. The work itself is always something I enjoy. It doesn't matter if it's digging ditches or doing a fine piece of cabinetry—it's honest work that I can be proud of. The problems I've had have always come from the attitudes of the men I work with and for.

I worked for union general contractors for over eight years doing every conceivable job, from concrete work to finish trim. I considered myself to be a good all-around carpenter. Then six years ago, I got a job as a maintenance carpenter for the City of San Francisco. During my first year working for the city, I felt like an apprentice again. I had to learn how to use all the shop tools such as shapers and jointers and routers and lathes and the various drill presses. On my previous construction jobs, I had used radial arm saws and table saws as well as an assortment of various power hand tools, and that was it. But I loved learning so many new things, even if it felt like starting over. I became a cabinetmaker of sorts and had bizarre tasks like making oars for boats or crates for sending hippopotamuses to China (me, who could never manage to get a package of books intact to Chicago). I still work for the city and still think the work is interesting and quite varied. We repair locks, board up windows, frame new construction, form concrete, repair ping-pong tables—and many other tasks impossible to enumerate. We often go to two or five places in a single day to take care of emergencies or work on small, needed community projects. Although priorities are set by our bosses, we have a modicum of independence. For example, we generally have so many work orders that if it's cold and rainy, we can choose to work on an indoor project; or if the temperature soars, we can usually find an outside job. I still love the smell of wood every morning when I enter the quiet shop and feel a lift of pride in my work.

Well, the more things change, the more they stay the same. After three years of working on a "temporary" basis for the city and scoring quite high on the civil service exam, I found myself in the position of fighting for my job once again. The same fellow who had hired me and given me good evaluations now vowed that he would not hire me on a permanent basis. Three other women (in different departments) had also been working as carpenters on a temporary basis for the city and also scored high enough on the exam to be assured of permanent jobs. We conferred and found that all of us were asked illegal and sexist questions that no man had been asked, and that none of us thought that we would be hired. At that point, we consulted a lawyer who wrote letters to all the city departments for us, and we also pursued a number of other pressure tactics. I went through most of the chain of command, ending up with the top boss, who was furious after hearing (and checking) my story and ordered that I be hired as I deserved. After that, I was subjected to a humiliating meeting in which I was warned that I would never pass probation.

I did pass probation and the fellow who vowed to never hire me was passed over for a promotion and retired. The other three women were also hired on permanent jobs eventually, but nothing else has changed in the past three years. The first four women carpenters for the City of San Francisco (ourselves) remain the *only* women carpenters who have been hired in the last six years.

How the men on the job see me hasn't changed over the years. What has changed is me. When I first got into the trade, I watched my body develop, seemingly without limit. Recently however, I had a serious accident: I fell two stories (on vacation, yet), fracturing a vertebrae and, more seriously, breaking about half the bones in my right foot. I'll never walk correctly again nor will I walk without pain. But I can walk and I can work—with pain. Now I no longer disdain carts and carry the lumber into the shop myself, as I always used to do. I no longer turn up my nose at the light-duty, repetitive tasks.

Even though I know that I still produce more than most of the carpenters in my shop, I feel "less" than I was before. It has been hard enough to fight the consistent message that I can't do the job because I'm a woman; it's even harder now when I'm less than able-bodied.

My task for the past year has been to come to grips with

aging and minor disability in a positive way. Because I am in civil service, I have a secure job and will be able to support myself as long as I am able to work. If I worked for a general contractor, I could expect to be dumped just because I looked too old. Another difference is that I will be working with the same men for years to come. Every now and then, someone will retire and a new younger carpenter will take his place. Dealing with one young man's attitudes every few years is vastly easier than dealing with whole new crews every time you change construction jobs.

Before I got this job, I used to worry constantly about what I was going to do for a living when I got into my fifties and could no longer get construction jobs. Not that I wouldn't be able to do the job, but that I wouldn't get hired. Older men have a hard time getting hired and I couldn't kid myself that it would be any different for me. I knew I would have to make a career change again, something I dreaded. Besides, I really loved carpentry and didn't *want* to do anything else! Now, those worries are over. Assuming good health, I'll be able to retire in sixteen years at age sixty-two with a pension and social security. I imagine there will be some difficult times, but that won't be unique to me—that's life. I have many good tradeswomen friends and we will see each other through.

Trudy Pax Farr • Steelworker

My first day. The BOP (Basic Oxygen Process) Shop towers some six or seven stories. Everywhere there is equipment of gigantic proportions. Ladles, cranes, transfer cars. We workers are dwarfed beside them. Forklift trucks and bulldozers run around like beetles.

I stand mesmerized when the huge furnace tips and slowly pours out its liquid fire—what other name can I give that brilliant soup? "Don't look at it," another worker says, "you need these," and he gives me some small blue-lensed glasses that I can clip on my safety glasses and flip up or down as I need. As the steel flows from the tap hole of the furnace into the waiting ladle, a sunset glow sweeps over everything and, for a brief moment, there is color in this drab, relentlessly gray building.

Many feet above—I can barely make out the operator in the cab—runs the crane, its runway spanning the width of the building. It comes now, and with much creaking and straining, laboriously lifts the filled ladle. When it does, some steel sloshes over and a glowing puddle sits on the ground after the crane glides away.

I become a burner. I don a stiff metallic-like coat and leggings, strap leather gaitors over shoes. A welder-type shield over my face, leather one-fingered mitts for my hands. All to protect me from the "sparks" (in fact, small droplets of hot steel) that shower down when oxygen, flame and air meet molten steel. Still, those sparks find their way down my shirt front, into my gloves. At first, I stop to inspect each small burn, but before long I do as the seasoned burners do: simply shake the spark out of my glove the best I can, hold my shirt away from my body and let it tumble down, and continue at the job. Under all that fireproof clothing, my t-shirt and bra are filled with small burn holes. My hands are pock-marked.

Steel: durable, impregnable, indestructable. I cut through it like butter. At a touch, the flame of my torch turns that sturdy mass of steel into flowing liquid. What power!

Sometimes I cut scrap—old rods from the stoppers that close the opening on the ladles. Sometimes I help prepare molds for the next batch of steel—I cut off the steel that has spilled over the edges and has hardened there. Sometimes I'm called to the ladle-liners—steel has worked its way in between the bricks of the ladle lining and now they need to get those "frozen bricks" out. (This is tricky: cut the spilled steel, but not the ladle that it's attached to.) Sometimes I work the mixers (large heated drums that hold the molten iron until the furnaces are ready for it)—then it's iron, not steel, that we cut away. It has sloshed around the opening, building up layer after layer until we need to clean away big chunks. Sometimes there are spills on the railroad tracks—a mold full of molten steel has toppled and the hardened metal has to be cleared. All these jobs are small and are done with a hand-held torch.

But more often than not, I work in the "strawberry patch." What a colorful name for yet another ugly spot: an area just outside the BOP Shop where they dump the leftovers from ladles—big bowl-shaped chunks of steel and sediment that must be cut in half before a crane can lift them. Then I work with an unwieldy fifteen-foot rod that can reach far into the crevice I create as I burn. Out of that crevice comes a waterfall of fantastic colors. Through my blue-tinted glasses (now I use those glasses my fellow worker gave me on that first day), I watch it flow like candle wax: red, bright orange, magenta— snaking out, layer upon layer, each quickly fading to a paler shade. A thing of beauty. The only beauty in this gray and dusty place.

One day I meet a photographer—he's come to make an ad for Ford. It will show a spanking-new car springing effortlessly and ready-made from the molten steel. He is surprised to find women working in the mill and asks about burning. I proudly explain the process. Then, "Tell me," he says, "how do you breath in here?" How indeed? I develop a chronic cough.

Little by little, I begin to feel like a real part of the mill crew. I know I have made it when I begin breaking in new workers. Occasionally the new worker is a woman. On those days, the mill seems different: less austere, more hospitable. We relax, work smoothly; we have to answer to no one, have nothing to prove.

I try to befriend some of the old-time women—those left from the days of World War II when women did so many of the mill jobs: welders, track gang, crane operators, observers. I am fascinated with their life stories: How they came to the mill during the war; how they managed to stay on after everyone told them that their patriotic duty of taking a job in the mill was over, that their patriotic duty *now* was to go home and be a full-time wife. But, for the most part, they seem to resent us newcomers. They complain because we have it easier than they did, because we don't work hard enough, because we demand too much. And sometimes because too many of us are black.

We—all of us in the mill—work around the clock. There are no weekends, no holidays. Steelmaking, they tell us, can take no rest. We come and go—at eight, at four, at midnight. We meet briefly, passing the baton, so to speak, of our particular job. If no relief shows up, we stay for an extra turn (shift).

For single mothers with small children, the schedule is pure hell. Some might call it irony; I call it injustice: Single mothers who so desperately need these relatively well-paying jobs have to face impossible conditions. And no exceptions can be made. (Although I've seen a man get a "special schedule" to accommodate his working wife.)

Each week, people cluster around the bulletin board to decipher their schedule for the coming week. Some read it and are silent: pleased or perhaps resigned. Others object. "Sunday, first turn! No way! Let me talk to that scheduler!" And off they stomp to Nurven's office—a small shanty next to the general foreman's. More often than not they soon come back, sit glumly and silently in the shanty. Nurven is not easily persuaded.

Accidents happen everywhere in the mill. But none so gruesome as those in the BOP Shop. I am on the midnight turn when the first fatality happens. I am working in another area, but hear the voice on the intercom. I don't suspect death—the voice is urgent, but not panicky: "Get a foreman down here. We have a problem." In the morning, I learn it was amiable, deliberate, soft-spoken Slow Joe, his forklift truck tipped over by a railroad transfer car. Not long after, there is the remote-control train operator, squashed by the very cars he is manipulating. Then the millwright caught in the huge cables of the crane he was working on. Another millwright crushed when the equipment he is repairing collapses on him. A man burned to death by steel that spills over the edge of the ladle. Each death wrenches me, twists my heart for days. But despite it all, I feel immune. Confident no such thing will happen to me.

Confident, until it happens to a burner.

They tell me about it when I come into the mill for my afternoon turn. A freak accident, they say. He was working on a strawberry, cutting it in half as usual, when the molten steel that had gathered in the crevice "backfired" and spewed out on him. He has third degree burns on most of his body. He is still alive, they say, but barely. Better to die, they say.

I go to the spot where it happened. I stand looking at the half-finished strawberry—a strawberry like any of the dozens I had worked on. I nudge a piece of something on the ground with my metal-tipped shoe. It is a portion of the burner's safety glasses, melted and contorted. And I think: The only reason I'm standing here and not lying in a burn unit somewhere in the city is a question of schedule. I decide I no longer want to be a burner.

I put aside the tools of the burner: torch and striker, rods and hoses. I put aside my fireproof clothing. I take up a trowel and hammer; I become a ladle liner.

The ladle liners' job: build a floor and wall of fire brick inside the ladle, to keep the molten steel from burning right through the ladle. I heft the eighty-pound bags of cement, mixing it in big drums to make the "soup" that will seal the bricks together. I climb down into that huge container, big enough to hold two hundred tons of molten steel. I slap the bricks in place—clack, clack, clack—one layer, two layers. A wall to hold in all that heat and fire. Like a mason, I tap the brick with my hammer to make it break just so, the exact place, the exact size I need to fit this space, to snug this row.

Some of the ladles come to us direct from the teeming aisle, still hot from the recently poured steel. A pleasant thing on a cold night; not so in the summer.

Steelmaking—that's the heart of it. But the process, despite all our technological know-how, is still a surprisingly seat-of-the-pants operation. The final product is always iffy, and the furnace men are always nervous, often frantic. We try to have as little as possible to do with them, but all our work revolves around them. The ladles we line will carry the steel they create, poured fresh and boiling hot from the furnaces.

A good day—things are perking along. One after another, the torpedo-shaped railroad cars come rolling in, bringing iron from the blast furnace. Iron, scrap, a few bags of this and that dumped into the furnaces. Then what wild rushing sounds: flame and fire, roar and grumble. Steel is being made. Frenzy everywhere. Prepare the molds. Are there enough? On what track shall they be put? Send for the crane: Take this ladle here, bring one from there. Workers pull on their metallic-like coats, ready to approach the heat and fire. On the platform, the steel pourers crook their arms over their faces, a futile attempt to shield themselves from the heat, the glare. They move in quickly, manipulate the flow, take a sample and move away. Mold after mold is filled with the molten steel.

But not always—things do not always perk. Some fuck-up

somewhere: no iron from the blast furnace; a torpedo car "frozen," the iron crusted and unpourable; a furnace down. No steel is made for hours.

Then there is time to sit. We gather in the shanty. (A name that reveals historical origins. Now it is no more than a room to the side of the foreman's office). We talk about many things. (How Americans never live to be a hundred. "Speak for yourself!" says Love, indignant.) About the general foreman. (How he gives you days off, at the drop of a hat. "He don't know no number smaller than three," says Medicine Man.) Stories of the mill, perhaps already told too often, but part of our culture. There's always one newcomer who has not yet heard them. (How Beefco's dentures fell down through the opening in the ladle he was working on, landed in a bucket of mud and slush in front of Casper, who went running to the office, pale as the ghost for whom he is named. How Beefco went to retrieve them, wiped them on his pants, put them back in his mouth... How they tied Potato's shoes together while he slept... How Richie the foreman got fired for stealing... How....)

On those slow days, there's time for a leisurely lunch. We put packets of tacos, jars of soup, and foil-wrapped ears of corn on the salamanders, and stand around those drums of burning coke while the food heats. Once there was even a whole fish, wrapped and cooked, then spread open for everyone to feast on.

In summer, the heat is unbearable: In addition to nature's heat, we have the steelmaking heat and our heavy protective clothing. Everyone has their theory on how to combat it. Ice cubes in drinks, under hard hats, down shirts. The ice machine they installed in the shanty works overtime. But College Joe makes pot after pot of strong coffee on his little hot plate. "The hotter it gets," he insists, "the more coffee you hafta drink."

Seasons come and go in the mill. As far as I know, they will go on forever.

But one day, when the new schedule appears on the board, my name is on a separate list—the one entitled "furlough." I don't mind. This has happened before, and it is a welcome break. A chance to forget about shift work, a chance to live a normal life for a week or two. There are rumors that this layoff is bigger, farther-reaching, but I dismiss those rumors. I have just invested in a pair of new metatarsal shoes—I am sure I will be using them for a long time. I walk to the locker room in my new shoes, put them and the rest of my work clothes in my locker, walk out the gate, and never set foot there again. The big layoff has hit.

Reporters begin trekking to this far Southeast corner of Chicago—an area foreign to most of them. Nothing of consequence happens here. But now! Thousands laid off in one fell swoop. Mills closing with hardly a day's notice.

But what have they come to investigate? They nod listlessly, pencils suspended over their notebooks when we talk of women's hopes dashed, or returning to humdrum low-paying jobs. A Santa-less Christmas—that is what they want to hear. A starving child, foreclosures, suicides—these are the stories they drool over. And there *are* those stories. When one surfaces, they perk up, smile. They begin scribbling in their notebooks.

Despite all the attention, we feel invisible to the non-steelworker world. For some time, among ourselves, we keep our identity: We continue to meet at the union hall; government cheese, milk and honey are distributed; a job training program is started. But there is not much hope. Other mills—and other industries, too—are closing. Even workers with training—machinists, plumbers, welders, electricians—find it hard to get a job. Workers are being shepherded through a funnel into the shrinking job pool. A few make it through. Most are left to flounder. There is a feeling of life having come to a halt; a feeling of depression: What will become of us, our community? A feeling of betrayal: So many loyal years given to the mill; now the company turns its back.

Little by little, our ties weaken, and we scatter.

What has happened to that small group of women who

once called themselves steelworkers? I have lost track of all but a handful.

Some sought jobs similar to the mill—construction, apprenticeships. A few succeeded; most didn't. Some went back to previous jobs. Jobs that, when you came right down to it, they preferred all along. Jobs that pay less, but are less dirty, less dangerous, and, most importantly, have a decent work schedule—a schedule more compatible with raising kids. Some (like me) went back to school, seeking security and stability in nursing, computing, word processing, teaching. A few fled the Rust Belt, along with the industries, looking for the much-touted jobs in the Sunbelt. I don't know what happened to them.

Sometimes, when I go past that deserted parking lot, now overgrown with weeds, the fences battered and falling, and I see the BOP Shop looming there just beyond, I recall the days at the mill. Then a part of me signs with relief—the part of me that hated the midnight turns, the dirt, the danger, the harassment, the chaotic life. But another part of me is rather nostalgic—the part that felt the satisfaction of overcoming trepidation, that liked being a part of something BIG. The part of me that enjoyed so much the banter, the camaraderie, the oneness of the mill life. And if today, I were offered a chance to do it all over again, I'm not at all sure what my answer would be.

Fai Coffin • Drywall Rocker and Taper

Recently I was invited to speak at a workshop for women who wanted to enter the non-traditional job market. Of the participants, more than half were women in their forties who were raising families in poverty. They desperately wanted to find a job that would improve their family's economic status. Many of them had no college degree. And somehow, through a friend, a newspaper article or the radio, they had heard that the community college was running a class about non-traditional trades for women.

I enjoy sharing my experiences in this area of my life. When I was forty I realized I was no longer willing to be a secretary, to sit at a typewriter and stare at the four walls of my little cubicle in the heart of an enormous university. I was itching to try something new and challenging. I was also a single mother with growing economic responsibilities.

During the question and answer period several women asked, "Do you really know how to do sheet rock? Can you really lift that stuff by yourself?" (A piece of sheet rock is generally four feet by eight feet and can weight between fifty and eighty pounds, depending on its thickness.) "Yes," I would reply, "I know how to 'do sheet rock' and no, I can't lift a piece by myself. Some women can, although it's not usually necessary."

The workshop ended with a comment by one of the women

about how old dogs can learn new tricks. I had never thought about it like that, but there are a number of women who at forty, fifty, sixty and older have taken on entirely new challenges in their lives and survive, even thrive.

I entered the trades through knowing two men who had a sheet rock business and were looking for a helper. When I started, the tools were completely unfamiliar to me. I didn't even know how to hold a hammer the right way. Anyone who's ever trained with me has heard me say, lots of times, "You're choking up on the hammer." That means you're gripping it up near the hammer head—therefore using more of your energy than necessary, slowing up your work, and possibly causing injury to your arm. I learned it all from scratch with these two guys.

After a month, I was on my own. I don't recommend to anyone that they start the way I did, with no savings. But, on the other hand, I survived. Sheet rock work or house painting doesn't require a big outlay of cash to get started. Trades like carpentry and plumbing take a larger cash outlay, and they require much more training.

Getting started involves buying tools and supplies. I got my tools secondhand, for about 150 dollars. Supplies are usually covered by the advance payment on a job. You also have to begin selling yourself—otherwise known as advertising. Advertising can start with xeroxed hand-outs, but business cards are really helpful. You can also place ads in newspapers and community bulletins. One very useful advertisement can be a sign for the lawn of the job you are working on. But, most of all, you have to hustle. Hustling—that's dealing with the reality that you are out there on your own. I've received calls from ads placed in women's papers that have made it clear to me that many women don't really trust that I know what I'm talking about. It's hard for them to believe women can actually do dry wall, plumbing and carpentry work. We've all been conditioned to think that only men can do construction work and think rationally—women are supposed to take care of babies, be nurturers, mop floors.

But many women are willing to take a leap of faith and hire us to work in their homes. Me, that's how I earn a living, and I've been doing it for eight years now, which is longer than any other job I have ever had.

When I'm invited to speak to classes, it's usually in the middle of a workday. I wear my work clothes: grubby old overalls (painter's whites), T-shirt, white oxford-style shirt from the thrift shop, thermals if necessary. I wear my workboots, laces usually hanging on by a couple of threads. My eyeglasses and my watch are covered with a fine spray of paint. And usually I am too. I mention this because when I first started speaking in public I was worried about my appearance. If I had an appointment in the middle of the day or a luncheon meeting, I would change out of my work clothes. It took me a long time to stop being ashamed of my work clothes outside of my work place. Now I am proud.

The very first time I was asked to talk about my work, I was very nervous. What did I have to say that anyone would find useful? I spent four or five hours preparing for a twenty-minute presentation at a community college class. The presentation was scheduled in the middle of my work day and I didn't have time to change. The class instructor, Jan Denali, had been a journeylevel union carpenter but had to leave construction work due to onslaught of severe arthritis.

Jan introduced me and went to the back of the class. I started to speak, but my hands were shaking so hard I thought the sound of the paper rattling would drown me out and I kept forgetting what to say. Then Jan came up to me, offered some miraculous reassurance—and I relaxed.

When I finished, that whole group of women actually clapped. I felt deeply honored, and surprised. Most of all, I finally felt that all the hard knocks of my first six months as a self-employed dry wall finisher had been worthwhile.

There were some really hard times in the beginning. Maybe the worst was when I got ripped off by a contractor who skipped town before paying me the 440 dollars he owed me. I had to apply for food stamps and borrow little bits from my friends to help me get through that period. Another time I was working in a man's house, taping the newly hung sheet rock in a large living room. I was up on the ladder, sanding—when suddenly I felt a hand on my thigh. There was the owner coming up my ladder, pawing at me. I was furious and, briefly, petrified. I took a deep breath, put my foot down on the hand he was using to hold onto the ladder and said something like, "Not only are you going to get off this ladder right now, but you are also going to pay for the rest of this job in advance." He mumbled something like, "You tough bitches ain't no better than men," climbed down the ladder and left the room, slamming the door. A few minutes later, he slipped a check for the full amount under the door. That was really amazing.

After I'd been in the trade for about two years, I was invited to speak on a panel with three other women for a local Women in the Trades Fair. When I got there the hall was full. The organizers had a sign made for each of us, with our name and trade. There it was—FAI COFFIN, ROCKER AND TAPER. It was now official. I had survived. I don't remember much of what I said—except that I started by talking about how it felt to be up there with that sign. I was a very proud survivor at that moment.

Recently a small group of us set up a hands-on exhibit at a local home show. Our group of four women included a plumber, a carpenter, a home energy auditor and myself. Lots of people came and stared. We encouraged women to pick up the tools and try them. It was great watching women (who said they had never used a hammer) drive a nail deep into a two-by-four. I set up a sheet rock exhibit so people could see how it was done, drive in a couple of nails and try using the mud. (Mud is the trade name for joint compound.) Kids were the most enthusiastic, but some of the parents would encourage their sons and forbid their daughters—saying it would ruin their clothes. After explaining that mud washes out of clothes easily, I would make a deal—I'll show your sons if you'll let me show your daughters also. Mostly it worked. At some point an older woman came up to me and told me she was amazed to see women doing this work. "And of course I see that you have lots of gray in your hair. How old are you?" When I told her I was forty-four she was surprised. She had heard there were some women working on a construction site in her neighborhood, but they were much younger. She finally asked me if I worked in people's homes—she needed some work. Would I come look at her house?

I did and she hired me. While I was doing that job, she told me she was a writer for her local senior citizen's center paper and that she wanted to do a story. She also asked me to come to the center and show the film *Rosie the Riveter*. That was a wonderful experience. The group loved the movie and we had a great discussion. Afterwards, when we were having a snack, one of the women came up to me and said that she was very sorry she hadn't discovered this work when she was younger. She had had a long experience of marital abuse, and now felt terribly vulnerable. She told me that I looked strong and proud, that I didn't look like a victim. I suggested that she get into a local self-defense class.

When I left I thought about what she said and realized that, of course, I feel very differently about myself now than when I was a secretary. I may someday go back to doing secretarial work, but I can't imagine taking the kind of shit that I used to.

Eight years ago, hundreds of buckets of mud, tons of sheet rock, nails and bandaids, miles of paper tape and endless gallons of paint later, I'm still at it. I'm not rich yet, but I have been earning a living for myself and my daughter. Now I'm helping to put her through college—with the assistance of scholarships, grants and loans. I have also helped to develop a training program for young, economically disadvantaged women/girls called GRIT (Girl Renovators in Training). This program provides instruction in carpentry, sheet rock, plastering and painting, as well as weatherization. It provides situations where students actually use their skills in rehabbing formerly abandoned housing. GRIT participants usually join the program because it offers a four-hundred-dollar stipend for summer employment, but by the end of the eight-week program, their self-image is changed—they have a set of tools to keep and some of them find work in the building trades.

During the course of my eight years, I have hired a number of women to work with me, one as a partner for four years. I have also hired several of the GRIT graduates, one of whom has been working with me for three years. Just recently this nineteen-year-old woman, Yvette Rivers, was notified that she passed the carpenter's apprenticeship test, and she will be moving on, making room for another GRIT grad to take her place.

I've had to train almost everyone who has worked with me, which has meant that I don't make as much money, but my work environment is the best possible. It also means that I can help more women develop marketable skills that might otherwise be inaccessible.

It's only been recently that I've found another woman to work with me, Chava Tuckman, who is at my skill level. I remember the first day she joined us. I showed her what had to be done and she said, "Okay, let me get started." When we took our lunch break I looked at her work. It was beautiful. Chava had worked union, been self-employed, done subcontracting, but had never worked with a crew of women. She was absolutely ecstatic. How amazing it was for her the day she came into work with premenstrual cramps and was dogging her way through the pain until one of us offered a back rub.

When I've talked to classes or groups about the work I do, one subject I always discuss is the "isms"—racism and sexism particularly. I am a white woman, a mother, of working-class background, Jewish, lesbian, forty-eight years old, and second-generation politically outspoken. I am very aware that as a woman, the odds are stacked against me in this job market. When I first started, people who called in response to my ad would ask to speak to my husband or the man who did the work. I would explain that there was no husband or man—that I was the worker. Often they would just hang up at that point.

I learned to avoid distinguishing pronouns: "They're not here." "We'll come out to do a bid." Sometimes doors would still slam in my face. That doesn't happen much now, but I don't advertise to the general public anymore. I advertise in women's papers. My business card says, "Hire women in the trades."

I have found the community of women, for the most part, to be a great source of support for this work. One of my few complaints, but an important one, has to do with racism among some of the white women. It is not very subtle. One of the most noticeable markings of it is that people who hire my crew are much more comfortable with my having the key to their homes than my co-workers, who are women of more color than me, but who are certainly as trustworthy as I.

One issue I haven't mentioned is age. I started this work when I turned forty, four months after a partial hysterectomy. I wasn't very strong, partly because of the surgery, but also because of sheer laziness. And, of course, most of my prior work experience had been deskbound. I asked one of my friends if she would work out with me for a half hour every morning. Without that workout, my aging might have become more of a stumbling block. Sometimes I look for the ways that getting older makes work harder. On the positive side, there have been a number of times over the years when I think my age has been a benefit. It has helped me maintain a certain amount of respect and assumption of wisdom. But salespeople at the local paint store sometimes refer to me as their little silver-haired lady. And I do stick out in a crowd of painting contractors, even in my painter's whites.

I no longer do much sheet rock hanging—but that's mostly due to a car accident in which I broke my neck and injured my back, causing residual pain that is aggravated when I have to hang a sheet rock ceiling.

I do grow afraid of the time when I can't do my work anymore. I have no pension or social security check to look forward to for financial security. I have always been an organizer and a networker, though, so I figure that I'll organize something. But that's indeed an area of real fear that I have not yet faced very bravely.

There's something I want to say about economic class and how it affects us all. I grew up in an immigrant working-class family with a strong focus on survival tied to community. I believe strongly in the right of all people to a decent standard of living. To me there is a terrible loss to all in the present economically exploitive system. I believe that we can learn to work together to build a better world—where not one woman has any less value than another. And perhaps if we can develop a new system of values lovingly among ourselves, we can turn things around. That's my dream.

Rose Melendez • Police Officer
Interview by Molly Martin

The process of entering the San Francisco Police Department (SFPD) started for me in 1973. That's when community groups got together and filed a suit to open up the job to women and minorities, and set up training programs to prepare applicants for the Civil Service exams. At that time there was no special recruitment policy for women, and as a matter of fact the title for the job was police*man.*

In its tests, the SFPD emphasized the importance of physical strength. The agility tests, as I saw them, had been set up to exclude women. The written test and oral interview were no problem, but the physical test was difficult for many women who didn't have the training. One community group set up "Project Agility," to train women to pass the agility tests. They got a federal grant to organize the training and they would put us through all kinds of tasks, including those that were going to be on the exam. For example: vaulting over a six-foot wall, and "body drag," where you had to lift a 150-pound bag of sand and roll it around in your arms. Some of the tests just weren't relevant; you never pick up a 150-pound person and roll him or her around in your arms.

In 1974, a thousand women applied for the job, and out of that about four or five hundred would show up for the "Project Agility" training. I participated in the training myself and also helped to train other women. Once we got involved, just knowing what happened to the other women helped us develop a camaraderie. Knowing that the Department didn't want us united us even more. The stronger women would help the weaker ones. Then minority men got involved in the training because they wanted to make it too, and they would help us. We became a huge group of people who were striving together for a goal that others were trying to stop us from attaining. We helped with psychological counseling; we'd have rap sessions where we'd ask each other, "Am I ever gonna make it? Is this worth it?" Most of us got through the test, and eventually the SFPD was forced to drop some of the agility tests that weren't relevant.

I had never been interested in becoming a police officer, although my brother was. My dad died when we were both kids, and as the older sister, I took over the household because my mother spoke no English. My brother has been very supportive of my career and has never spoken ill of any women. He entered the police academy with me and graduated in my class. He is still in the Department, and I think he's an excellent officer.

I was recruited by a Latino officer. I was working in the Mission (a predominantly Latin neighborhood) as a youth employment counselor and he said to me, "Someone like you would be great. You speak Spanish and English, you're young, you have the energy. Come on, you can do it." Finally I just showed up at one of the training programs. My interest was aroused, and also my determination was strengthened by the Department saying, "You can't do it."

The first two classes of sixty recruits, in July and November of 1975, included about thirty women each. The instructors let us know right away they didn't want us, saying, "We'd like to welcome you all here, even though we know a lot of you shouldn't be here." They weren't prepared for women. There were no locker room facilities. They put us in men's uniforms. At one point they tried making us shower with the men, then they split us up because it was worse for the men—they were shyer than we were.

The training techniques were developed more to set us up to fail than to train us for the job. In the physical training they set a standard that had never existed before. You had to complete a certain number of critical tasks to graduate from the academy. It was brutal. I remember people coming out of there with broken collar bones from being whacked, necks all twisted—men and women. Some of the takedowns and techniques they used were not properly developed or explained. You were told to just pick someone up and wham 'em down on the ground. All kinds of injuries resulted. I think in the backs of their minds they wanted us to get hurt so we'd quit. A lot of guys were fresh out of Vietnam, and some—not all of them—thought they were in a war zone. When the instructor said, "You grab her and throw her down NOW"—boom, there you were. It was like an order from the commander-in-chief. Eventually, many of the guys sensed that they were being used to get the women out, and they started working with us. But it was the sense of unity and the support of the other women that got us through those seventeen weeks in the academy.

After the academy training we were sent out to district stations for field training, which is like on-the-job training with a senior officer. We'd work the different shifts—night, swing and day. We spent three weeks at each of three different stations. I started out at Mission Station, and I trained with an officer there who was a good teacher. He told me right off the bat, "Hey, I know what they've been putting you through, but you've made it this far, and I'm going to help you get through the rest of the way. I'll teach you what I know." The next three weeks I worked with a guy who said, "Okay, kid, get out there and do it." Then he sat in the car and just watched, so I had to learn on my own. The third guy slept most of the time while I did all the work.

For the first year after my training, I worked the night shift at Potrero Station. None of the men would talk to me. That was the worst. If they had said something negative, I could have dealt with it, but when people just ignore you like you're not there.... We'd be driving around, midnight till eight in the morning, and my partner wouldn't talk to me all night long. Or we'd respond to a call and my partner—it was always a man then—would handle everything, and I'd feel like a little shadow, asking myself, "Why am I here?"

That was a question I asked myself seriously when I was assigned to work with an officer who had problems getting along with partners. That's what would happen to rookies—they'd make you work with the guys everybody else hated. One night he drove us to a secluded area and stopped the patrol car. When I asked why we were stopping, he said he wanted to shoot rats. Then he opened his shirt, pulled out a small handgun and pointed it directly at me. "I just want to see how fast you women cops can run," he said.

I was in shock. It was the first time anyone had ever pulled a gun on me—and it was a fellow officer. I couldn't believe what was happening, but I put my left hand up to get his attention and at the same time I reached for my gun with my right hand. In the most forceful voice I could muster I said, "Take me back to the station *now.*" He protested that he was just kidding, but we drove directly back to the station, and I let him get out of the car first so I could keep an eye on him. When I reported the incident to the sergeant, he just laughed it off. But I stuck up for myself and refused to work with that officer again. He's no longer in the Department. A situation like that wouldn't occur today, but that was before we began using psychological tests to screen out people with problems.

At first I was a novelty to the public. "Oooh, a lady cop!" After a while, they started accepting the idea. Sometimes they'd appreciate seeing a man and a woman. We'd go to a domestic dispute, husband and wife going at it, and we were able to relate to both people. He would deal with the man and I would deal with the woman. Two male officers might have just said, "Come on buddy, why don't you just take a walk and cool down." Instead, I would say to the woman, "Are you hurt? Has this happened before?" She'd be amazed that someone was talking to her. So the communication seemed to be better, and the image of police started to change once male/female teams showed up.

People didn't take advantage of the fact that I was a woman. They knew I was a cop. But I also had to deal with sexist attitudes. In an arrest situation sometimes men would say to me, "Well, what are *you* going to do with me." Then I'd have to come on strong and say "Hey, buddy, just cool it. Don't mess with me." I've always been able to take care of myself but now I had to develop a body language and presence that said: "No, no no, you're not hitting me; you might hit your wife, but you are not going to hit *me*." It took time, but soon I could walk in and gear my communication to the particular circumstances.

I found that I was having to control situations that I had never dealt with before, like a homocide. I had never seen a dead body in my whole life, let alone one that was all shot up. But I had to maintain control. You're dealing with emotion all the time in police work. People believe the popular image of police work promoted by TV shows—you rush out there, shoot-em-up, speed around in your car. It's not like that! We *can't* do that. I would lose my job if I ran around like a madwoman chasing and shooting everybody. These TV programs are just wreaking havoc on kids. If I were a parent, I wouldn't allow my kid to see something like that, because it's too violent. It's not real life.

The reality is that ninety percent of my job is communication. You have the five percent where you're in a critical life-and-death situation, and then another five percent when you have to be physical. But the majority is communication and you learn how to express yourself. Questioning a rape victim, for example, I have to be sensitive to what he or she has gone through. The hardest thing for me in police work—and I've handled all kinds of situations—is to make a death notification to a family or a lover. When I have to knock on the door and say, "Excuse me, but I have some bad news for you," that just chokes me up.

Since 1977, my partner has been a woman, Pam Wermes. Pam and I had graduated in the same academy class in 1976, and we both ended up at Northern Station, which is in the

Tenderloin, a rough neighborhood in downtown San Francisco. We had been working with different guys and finally I said to her, "I've been thinking about this. I'd really like to work with you as a partner. Why don't we approach the lieutenant and tell him we want to work together." When we walked into his office and told him, he started laughing. Well, my attitude came out right away. I said, "What's so funny?" We convinced him to give us a try, and he put us in the felony car. Now, Northern Station at that time was very busy, and the felonies there are likely to be homocides, knifings, shootings or bank robberies. They figured we'd botch up and probably leave. Well, of course, we loved it.

We made fantastic arrests. I remember one midnight shift while patrolling Union Street, we routinely cruised down an alley. We saw a disturbance, but couldn't really tell what was going on. It looked like three or four guys fighting. Poor visibility is a problem that goes with night work. As we got close, we heard one of them shout, "It's the cops!" and two of them took off running. Pam jumped out of the car, and the other two took off. That's when I saw one of them had a gun. This all happened in a matter of seconds. Pam was on foot, I was driving, and at the same time working the radio putting out information and calling for help. Just as I turned the corner, I saw the guy pull his gun and point it at Pam. I didn't have time to get out, so I ran over the curb and hit him with the car, pinning him against the wall. When he saw me coming, he panicked and dropped the gun. We made an arrest and he was convicted.

When Pam and I first started working together, it was very new to see two women officers. We would respond to some calls from women who just wanted to have men around. I'm serious—you know, women who live in hotels by themselves and want to have the guys over for a drink or whatever. We'd knock on the door, "Police," and she'd answer the door, "Police! I called for a man!"

Men were not used to being arrested by women, so at times we'd have to fight. Our academy was real hard; I mean, we learned to fight. So whenever anybody challenged us on the street just because we were women, it was like we were back at home base. Here was somebody telling us we couldn't do it. The poor individuals would be laid out in a matter of seconds. The public learned quickly, but there were always some individuals who still wanted to talk to men; they didn't think women could handle it. I found that Third World people were much more accepting of women with guns. We had the most problems with white, middle-class men. They were rude, and we'd just have to be really blunt.

Feminists were not necessarily supportive of women in the police force. In the beginning, my women friends said, "Why do you want to be in police work? That's sick. You're arresting people and putting them in jail." But I'm also helping people. *They're* calling *me*. I'm not going to their homes and forcing myself on them. When I can help them in an empathetic way and provide them with referrals or whatever it is they need, I feel satisfied.

The negative attitude toward police did cause problems within the women's community. When we first started, women had no support in the Department. So we set up a women's support group where we could meet and talk about our problems and how to approach the administration with some ideas to better our working conditions. We didn't want to meet at the Hall of Justice or at one of the police stations because we wouldn't have any privacy. The San Francisco Women's Building, a four-story building in the Mission, was a new project of the women's community, and we thought it would be an ideal place to meet once a month. When we approached them about renting a room, I was flabbergasted by the response. They said, "No way, because you're representing a segment of society we don't approve of." "But," I said, "we also represent women—Third World women—all kinds of women who are in a non-traditional job." They responded, "We have nothing against you personally. It's just what you represent." And I said, "My job is more important than me?"

We finally found a church where we could meet. But the incident split the women's community down the middle. Some were very against us meeting at the Women's Building, and others said, "Hey, that's not fair. We're women, we're the ones who fought to get them in the police department, and now you're not even giving them space to meet in our building?" Then the whole thing got in the papers, and I got called into the chief's office; he was worried it would reflect on the Department. Finally, the Women's Building told us they would give us free space, but we declined—we were fine in our church.

The women's support group kept going for about four months, but eventually broke apart internally. In 1984 we started up again, and now we're going pretty strong. There are thirty to forty women participating. We have single women, married women, lesbians, single mothers, every kind of woman. We deal with getting the Department to provide better facilities, medical care for women, pregnancy care, and many other issues.

Another group of us got together to address the sexual harassment that was causing life-threatening situations on the street. For example, when you're calling in for help or you need backup and somebody cuts you off, or starts talking so you can't get through, or they don't show up when you call for help. Some of the men got tired of this too; they were getting cut off on the radio just because they were friends with or worked with one of the women. Until recently, harassment had been tolerated. But the chief took it seriously when we approached it as an officers' safety issue. Our point is that we should be able to do our jobs with mutual respect, and work in a safe environment where we can all get along.

We developed a professionalism panel—men and women—who had experienced sexual harassment, and now we're providing awareness training. We discuss different types of harassment that occur subtly: the ignoring, the obnoxious comments that aren't meant to be heard by anybody except you. The training is working; it's changing attitudes. It's opened up communication and allowed us to confront the issue. You can say, "Hey, Joe, cool it. I don't like that," and he knows what you mean.

Reports of harassment are now heard by the professionalism panel and directed to the chief's attention for disciplinary action, and the number of incidents has slacked off as a result. Offenders get pulled from the street and get stuck doing a detail somewhere in communications. Nobody wants to work inside pushing papers. The administration's behind us, and I think our efforts are improving working conditions for everyone on the force.

Police work has definitely come a long way since women entered this job. In the years that I've been in, I've seen dramatic changes in the Department—in training, in dealing with the public, in communication between co-workers, in equipment, in facilities, and so on. There are now close to 200 women on a force of 1800, and more women are coming in all the time. In the last five years the composition of the Department has totally changed. It's more educated, more professional.

It's hard to categorize police work—is it a trade or a profession? Is it white-collar or blue-collar? It's a very physical job, but it's also a very legal, technical job. When we're out there making a case, if we don't write it up properly it's thrown out. Sometimes we know the law better than the attorneys. There are many technical tasks that we accomplish on a daily basis. I think one of the hardest things for a young person coming into this job to grasp is all the little technicalities. Let's say you have a homocide. What do you have to do? First you have to find out if the person's dead, so you have to touch the person. Then you have to get the ambulance there or a medical doctor. They're the only ones that pronounce death; you cannot. Then the coroner. If it's a homocide, you have to call in the proper investigative units, the photography, the lab. You can't let anyone else touch the scene. You have to coordinate all of this. And then, you have to write the report.

I'm a training officer now. It's only been in the last several years that women have started to train new recruits in the field. There are people who come in who shouldn't be doing this job. Some people have communication problems, some are afraid and not in control of their own emotions. Some people are poor learners, they can't hear what you tell them. It doesn't matter how big you are. It has nothing to do with strength or size. I trained a woman about four-foot-nine who was one of my best recruits. Some women think they're guys. That's just as bad as being cutesy and going out with all your co-workers. I never tried to be one of the boys, because I never wanted to be. It's taken years to be able to kid with the guys and not expect them to come back with some sexist remark.

Personally, racism has affected me less than sexism. I've never been seen as being Latina because I've always been *woman*. That also seems true for Asian women. We're more invisible than blacks. Black women have had a harder time. They have a double-edged sword to deal with: sexism and racism. The older black men have always kept their racial identity. They have also been very supportive to women. And I've never forgotten my roots. I was born and raised in San Francisco, but I'm Puerto Rican.

Sometimes I think this job does reinforce racism. You see a side of life that you've never seen before. The blacks, Latins and Asians that most police officers deal with on the job may be the only ones they ever see. I can't stereotype people because I keep my connection to Third World people. My friends are mostly Third World. Police often associate mostly with police. I don't. The only way to change a person's attitudes is to expose him or her to other groups.

I love my work. I enjoy the diversity of dealing with people. You never have the same situation. You can never be complacent. After my first two years, I might have said, "I don't know about this." But now I'm doing just what I want—the women's support group, the professionalism panel, working with the administration. I like feeling that I'm changing things from within, and having the satisfaction of seeing young women come into a better working situation.

Mari Lochhaas • Fisher

0430 It's so hard to tear my body from that warm bunk, muscles aching, hands burning from a hundred tiny cuts, to roll out into the chill, damp morning. The steady drip from the camper roof forecasts the weather for today: FOG.

Not your common garden-variety fog, but blanketing, muffling, permeating Oregon coastal fog. The type that falls from the rigging in great dollops, stinging my eyes. It seeps through raingear, wool sweaters and long underwear. The casual observer might call it light rain or even "Oregon mist," but rain comes down sideways here, and the complete lack of visibility qualifies it as fog. My enthusiasm, such as it wasn't, wanes.

I slide down the ramp and sleepwalk down the dock. The ghostly boats float dreamily in the fog, awaiting their masters' awakening. I step aboard my dory by habit, assuming it's in the same spot. If someone else tied up here I'd probably fish their boat until noon before I realized why everything was out of place.

The engine coughs and rumbles, then purrs. I thaw out the day's bait and put on my damp raingear. It's better this way, damp. I'll be soggy in an hour, anyway. I may as well start out that way.

I wipe the fog from the inside of the cabin windows. The open-backed overhead cover, common to dories, can't keep the fog out. I'll need to be sharp with the loran this morning. I wait for its blinking yellow lights to settle on coordinates. My loran is outdated; its LED shows only two five-digit numbers, which correspond to my position on a grid that I've superimposed on charts of the coastline. I must depend on my water-logged, fish-blood-splattered notebook for the coordinates of buoys, jetties and other fixed objects.

Beside the list of coordinates for navigating the channel are compass courses to steer for the next buoy. This technique of navigating with compass, loran and notebook usually works, providing I compensate correctly for current and wind. This is a broad provision so early in the morning.

Other pages of the notebook list the coordinates for the other ports from which I fish. Wildly strewn in between are isolated coordinates with "pinnacle," "crab pot" or 🐟 next to them, indicating their value.

The numbers on my loran are now a constant display and correspond to the ones in my notebook. I strain my eyes in the dim compass light to make out the hen scratch scribbling in the notebook. Although I have the courses memorized, a quick review can't hurt. I think, for the two thousandth time, I should get a new loran.

Casting off, I feel my way down the channel, depending on my outdated equipment to make the dog-leg turn at the jetty, hidden in the fog. The ebbing tide humps up a bit at the bar, but it's not even rolling, so I'm off to the fishing grounds.

0930   I wake up. Somehow, someone set the trolling poles, ran to the grounds, set the gear and landed twenty-five Chinook and seventeen Coho salmon. As I am the only one on the boat, and it is a very small boat, I will have to assume it was me. I wish someone had told me I was going fishing; I would have brought a warmer shirt. It's wet and cold out here, but at least the wind isn't blowing. Yet.

I decide to run the gear, to see what I set while sleep-fishing. I engage the gurdy and its hydraulic spool begins pulling up the thin stainless steel cable, with its fifty pound lead, from thirty fathoms below. I have six of these wires, theoretically separated from one another by differing lead weights, floats, and attachment to the trolling poles. Occasional tangles due to the current, fish or bad timing attest to the reality of the system.

I watch the first line snap coming up the wire, like a stainless steel clothspin caught between the brass stops. A pair of these stops on the wire every three fathoms keeps the snap in its place and gives me an easy way to measure my gear as I let it out.

I peer back from the snap along the imperceptible monofilament leader to the bright spinning flasher. Behind the flasher darts the hoochie, a fake replica of a squid, this one painted with red-rimmed eyes and blue and yellow stripes that hide the hook in the white tentacles. I watch its action and make a mental note to increase my speed. Trolling at two knots, slight speed changes can alter a salmon's opinion of my gear. I remove the snap and coil and leader in the gear box.

The next spread, as each snap-flasher-hoochie unit is called, has a fish. A shaker, a salmon under legal size, futilely pulls at the hook. I pull the leader down, draw my gaff up on the barbless hook to slip it from the fish's jaw, and the shaker darts away.

There's a Chinook on the next spread, maybe a shaker, maybe a keeper. I hoist it aboard and lay it gingerly against the measuring line. It's a quarter-inch too short. The hefty fine that accompanies illegal fish decides its fate. I gently return it to its home. It leaps clear of the water then furiously charges the next flasher. I laugh at such arrogance. That one will be fun to catch when it grows up.

The following three spreads have no fish. The wire suddenly pulls back and I realize something strong has been sleeping on the next spread. I stop the gurdy as the snap comes up, place the gaff within easy reach. Slowly, I pull in the leader until I see a twenty-pound Chinook, only lightly hooked. I quickly check for any nearby boats, then concentrate on the fight.

This fish will bring sixty dollars at the dock. I must strike exactly right with the gaff, its sharp steel point must hook to hold. I balance its familiar weight on the two-foot-long wooden handle. My favorite gaff, don't fail me now! I gently play the fish up to the boat; it veers and sheers away, I play it back again. It runs twice more, then, in a moment of fatigue, it slows a little too close to the boat. I plant the gaff, full force, in the gill plate and haul up with both hands as the fish thrashes to break free. I drag it over the transom and it's aboard! For a moment I atavistically rejoice in the triumph of the primitive battle, then I mercifully dispatch my opponent with a sharp blow to the head.

Still thrilled with the success of landing such a fish, I go back to running the gear. I pull up the next spread and quickly land a nice ten-pound coho. As it hits the deck, it spits the hook, slithers away from the gaff blow, flops its way forward, over the other fish, over the coaming and into the cockpit, splashing blood and slime everywhere. Disgusted with the extra trouble this fish is causing, I climb out of the gaff hatch to retrieve it.

A boat suddenly looms ahead, seemingly inches away. But it's an illusion. We are really several yards apart, probably a full minute from complete disaster. I pull the old "dory doubleback," spin on my gear in a 180-degree turn. It's my friend, Big Boat Bill. His schooner is three times bigger than my boat and not nearly as maneuverable. He apologizes for the close call. Apparently, he hadn't picked me up on radar. Over the radio, he admonishes me to get a radar of my own.

I know, I know. Last year I bought a new engine. I'm just getting enough ahead now to buy new electronics. They will do everything for me: lorans that store a hundred waypoints, tell my course and speed, my ETA (estimated time of arrival), my sister's birthdate, and how many calories in my last meal; radars that plot the true course and speed as well as sexual persuasion of the captain for every boat within sixty-four miles. Marvelous technology which I can hardly wait to own.

But when was my last meal? No dinner last night, too tired, no breakfast yet. Let's see what's dry and easily available. I still have to keep a constant vigil for fellow fishers. No, I'd better run through the gear, I see a few fish shaking the lines.

1340 At last, the hot bite has tapered off, the fish are all cleaned and the fog has miraculously lifted. I can see now that forty boats have been working this thirty-fathom curve, yet I had seen only seven in the fog. Of course, I had a distressingly close look at the rigging of each of those boats. With the improved visibility, the boats work closer together, plying a glassy sea beneath an impossible blue sky. A rare day on this coast.

I dodge a crab pot, long stuck in the sand and lethal to my gear. That pot could strip my lines of flashers, leaders and leads, costing me hundreds of dollars and a couple of hours re-rigging (a write-off I could do without), yet I have fished around it all day. Lucky. I write down the loran coordinates to increase my luck in the future.

I finally wolf down a dubious-looking cheese sandwich and some slightly fermented juice (I really should get some groceries soon), while chatting on the radio. There is always a fisherman willing to talk in times of boredom or panic. They have always been such a help, advising on mechanical difficulties, or offering hints on what to fish with, or how the weather is, or who is really catching, most of it lies. And they *never* offer "where."

Everyone must learn "where" alone. It's part of initiation. If I survive long enough to accumulate a few fishing holes, then locales will be exchanged, in limited quantities, with liberal embellishments, misleading hints and probably in code. It's all part of the game.

I finish lying on the radio and return to running gear in the glorious sunshine. I've wandered into a patch of hake, a ubiquitous junk fish. I wander out of them, stripping the squishy fish from my gear. As there is no reasonable market for them, I leave them floating in my wake. I feel badly about the waste of time, bait and fish, but not as badly as the hake feel when seagulls swarm down to shriek last rites.

1930 The salmon start biting in earnest again. I've been trolling towards home, but must back tack to return to the best fishing. I warily watch the fog bank, crouching offshore, awaiting its return with the night. I don't want to get caught out after dark in the fog. The hours it takes to grope my way back into the channel without a radar are a bad memory of times when greed kept me out too late.

The fog bank holds steady. The fish continue to climb aboard until the sun vanishes into the encompassing shroud on the horizon. I pull my gear on board and push the throttle—WIDE OPEN!

I feel great now, flying across the still water, burning past larger trollers in a flash of fossil fuel fury, fish hold full and planing over the bar. Around the corner by the small boat docks, I slow to haul my trolling poles. An older woman tends her crab ring in the twilight. She smiles and raises her hands in question. I flash seventy-five fingers and call out, "A great day!" Then I spin the wheel and race to the fish company.

While waiting for another boat to unload, I wonder about the woman. Did she once work a job, rewarded with pay and benefits? Did she work at home, rewarded with fine children and love? Or did she work, like so many, for no reward at all? I wonder if she was one of the forerunners, the few women who broke the ground for me. They walked a more precipitous edge and made my break with tradition a little easier.

It's my turn. I whirl to the dock, jump off, tie up, swing open the hatch. A couple of loitering fisherman groan. The buyer rolls his eyes, his helper comes down to unload. I accept the proffered beer and the compliment, in a soft foreign accent from the helper, "You've done the best today, so far." I thank him, and glide over to the slip. Exhausted, I tie up the boat, clean the fish hold, turn off the electronics. I stumble up the ramp, pick up my fish ticket and another beer, and crawl into my camper.

2230 Contemplating the effort required to cook the snapper I filleted this afternoon, I opt for more sleep. As my mind quits churning with the thousands of projects to be done, I question my motives for choosing this line of work. A thousand-dollar day does add incentive, but most days aren't this productive. I'm not working for the rent and I'm certainly not here because of the fantastic lifestyle of working and sleeping as total existence. Maybe I'm working to fulfill the dreams of my aunts who read my letters, vicariously living the adventures they missed. Perhaps it's for the men and women who financed my operation or generously taught me their trade. Or maybe it's for my friend's young daughter, who, when told by the boys, "A girl can't be the fisherman in the 'Fishing' game," adamantly stated, "Well, Mari's a girl and she fishes."

As I drift off to sleep, I hope I bring a warmer shirt, tomorrow.

Gloria Nelson • Operating Engineer

The trip across town seemed to take forever and my apprehension was growing by the minute. I'd never before applied for a job I wasn't fully qualified for—I was used to knowing the answers to every possible question the interviewer might ask. I wasn't enrolled in the school of engineering nor had I taken the required surveying courses. And I wasn't male. It seemed foolish to be driving my motorcycle across town when I was so under-qualified, but I really wanted to work outside. After a winter spent in organic chemistry labs and libraries I needed to feel the earth under my feet.

I was ready to turn my bike around and go home when a severe thunderstorm broke out. My entire being concentrated on keeping my bike on the road and I continued on to the city's field engineering offices.

I didn't even merit a glance out the window as I parked my bike. When I got inside I found there was no women's bathroom, so I took off my rain gear and fluffed out my hair in the huge entrance room that was filled with coat racks and dozens of picnic tables. Adjacent to this room were offices for the field engineering staff and the garbage collector's supervisors and dispatchers. By the time I'd gotten my waist-length hair out from under my helmet I was already receiving curious looks from men strolling past the open office doors. Sid, the city's head field engineer, came out and graciously escorted me into his office. The interview was a casual conversation. After a while Sid said that he found me sincere, but that I wasn't qualified for the job. However, he pointed out that the following year the city's affirmative action office would be making his department hire minorities and women—and that he'd rather hire someone with desire and determination now than hire someone later that the affirmative action office picked out.

Then he told me that there was something I should know before accepting his offer, something about working with an all-male crew. The way Sid was blushing and stammering as he searched for an appropriate way to phrase it, I began to think that maybe the men started their day by jacking off or something equally crude. Finally Sid found his way to explain that when men are together in a group they have a tendency to use rather "flowery" language. I'd have to be prepared to ignore it since it was probably impossible for them to change.

I explained to Sid that my dad had raced amateur stock cars, so I was familiar with how men talked when they were in a pack. I could ignore it. With that settled he promised that the department would provide plenty of on-the-job training. I was to start the next day.

In the morning I came zipping in only to be stopped dead in my tracks by one hundred male garbage collectors and laborers that were assembled in the large room I had to cross. They were all ready for me with catcalls and whistles. I escaped into the engineering offices, only to be glared at by every inspector and survey crew man working for the department. Normally they would go straight to their assigned jobs, not to the office, but since the word had spread that a "girl" was starting, they had all stopped by the office to requisition more paper clips, rubberbands and other essential items. Sid introduced me to my crew chief and hustled us out.

The first day I pounded stakes until my hands bled. We did more work that day than we did on any other day during my three seasons with the city. The reality that even the men were dragging didn't sink into my brain. I thought every day would be like that. The first day of haying season on my uncle's farm made me feel that bad or worse, so I knew the muscle aches were temporary. What I didn't know then was that the crew had spent the previous afternoon preparing for my first day. My first day wasn't normal; they had tried to break me.

I was in a daze when Sid asked me if I'd be back the next morning.

And they were shocked when I arrived the next morning, leather gloves in hand.

I started out as the stake pounder, but in two seasons I'd worked up to alternate crew chief. The third year when Sid called to invite me back to work, he started out by apologizing: He'd already filled all the survey crew positions before calling me. I started freaking out, but then he continued explaining that he thought I'd be a good inspector. He wondered if I would be willing to be trained. What a silly question!

That summer working as an inspector I nagged the operators to show me how their machines worked. Every now and then they'd let me run the bulldozer and dig a few buckets with the backhoe.

The backhoe operator treated me like his tomboy daughter. He thought we were almost family since he and my dad had raced stock cars together when I was five years old. He asked me why I didn't get my own piece of equipment. I told him I didn't know how, so he explained his union's apprenticeship program. I didn't know that he was so knowledgeable because he was on the union's board of directors. The next day he arrived with the apprenticeship papers in hand and helped me fill them out.

When I took the application to the union hall, the office woman told me that they weren't accepting applications until November. She said that she'd note that I was in early, but that I should send in the application later. I took that to mean that I should stop in often, so I did. After a while she kept telling me not to worry, that I was in. That was before I'd submitted an application, taken the test or had gone to the interview. I thought she was trying to get rid of me. I did slack off a bit in my calling, but she kept assuring me that I was accepted.

Sure enough, the next April found me reporting for training at the apprenticeship center along with eighteen men and one other woman. The teachers at the school weren't pleased to have me as an apprentice and they made my first day especially difficult. As I left that day the director ever so sweetly asked me if I'd be back the next morning. Didn't he know I'd heard it all before?

Although one of the instructors at the school did his best to get rid of me, he didn't succeed. I was sent to my first job as a first-year operating engineer apprentice. The company I was assigned to was a general contractor with a very large city contract. We were remodeling a historic downtown theater, transforming it into a civic center.

In other trades a first-year apprentice will spend her or his days sweeping floors or moving material by hand. A first-year operator is expected to do everything that needs to be done with the machine she or he is assigned to. If you don't know how to do a task, there should be journeyman assigned to you to explain. In my entire year with that company my journeyman refused to answer my questions or do anything for me, except to make my job harder for me.

My job was primarily to move material. I'd go to the storage yard, pick up the material and deliver it to the appropriate area. In theory it's simple. In reality it takes a lot of knowledge to know what the object you're after looks like, and it takes skill to safely deliver it. It can be tricky putting a pallet of blocks up on scaffolding, especially if you want to leave the scaffolding intact.

Now if you were a laborer whose main duty was to keep the brick masons supplied with materials, you would normally hop on an empty forklift whenever supplies were running low. But if the forklift was occupied by an apprentice operator like me, you could do one of two things. You could act pissed off and refuse to advise the novice. (This would put your life in jeopardy.) You could do everything you could to teach that person. (This would insure your life.) Luckily the people with me that year were wise enough to help me.

A first year apprentice gets to do all the jobs that the journeymen don't want to do. Operating engineers who work in the building trades don't like to get dirty, so that year I gained a bit of experience digging footings with a backhoe and grading areas using a bobcat. Once in a great while, thanks to a sympathetic superintendent, I'd get to run a little twenty-ton crane. I got just enough experience to gain some confidence in myself. The ironworkers, whose fingers and toes were always in constant danger when a rookie like me was at the controls, also developed a margin of confidence in my skills.

The theater renovation job was special in that all the subcontractors had their female workers assigned to it. There were seven first-year apprentices and one laborer. We banded together and started going out after work to discuss our mutual problems. It didn't matter that we didn't share a specific trade—the problems we encountered were with the men, not the trades. It became apparent right away that going to a bar wasn't suitable, so we began having potlucks at each other's houses. Whenever we'd see new tradeswomen we'd invite them. The potlucks have grown over the years and are now hosted by an area employment agency which specializes in nontraditional jobs for women and minorities. Of the original eight women, four are still working in the trades, one has retired due to a severe on-the-job injury and the other three have drifted away.

In the fall, when the theater renovation was nearing completion and the excavating work in the area was slowing down, a worker I knew named Scott came to work for my company. When I was an inspector the previous summer, I had supervised the company he then worked for. I was comfortable working with him and considered him a friend.

One day Scott, Vaughn, who was the laborer's foreman, and I were discussing why one of the women had reacted very hostilely to being called a cunt. I told them that was where I also drew the line. I thought that I made many good points in behalf of my woman friend. I didn't know I was leaving myself wide open.

A few days later the little crane was ready to be picked up from the repair shop. I jumped at the chance to drive it back across town. Vaughn and I drove to get it, but the mechanics wouldn't release it to me. I had to take out my union card to prove that I was an operator. There was no way that I was going to let Vaughn have the fun of driving it back to the job so I took over.

Upon our return we found a semi-load of iron waiting to be unloaded. I set up the crane and got the rebars up to the roof. Paul, the ironworker signaling me, was all grins as his star pupil (me) made the tight picks safely.

After work I floated happily into the tool room to put the crane's keys away and to get my lunchbox so I could go home. Scott was picking up tools in the gutted theater auditorium. It was the perfect echo chamber—any sounds from that area could be picked up all over the building. So everyone heard him when he bellowed, "Hey guys, did you see that cunt in the crane?" Instantly I jumped on his case. We headed to the tool room verbally assaulting each other. I was really upset that someone I had considered a friend had violated my confidence and had publicly cut me down. I was pretty out of control by the time everyone crowded into the tool room to retrieve their gear. As I turned to join the line filing out, there was Scott right in front of me. He was mouthing off about all the "cunts" on the job and that we shouldn't be telling him what to call us! I couldn't help myself. I planted my foot as firmly and as accurately as I could between Scott's legs. No damage was done, however, except to his ego. He whirled around and grabbed me by the front of my coat. He would have hit me except that Paul reached over me and got Scott first. I hadn't known that Paul was behind me, but it was lucky for me that he was. I escaped out the door and went straight to my car without watching the aftermath.

That night I went crazy. On-the-job physical violence was recognized by the union as an acceptable reason for instant dismissal, from your job and from the apprenticeship program. I had thrown the first kick. I was really worried and scared for my job.

The next morning Vaughn sent me out to the yard to pick through the used brick to find useable patching material. He uncharacteristically went along. He had heard everything that went on the day before. We talked at length and then he asked me if I wanted Scott fired. I felt that firing him would give Scott one more chip on his shoulder—then again I never wanted to see Scott again. Fortunately, Vaughn had just the right work detail in mind for Scott. In the stage area the masons were rebuilding an eighty-foot-high wall. There was no way to get materials to them except by a well wheel and a rope. Scott was put in charge of keeping those masons supplied. He quit a few weeks later. Vaughn brought out an electric winch for his replacement to hoist materials with.

The next summer I was sent to work for a masonry contractor. Once again the company had a big contract coming up where they would need a woman or a minority. The company didn't own any equipment except for forklifts and bobcats. I was furious at the prospect of spending my second year of apprenticeship running a boring forklift. I tried everything I could think of to get rotated to a dirt contractor. My business agent told me that if I didn't like my job I should quit. He claimed there wasn't much work in my area, but if I quit maybe in a few months I could work at another site, which was about ninety miles from my house. I decided to stick it out close to home.

I worked in town on a few small jobs while the masonry company decided if I was suitable. Then I agreed to go out of town to work on a job in a small community about thirty miles away. The foreman's name was Tuffy, a name which I was warned he lived up to. When I arrived at the job an hour late due to really poor directions, I found a five-foot-tall, red-haired guy screaming at a laborer. The laborer had the forklift nearly bottomed out in the mud. I walked up and the laborer looked so grateful—he knew that he was off the hook and that I was on it. Tuffy asked me if I could run a forklift. When I said of course, he looked like he didn't believe me, but he told me to get the bricks up on the scaffold as quickly as I could.

I hopped on the machine, put it in four-wheel drive and churned through the mud to the scaffold. The masons weren't working very high up, maybe twelve feet off the ground. All I could see from the operator's seat were the planks, the scaffolding and the masons' feet. Generally the masons' feet would be turned in towards the wall they were working on—but this time all the feet were turned towards me! I delivered the bricks, set them down and retracted my forks without jarring the scaffolding. I tried not to grin as Tuffy launched into a tirade aimed at getting the masons back to work.

Tuffy always wanted everything done as quickly as possible, yet done perfectly. We got along fine, which won me a lot of respect from not only my co-workers, but also from the always observing subcontractors.

When this masonry company had started, the owner did the bricklaying, his brother worked as his laborer and his wife did all the clean up. Cleaning up after masons is not any easy job, so doing it made her a full-fledged partner in the minds of all the long-term employees. In terms of harassment I had absolutely no problems while working with this company—a fact nearly unbelievable for any person who has ever worked with masons. I attribute it to the high regard the foremen had for the owner's wife.

In late summer I was sent back to town to the job I'd been hired for, a state office building project. As it turned out, I was shared with the general contractor. I ran their materials hoist and our forklift. While I gave priority to our materials, I had to keep all the subcontractors satisfied. I worked all through the winter, nearly freezing to death while standing on the ground running the controls.

At the end of my second year of my apprenticeship my business agent wouldn't rotate me to a different company. His theory was this: why should he rotate me off of a year-round, "cushy" job to a seasonal, dirty, heavy job. Luckily he went to a labor conference in Hawaii, and another business agent was put in temporary charge of my county. The new agent had been operating equipment for a subcontractor on the job where I had worked for Tuffy. He was sympathetic to my cause and pushed through my transfer to the dirt contractor he had worked for.

After two weeks of running a compactor back and forth in a sewer main trench for my new company, I was told that I was being reassigned to a little loader. The next morning I reported to the new jobsite. The only piece of equipment I saw there was a "little" 966 Caterpillar endloader. Its tires were nearly as tall as I was. I had to climb up three steps, step up on the fuel tank, and then step into the cab. In the cab I found a grinning superintendent, Roger, who took me out for a spin around the jobsite. He showed me how the machine worked and told me quite a bit of the theory behind what I'd be doing. I was terrified of heights. I couldn't bear to look down. My knuckles were turning white before I even took over the controls. Roger explained the day's game plan. I was to level off the material that a truck would be hauling in. If I had time I could sort out the big rocks. It was so very simple. Today in the same situation I can keep up with a dozen or more trucks.

The only thing that kept me going was that before Roger left he had looked me in the eye and calmly stated that he had every confidence that someday I would be able to run that machine with peak efficiency. For some strange reason I believed him.

Winter came and I was thankfully laid off. The company promised that they would call me back to work in the spring. Sure enough, one spring morning at six o'clock they called me and asked if I could come to work that day. There I was, back in the saddle again.

It was a big year for me. I got my journey card, got married, and got pregnant, in that order.

Roger came to our wedding. At work, he was the first one I confided in that I was pregnant. I hadn't planned on telling anyone for months, but then a fire extinguisher discharged in the cab of my loader. I didn't know what effect it would have on the baby, so I told Roger, and I naturally assumed that he would tell the dozen other superintendents and foremen the company employed—but he didn't.

Weeks later as I was leaning on the loader's back tire, retching my guts out from morning sickness, the foreman came up to me. When I was done he put his arm over my shoulder and asked if I was having problems at home. He said he knew newlyweds often needed help adjusting. If that was why I was being compelled to drink so much that I was vomiting all day, three days in a row, then I should know that I could talk to him. After that I decided it would be better if everyone knew I was pregnant than for them to think I was becoming an alcoholic. Nearly everyone in this area of Wisconsin who works in construction has a farming background. All of my co-workers seemed to know someone whose wife or mother had driven farm tractors while pregnant, so it wasn't a big deal with anyone.

My husband and I had planned my pregnancy so that I'd be laid off through the "biggest" part of it. What I hadn't planned on was the constant nausea I had for six months. It became a hazard when I was sent to run a loader with a faulty safety brake: I had to lean over the side of the machine to throw up while trying to keep my foot back in the cab on the brake pedal. And, of course, the job was in a hilly area! At one point my partner got the flu. It was comforting to look over, expecting to see the guy smirking at me as I vomited over the back of the machine, and instead see him bent over in back of his, also vomiting. He was out sick for a few days after that. When he came back he very loudly brought up at lunch how awful and wiped out he'd felt. He asked me how I could stand it, throwing up all day, yet working so hard? I told him I was used to it, but that I'd hoped to have been laid off weeks earlier when the company had done their winter layoffs. The foreman looked nervous. He said that I couldn't be laid off and I'd have to talk to the owner of the company if I wanted to be.

That night it rained. The dirt was too wet to be worked, so I had the day off. I went right in to the office to talk to the owner. He hedged, but I gathered that he was afraid that I might sue him if he laid me off. He thought I might claim he laid me off due to my pregnancy, not the weather. I convinced him that I had planned to be laid off and that I wanted to be. He said he'd check into it to see if he could arrange it. The next day I got my layoff slip in the mail.

Matthew was born three weeks late and via a C-section, which threw my schedule off for returning to work. Because of the C-section I was able to collect disability payments uncontested. Before his birth my business agent had told me that I would not be able to collect payment for a planned illness. I told him that he'd better contact the union's lawyer because I'd be contacting mine. I actually never called a lawyer because I felt that until I had been officially turned down by the bureaucracy of the union, there was no point in getting upset. Not only was my claim approved, but the union explained to me how to apply for free dues while I was "disabled."

It was midsummer before I found myself back in Roger's truck heading across town. My oversized thermal lunch box and gallon water jug didn't arouse any curiousity, but the stack of a half dozen bath towels behind them did. The question was shining in Roger's eyes and I debated what to tell him.

I was still nursing Matthew and wanted to continue. My Plan A was to go sit in my car at lunch and quietly express milk. That plan was wrecked when I found out I was to work as a floater—I'd be traveling around all day filling in wherever extra help was needed. Plan B was to hang towels in the loader's window, thereby giving myself some privacy and express milk while in the loader. I didn't know if the plan would succeed. I hadn't even practiced in advance with my breast pump.

So there I was in Roger's truck at six a.m. My breasts were already feeling full. I was worried about my husband's transition from roofer to full-time dad. My stomach was already sore just from lugging around my lunchbox full of ice, and Roger was dying to know why I was dragging around a stack of towels. He had always come through for me before, so I decided to trust him. His eyes widened when I told him, then he simply said that in life a person has to do what a person has to do, and drove off to check on a different job.

The job I was sent to that first day was the tail end of some underground work on a street job. Don, a working foreman, Studs, a laborer, and I were to do all the bits and pieces that remain after the full crew has finished. The guys were easy to lose at lunch time. The towels kept falling down and the passersby were really intrigued by them. My T-shirt and bibs mostly covered me up and the clear cylinder of the pump couldn't readily be seen at a distance. Sitting there quietly in the loader no one even glanced my way after I gave up on hanging the towels. I thought it would work.

On the third day I again ditched the guys at lunch time and parked under a shade tree. I set up all the paraphernalia. Feeling like a pro I adjusted the pump's pressure, put my feet up on the dash and had just started daydreaming of nursing Matthew when Don stuck his head into the cab shouting about my being so suddenly unsociable. Why did he and Studs have to chase me halfway across the job just for some conversation? It finally soaked into his brain what I was doing and he nearly fell backwards off the loader. There he was, fifty years old, married for thirty years but no kids. And there I was, covered with my bibs but with the pump half full of milk sticking out. Meanwhile Studs was standing on the ground wanting to know where we were going to eat. Since Don couldn't talk right then I suggested that they sit by the tree's trunk. I shut off the engine but I kept discreetly pumping on the opposite side of the cab. Never once did the guys look anywhere close to the loader, let alone up to my level. It ended up being a surprisingly nice, congenial lunch.

That was the last time that summer that anyone came near me at lunch. After that the word spread, and instead of signaling me to shut down for lunch, my foreman would generally signal me to head out of the area.

Five years and another baby later I was again working with Studs on a very wet, swampy job. At lunch the stories were rolling along about various de-watering procedures used in the past on other jobs. Seeing the twinkle in Stud's eyes I braced myself. But he only casually remarked that I was the gutsiest pump operator he'd ever seen. With that comment he gave me a wink, grabbed his lunchbox and headed back to work.

Now in 1988, after living through ten years in the trade and hundreds of war stories, I still enjoy both sides of my life. On my winter side I'm a laid-back, laid-off, full-time mom. I cook and bake from scratch, cuddle my kids, and work at training my dogs. On my summer side I'm a juggler. There's never enough time or energy to do everything I want to do. I'm up and long gone before my husband Curt wakes up. He does all the morning chores on our small farm, gets the kids up and takes them to preschool. At night after dining on carry-out food I'm often in bed before the kids are, so Curt often has to tuck them in.

Not only is Curt's job flexible enough for him to stay home in the summer if the kids are sick, but he personally is flexible enough to cope with the craziness of our summers. Our marriage is a partnership in both theory and practice.

People think it must be incredibly hard to work in the trades. They're right, it is, but isn't it also difficult to be a waitress? At least when I'm working I can afford a good, white-collar preschool for my kids. It took a lot of searching to find one willing to be flexible. We're their token blue-collar family.

When my son Jonathan got a new teacher this fall, she watched me pick him up every day for a week. It was a wet week. We were trying to finish a job, so we were slopping around in the mud. I'd come in at night muddy to at least the knees. The teacher finally asked Jonathan, while I was collecting my welcoming hug, if he could tell her what his mommy did at work. He replied, "Oh, she just plays in a big sandbox." He's right—the essence of what I do is kids' play. To sculpt the earth takes the imagination little kids display playing in a sandbox.

When I do my job I'm in my own world, working as a team with my crew but responsible for my share. At the end of the day, the result of my work lies out in the open. If I've fallen behind, kept up, butchered the job, or polished it to perfection, it's all right there for everyone to see and judge.

Each year as winter winds down and spring approaches, I

look forward to returning to work. I'm fortunate to be among the group of people who really enjoy their work—though I always tease my friends that the only reason I work construction is that I get the winter off.

Being a basically optimistic person who prefers to address life's good points, I have survived. More importantly, I've had fun.

Fran Krauss • Ironworker
Interview by Nancy Powell

I'm an ironworker apprentice in the San Francisco local. I can't say I thought of doing ironwork specifically when I first considered getting into the trades. I'd been doing office work for about seven years and I was tired of it. I knew I wanted something different. I wanted to work outside and I liked the idea of working high and making lots of money! I was watching the paper and saw an ad for the ironworkers apprenticeship. It sounded like something I could do, so I went to the sign-up. At that time you were called in the order you signed up. Now you go to the apprenticeship office and put in an application and then they call you.

After the sign-up, I quit work and started working out at a gym. I was really committed to getting in shape and proving that I could be an ironworker—to myself and to them. Eight months later they called me to start. It sounds like a long time, but I was lucky because there were people who were still waiting from the previous sign-up about a year and a half before.

I started working in the summer and then started school that fall. You had to go to school two nights a week for two and a half hours, or sometimes, as with my class, you had to go on Saturdays for five hours. School runs for the duration of the community college term—early September through about mid-June—for three years. The pay periods run every six months. In each six-month period you have to maintain your school attendance, pass your exams and work a minimum of six hundred hours. The requirement on the hours is pretty liberal because it averages out to only three days a week. If you make a lot of hours early in the pay period, you can take time off later on—if you can manage to do it without getting fired! You're always dealing with three separate entities—the union, the employer, and the apprenticeship program—you figure you're cool if you can keep two out of three off your back at a time.

I started out at sixty-five percent of journeylevel wage, which at that time, 1980, was about eleven-fifty an hour with vacation and benefits. One of the really nice things about the apprenticeship program is that if you hang in there for six months your wage level increases from sixty-five to eighty-three percent. Somewhere along the line you get sworn into the union. You're technically on probation for six months or one thousand hours. You can only make one thousand hours if you work every day for six months, so they can extend your probationary period past six months. After you've passed your probationary period, at some point the union will invite you to join. I know people who are in the last year of their apprenticeship but they still haven't been asked to join the union. It's all very political—if you know the right people and they think you're cool, then they'll ask you to join. Technically as an apprentice you're supposed to have the support of your union, but there are certain benefits that you won't qualify for if you're injured and you're not yet a union member. You also don't have any way of knowing what's going on at the union meetings. Fortunately, I've gotten a lot of support from the union; I've been lucky in that respect.

The trade is broken down into several areas: rebar, structural work, rigging, bridgework and miscellaneous. Rebar is putting in place and tying off the reinforcing bars that are put in concrete forms before the concrete is poured. It's probably the most grueling and least rewarding part of the trade because you put in your iron, they pour concrete and it's gone! It's also the heaviest work because in other areas, even though you might deal with iron that's heavier, most of the lifting is done with a crane. No one expects you to walk off with a two-ton beam, but there have been times when I've been working with rods and I've seen people—I've *been* people!—walking off with a sixty (a number eleven bar sixty feet long)—and that's about 350 pounds. Working rods is the most hazardous job, not in terms of single accidents, but in terms of the overall wear and tear on your body. Sooner or later something gives. Guys that have worked rods for a long time usually have bad backs, bad knees, bad shoulders—something. A lot of them either drink or do speed all day so they don't feel the pain. If I'd started out in rods, I probably wouldn't have made it in the trade. A couple of other women that began the apprenticeship program with me did start in rods and they didn't last long.

Rod companies are known for abusing safety standards. One day we were putting in sixties at the top of a fourteen-foot wall—the wall was all rebar so it was like climbing up monkey bars. Two of us ended up carrying the bars up. When you climb up a wall with rebar you have to put it on your knees, so all of the weight is on your knees, then you kind of pull yourself up with your hands. It was hairy—a 350-pound rod and there were just two of us. That's the type of safety standard abuse that only the rod companies get away with. They have no regard for the workers and the union doesn't get on them about it.

Structural—putting up columns and girders and walking the high iron—is another big part of the trade. They don't send women out on structural jobs very frequently. Some people find it kind of romantic and some people find it just plain scary! When they first started putting up skyscrapers, they used to call the guys who did that work "cowboys of the sky." Guys who do structural work tend to be as macho as the rebar guys, but they work more cooperatively, because if they don't they're dead. Structural has the highest percentage of fatal accidents in the trade. When you're connecting—that's the part you always see on TV where there's a guy up there putting bolts into a girder—you can't tie off to anything because you're moving around all the time, so it's high-risk work. After the columns and girders go up, the decking crew comes in and puts down the large sheets of corrugated iron that span the girders. This is also very hazardous! The sheets are heavy and it's windy up high. When they put the first sheets up, the workers don't have any more to stand on than the beams. The sheets are eventually welded together, but until they are it's real easy to step on a piece that can drop right down. A lot of the guys that get hurt on the iron get hurt when they fall through decking that's not secured yet.

I've never worked structural, but someday I'd like to be able to walk the high iron. I think you have to not allow yourself to freak out—like look down and get dizzy—you just have to clamp down and say, "I'm going to walk this iron or I'm going to be here for the rest of my life—which will be short!" I've heard that structural can really give you nightmares, but I think it would be a challenge like anything else—and I like challenges.

The work I'm doing now is part of what's called miscellaneous. We're putting in stairs. Part of the job involves going out on girders carrying pieces of iron called stairway supports. We hang the supports off the girders, then we hang the landings off those and then put in the stringers connecting the landings and the floor. I'm the one in charge of the layout of the rails, which is a lot of measuring and technical work that must be done right. You get these big brawny macho guys who might be able to throw a lot of iron around, but when it comes to putting it in the right place, they don't know what they're doing—and they end up having to throw it around a lot more. Miscellaneous covers a broad range of work and different phases of the job. Putting in stairs, for example, is something that happens at the beginning of a job, while putting in handrails, another part of miscellaneous, happens right near the end. There are also a lot of small structural jobs, like working on elevators or earthquake proofing.

Another important part of the trade is rigging and crane work. It's a part of the trade that I really love. Cranes just fascinate me. Just recently I got to do a rigging job that was really fast-paced and I had to look at the prints, know what iron had to go up, lay it out and put it on the crane. Everyone else was ready to drag up (quit), but I loved it. Learning something about rigging and crane signals is useful in other trades too. The signals are painted on the side of a crane, so if it's not part of your school program you can figure them out yourself. Even if you never actually get to do any signaling, you'll be able to tell if someone else is giving a signal that might endanger you and you can get out of the way.

The last part of ironwork is bridgework. Bridges are at the very heart of ironwork. Before there were skyscrapers, the trade was almost exclusively involved in bridge building. Ironworkers then were called bridge men and they'd travel around the country to wherever a bridge was being built. Though the trade now has evolved into all these different areas, bridge work is still a very high-status job. If you're really a good apprentice and they like you, you might get to go out on the Golden Gate Bridge. There's a constant crew of ironworkers out there—somewhere between ten and fifteen—because there's always repair and maintenance work needed on the bridge. I'm hoping I'll get to go out there. Before I ever considered being an ironworker I had bridge fever. When I first got to San Francisco and was thinking of living here I looked at the bridge and the city and said, "This is it." I guess it's in my blood. I once saw a TV program where they interviewed an ironworker who had worked on the Golden Gate Bridge in 1937. They brought him back up to the north tower and showed footage of the view from there. That's when I thought, "Wow—how do I get that!"

One thing I love about my job is learning how to use tools. I like knowing I can move a 3800-pound precast panel with a five-foot crowbar. Most of our work involves wrenches and cutting torches. I've also learned a lot about all kinds of cranes and winches and come-alongs to raise large weights. There are very specialized tools for each part of the trade.

Any woman who wants to be an ironworker should enjoy physical challenges. It is a very physical job—if you're not actually carrying things, which you usually are, then you're going up and down ladders or stairs. Learning to lift properly is very important. You have to learn how to use your body in the most advantageous way, and that doesn't mean lifting things the way men do. The only practical way to do this, if you haven't already had some type of lifting job, is to go to a gym and train with weights. That way you can get an idea of what your capabilities for physical work are—and you can also find out if you like it. In addition to a good weight-training program I think women should concentrate on improving their sense of balance. If you're walking down the street you can practice walking on the curb—keeping aware of how your speed is affecting your balance. I try to think of tightrope walkers when I'm walking iron—all they have is a rope that's swinging around to balance on, and here I have this iron—it's not going to go anywhere and it's nice and big.

Women entering ironwork also have to be ready to face some harassment. Luckily I have a big mouth and if guys start harassing me, I can outtalk them. In my experience, it's mostly the young guys that get on you, which is surprising. When I went into the trade I expected a lot of shit from the old-timers, and they are actually the ones that will treat you more decently and give you a chance. They know that the work is there—it was there when they started and it'll be there when they retire. They aren't as threatened as the younger guys, who feel like they have to outmacho everybody. It's slowly changing—I'm seeing more young guys coming in now who accept women being in the trade.

I was harassed the most when I was working rods. They'd send me wherever the heavy, heavy work was. As soon as I'd been with one crew long enough for them to accept me and work more cooperatively with me, the next morning they'd say to me, "You go over there." Then I'd have to start all over again with a new crew and go through the same shit. I was also burned when I picked up a piece of rebar that someone had just cut—I'm quite sure I was set up for that. The work I'm doing now in miscellaneous is definitely better, especially because there's less harassment.

The growing presence of women in the construction trades has already created a big change in the whole atmosphere on the job. When I get out to a new job the first thing I ask is whether there are any other women on the job. The support you get from other women is just incredible. That's one of the really good things about many of the trades today—there are just so many fine women doing this kind of work. I think the cooperative attitude we have, and not being competitive between trades—which is a macho tradition—will also have an impact. Those of us already in the trades see ourselves as a wedge in the door; we've got to hold the door open so that more women can come in behind us.

I hope more women get into ironwork. It's so beautiful up there early in the morning when the sun comes up. The air is nice and clean and you never feel boxed in. It's like being on a mountain without having to go to the mountains.

Polly Jerome • Rural Builder

I remember when I was nine, I used to look out from the coast of Maine to this little island with a lighthouse on it. My dreams of being a chimney sweep grew to include being a lighthouse keeper *and* a chimney sweep. I'd imagine myself out there pulling my little dingy down to the shore and setting out to work every day through the waves, my black hat on and chimney brush in hand. At night I'd return to my little island, where I'd eat the fish that I caught on the way over and fall asleep to the sound of waves crashing on the rocks.

Thinking back on this childhood dream, I realize how possible it seemed to me then. When I would describe my plans to my father, he'd just say, "Well, let's draw a picture of it," or "Just make sure you drag your dingy up far enough at night so the tide won't take it." No one ever told me I was crazy, or that I couldn't do that because I was a girl. I was always encouraged to mow the lawn, fix my own bicycle, and to try out for sports, coached by my mother who would play catch with me after supper.

When I was in the seventh grade, my parents gave me the choice of staying in school or dropping out and moving with them to a farm they had bought with the intent of starting a commune. Not that I was having trouble at school; I had good grades and plenty of friends. But given the choice, of course I wanted to quit.

I found myself one day playing my last basketball game at school and the next living on one hundred acres in Pennsylvania, in the middle of February. I was suddenly faced not only with my newly acquired independence (my parents weren't going to join me for another four months), but with the realities of using firewood and dealing with snowbound driveways. Not to mention living with grownups who didn't always get along and having no one my age to be best friends or enemies with.

I spent a lot of my first year there tagging along with Robb, fixing things and painting things and puttering around. That year he and his wife built a twenty-by-forty-foot log cabin. I eagerly stacked the limbs from the trees in the woods, hitched the logs with a chain to the tractor and peeled all the bark off of them. We then dug the holes for the foundation posts, built the first floor deck and started notching each log to fit together in the corners. After the walls, we set the rafters, sheathed them with plywood and nailed the shingles on the roof.

The next year, when I was thirteen, my parents, little brother and I went to visit some friends on another commune in northern Vermont to help with maple sugaring. We spent our days slogging around in three feet of snow, carrying buckets of sap to a sled that a team of horses pulled down to the sugar house. There the sap was boiled down into syrup. At night we hung our wet clothes near the fire and sat around the overcrowded kitchen, eating supper by a kerosene lamp. There was no phone, no TV, simple food, and lots of hard work. I hadn't wanted to come, but I sure didn't want to leave. My parents and brother stayed a week and I decided to stay on until the end of the sugaring season, a few more weeks. With my parents' blessings, and much understanding of my need for independence, I ended up staying fourteen years.

Farming with the horses especially intrigued me. We plowed and cultivated a few acres of vegetable gardens, made the hay and skidded the trees out of the woods for firewood with them. For those first few years we cut the wood with two-person saws, brought the hay in loose and milked our one, then two, cows by hand, making cheese and butter with the milk. This was the early seventies, when there seemed to be time for everything and ten people to do it!

Things did change: we bought a chainsaw, then a tractor with all the haying equipment. We built a dairy barn and milked sixteen Jerseys, sending our milk to the local creamery. It certainly wasn't as simple a life, but when I could mow down ten acres of hay in the time it used to take to do one, I felt a lot of satisfaction. There were also many discouraging days trying to figure out why the stupid hay baler wouldn't tie those magical little knots (a baler picks up the loose hay in the field and packs it tightly together into bales, then wraps it and ties it with baling twine), or whether the hay was really too wet to bring in, or if it was really going to rain. The shop became my second home, where I spent my time tearing the tractor apart and putting it back together for various reasons, replacing parts on a wide assortment of broken farm equipment that filled up the door yard, or just hanging out and telling stories with neighbors and friends. No project seemed too hard to at least try. The day even came when Lynnwood, our neighbor, came over and said, "Hey Polly, you gotta come get my baler going."

Eventually I turned eighteen and wanted a "real" job. I called a building contractor and applied at the local furniture factory on the same day. I'm sure I would have done just about anything, but at least I had enough sense to go with the contractor when they both called back.

The first day with the contractor I had to paint the exterior trim on an apartment building. I was standing on a shed roof, painting the trim above me. It started to spit snow (why was I painting?) and my fingers were turning purple from holding the wire bail on the can. Oh God! I didn't have any gloves and I was so cold I was close to tears. I was just too scared to go down and warm up, for fear of anyone thinking I couldn't do the job.

It was definitely a hard week. I knew somewhere inside that I had many abilities, but I wasn't in my safe little world anymore. I was so unsure of myself that I didn't even know if I could eat my lunch right.

I pushed myself to do whatever I could, and then more. I'd struggle to not let my aching back show as we unloaded truckload after truckload of fourteen-foot five-eighths sheet rock upstairs, or hauled shingles to the roof. One day while putting on vinyl siding, Ed, the foreman, asked me if I'd done much finish work. I thought of the equipment shed up the hill we'd just built, where there wasn't even any power. We'd used cedar logs for timbers, and the chainsaw for everything. "Well," I said, "I've done more chainsaw carpentry."

"Oh yeah," he said with a smile. He knew just what I meant. And the next day he had me measure and cut and nail up the trim boards for a window, by myself. It was a little rough, but I did do it. I saw him looking at it later as he passed by. He never said anything, so I figured that meant it passed.

It took a few months for all of us on the crew to start getting comfortable with each other. They admitted after awhile that they thought for sure I wouldn't even come back the second day. "It was so damn cold, nobody would have put up with that!" Mike, the boss said. So why did I have to do it? I thought, but I just laughed. And it was probably a good thing that I made myself do things I didn't know how to, or was really too scared to do. I remember on about the third or fourth day, Mike asked me to take some cement samples to Burlington, the largest city in Vermont, about three hours away. I gulped and just nodded. "Do you know Burlington?" he asked.

"Not very well," I said, not telling him I had been there only one other time, and that I had this strange phobia about going anywhere I didn't know. So he gave me his pickup, the biggest, newest vehicle I had ever driven, and off I went, with the directions scribbled down on a scrap of wood. And what do you know? I made it without even one mishap. Driving home I picked up a hitch-hiker. He was another construction worker and he talked on and on about his shitty working conditions. He obviously thought I was another working guy. "My boss can really bust my balls! You know what I mean?"

"Yeah, it's like that," I said.

That's one thing that ends up happening a lot. People assume I am a boy, without looking very closely. On that first apartment building there was a group of high school girls who would often stop and watch from across the street. One day I was outside picking things up and there they were. "Hi Paul!" I heard, and looked up to see them giggling and running away. And I began to wave back to them when they'd greet "Paul."

I don't know why I still seldom correct anyone. It has something to do with not wanting the embarrassment for them, and also not wanting to draw attention to myself as being different.

It seems that people often look at something else, besides you, when they assume they are talking to a man or a woman. It does have something to do with your appearance (I am five-foot-three with short red hair and wear jeans and work shirts most of the time), but even more with the way you carry yourself. If you swing a hammer with confidence, or walk like you know where you are going, a lot of people unconsciously view that as male behavior.

I remember one summer during haying, I went to town to get a baler part, and stopped to get a six-pack of beer on the way home. I was hot and greasy, and had on a tee-shirt. When I got to the line, there was a salesman talking to the guy behind the register, about to buy a pack of gum. He looked right at me and said, "Hey, let this young fellow go ahead, looks like he could really use a cold one!" (Could he be serious? I didn't have a bra on and I'm not particularly flat-chested.)

"Thanks," I said. "It is hot out." Now I probably should have corrected him. I had nothing invested in anything he thought, but I did feel conscious of not having a bra on and didn't particularly want him looking at my chest.

It can also be depressing when you are dealt with like a freak, because you are so different. A few years later I was welding on an elevator at a skiwear factory. It was just a repair job, so I was the only one there. I got a hot chip of metal in my eye and went running into the women's bathroom with tears and dirt streaking down my face. It was break time, so the bathroom was full, and all the women shrieked as I staggered to the sink and began rinsing my eye. Then they laughed a little as they realized that I was a woman and started to leave the bathroom, uncomfortable with being there with me. No one offered to help.

I have always wanted to just go along and do what I know and want to do, without making it a big deal. But I also am proud of what I do, and it seems I can gain respect for the quality and quantity of my work regardless of my sex. That it doesn't mean: "She's an awfully good carpenter, even if she is a woman." But rather: "Here is an awfully good carpenter."

On the other hand, I do want the world to see that a woman is capable of anything a man is, and if people think I'm a man, I don't make that point. There is a wonderful pride when someone thinks, "Wow, that's a woman doing all this!" But that takes away from the actual product. What is most important to me is that the jobs I do are done well, efficiently and with care.

On that same crew, we ended up building a lot of steel buildings, and most of them in the middle of winter. It never seemed to make much sense; it's just plain hard to keep your hands warm trying to pick screws out of your apron when it's anywhere from zero to thirty below out. One day I could barely squeeze into the truck next to three other guys; I looked down at myself and counted eleven shirts and jackets that I had on. Well at least I'd keep warm just trying to move!

On that crew I generally did whatever everyone else did. But I had to jump right in before they'd admit that I could do certain things. For instance, they of course assumed I didn't "do" heights, until one day someone needed another drill, so I just went up and walked out on the purlin (the cross pieces that the roofing is screwed down to) thirty feet up and handed it to him. I just started working and that was that.

Another time, there were some brackets that needed welding to the columns, and no one else was around, so I just thought I'd see what it was like to try welding. That went fairly unnoticed, but then another time a guy named Dave was having a terrible time welding some angle iron together. We were the only two there, so I offered to try. Nobody was around to make fun of him for letting me do his job, so he said sure. It came out great! The boss even asked me if I learned to weld at school. I admitted it was only the second time I had done it, but I became one of the welders anyway.

It felt really good to be accepted by my working mates as just one of the crew. It sounds kind of weird, but at the time it seemed good that they could make their dirty comments and jokes (and there were plenty!) in front of me. It meant that they were comfortable, and if you're going to work well with anyone, it certainly helps to be comfortable. Somehow it was understood that their jokes weren't directed at me. In fact, it helped me realize how empty those sorts of comments can be, how much they're just habit. But that's not always the case, and I have little tolerance for that sort of thing now.

I only had real trouble with one guy. It started after working together for three years. We were sort of a team and he taught me a lot. It began to get weird when he would barely let me out of his sight; he could do that because he was a foreman. At first he would just try to grab at me as long as some of the other guys were around, and it would always end in laughter. I began to get really sick of it and once when he grabbed my breast on a roof staging, had my foot connected, he would have been on the ground. But he didn't get the message, and his approaches began to get sicker. On one job, he decided that he had to hold onto my belt so I wouldn't fall as I leaned out the window to cut the metal siding away for the trim. Window after window, day after day, he began to put his hand farther and farther down in my underwear. Well, I was scared. Too scared to say anything (I kick myself now for not placing my knee in his underwear!) and I didn't know what to do. That Friday afternoon my boss told me that the next week Ed and I were to go finish up another job alone, no one else around. It was well below zero and dark when I went to get my car to go home, and I freaked. I walked out into this field, and just cried my eyes out. When I finally went back to the parking lot, two of the other guys were looking for me. They'd seen my car and figured something was wrong; it was too cold for me to just not be there. So I told them, sort of, and they admitted they'd noticed Ed had been doing strange things. They talked to the boss, and I never worked with Ed alone again. We never talked about it. I know I would deal very differently with this sort of situation now, but I was only twenty then. Although I felt I could do anything, I couldn't deal with that.

The company was growing very fast and there was a new rule that you couldn't take a company truck to a job unless you were a foreman. Where I was working, forty miles away, the company had hired a new foreman who lived down near the job, so I had to take my own car. On top of that, my boss told me to keep an eye on the foreman because he had never put up steel buildings before. So I couldn't take a truck and I was supposed to babysit some foreman who was making more money than I was! I had had enough, and gave notice. My boss offered me a dollar more an hour. That he couldn't have paid me what he thought I was worth in the first place also pissed me off, but I stayed on a while.

Things started going from bad to worse. On another job they had me running the roofing and siding crews. It wasn't the good old crew that I knew and loved anymore. This was a bunch of guys that had been recently hired and who didn't particularly enjoy being told what to do by some girl. I just wanted to do my work; I wasn't interested in making any points. So I gave my notice again. This time my boss offered me a chance to "work my way into a foreman's position." (Hadn't I already done that?) He wasn't able to lure me with my ego, nor with more money. He finally tried threatening that he wouldn't pay me my vacation pay unless I stayed until the end of the job, which didn't work either. I ended up leaving with my vacation pay from the previous year and a certain amount of bad feelings. It was time for me to move on with my life: My job had run its course, and big time construction wasn't really what I wanted to do.

That was seven years ago and I've done a variety of things since: building and installing air-to-air heat exchangers, apple picking, making and selling metal wind chimes and continuing to dairy farm. But I've mostly been building. I've worked with a crew of anywhere from two to four people building houses, additions, barns, garages, decks and roofs (one summer we re-roofed ten houses and a church). Winters I've done a lot of work on my own, including two complete houses for women friends, right down to all the wiring and plumbing.

Although I assume I'll be building for a long time to come, I do worry about the future. Not only is there the retirement question (you'd think I was old at twenty-eight), but I worry about how my body will hold out for another thirty years. I've worked myself hard, and I realize how much I have always relied on my physical strength and how vitally important it is to my trade. There are times now when I dream of a less physically demanding job; I appreciate how much easier it is for someone else to reach that last nail because they are closer to six feet than I.

I think in rural areas there are often broader views of what women can do physically, partly because there are women that do everything from running the farms to working in the woods and it's been like that for hundreds of years. Unfortunately, they don't always get the credit for it. There are farms where the wife does most everything, but the sign out front says, "Donald Smith and Sons." But no matter how much or how little recognition they get, these women know what they can do. They have always been a great inspiration to me, as have the women who've turned from waitresses to electricians and have proved to the world that they, too, can be anything they want.

Johnnie James • Miner
Interview by Lisa Parnell

Johnnie talks a lot about working on the belt. If there's one redeeming quality about shoveling, it is that it's mindless; and if a belt cleaner is lucky enough to be working alongside a buddy they can talk, talk, talk. It's dark, it's hot or cold, never comfortable. Belt cleaners can feel as if they are all that's left in the universe, except for the incessant clanging of the belt's metal splices. And that's how Johnnie and I became friends, she and I and our shovels and the belt clanging and clattering along.—L.P.

I was born south of Tuscaloosa. My parents had twelve kids. There were two sets of twins. We were rural people. My father and my brothers, they farmed for a living. My father also worked in Mobile on the docks, in earlier years, back in the fifties. My mother, she never worked outside the home much, she was basically at home with us.

I went to rural schools, segregated, black and white. I feel as if we got a decent education. As far as books were concerned though, they badly needed upgrading. When I was fourteen years old, my sister and I left Alabama for the very first time. We stayed a year with another sister in Canton, Ohio, a small industrial town. We both attended public schools there. Ohio was quite different from the South, like night and day, really. Everybody was extremely friendly, eager to help us, and at first

I was lost quite a bit, especially at school. It was a pretty large school, and it was integrated. The teachers were really nice, and they took a personal interest in me. I don't know if it was because I was from the South or if it was due to the standards of the school. If I was out of school one day, the principal or the assistant principal would call my sister and would want an explanation of why I was not at school.

I finished high school in Greensboro, North Carolina. It was a segregated school, like the ones in Alabama, and the teachers didn't take that much interest in you. A lot of kids didn't show up for school until December or January because they were at work in the fields.

After I finished high school in Greensboro, I went back to Canton. I worked there for a few years, and I came back to Alabama at age twenty. I completed an eighteen-month business course at a technical school and for the next ten years I mainly worked at clerical jobs.

I applied for a job with Jim Walter's Resources, the coal company here. I thought it was great at the time. I'd make more money. Well, it hasn't been easy. It's been a long, hard struggle. Like many other blacks, I'd never worked in a coal mine before. I had no idea what I was getting myself into.

I've learned a lot since I've been here. Sometimes I've felt like everything was directed at getting rid of me. Partly it's because I am female. I've been written up, which means they say you broke one of the company rules. You can file a case and challenge them, so that's what I did. I won most of the cases. And I can tell you that didn't go over very well with the company. I'm not considered one of their most favorite people. Company people, even a lot of union people, want you to go along with what the company says and does.

I once bid on a scoop operator's job and was turned down because they said I couldn't perform the job, that I'd never performed the job before, which was a lie! The company themselves had been forced to give me some experience on the scoop when I filed a grievance, sometime back, and won it. I had been working on the beltline and wanted to get moved to a better job. Being on the beltline is just shoveling. You're either at a header (the location on the beltline where coal is transferred from one belt to another) or on the belt, cleaning up any of the coal that spills. The belt conveyor takes the coal out of the mine eventually. Shoveling is noisy and dusty work. You don't get a chance to see a lot of people. If you're not used to working other places you wouldn't know what was going on in the rest of the mine, especially on the faces (the area where coal is being extracted).

I worked on the beltline for at least one year and a half, maybe even two years. I always noticed that other people—white females and males who got hired after I did—got a chance to work on other jobs in the mine, even if they came back to the belt. I felt that it was my right and my privilege to learn to run equipment, and to learn what was going on around me in the mine. I felt the company was denying me this right. I decided to ask for training on the scoop. When they turned me down, I filed a case. The grievance procedure has four steps, and it can be settled at any step. The company always lets it go all the way to the third step, even though they know you're right. They hope you'll drop the case, but I didn't give an inch. Eventually they put me on a section (an area where two or more faces are located) where I got a chance to learn how to run the scoop and also learn the workings of the mine.

I've not made a lot of friends in the company. I realize my rights and I stick to 'em. I do what I'm supposed to do. I don't violate any of the rules. I'm now a classified scoop operator. A scoop resembles, to me, a road scraper. I always say that 'cause we lived in the country. We had dirt roads and the road scraper always came to scrape the roads. The scoop has about five levers, which move the different parts of it. And of course it has a tram peddle and a brake peddle and parking brakes. A child could learn to operate it is fifteen minutes, let alone a high school person with an education or whatever.

For a long time I really felt left out. I'll give you an example. Most of the people on the belt didn't know how to drive a manbus. You really don't have a chance to learn. You either walk to the bottom of the mine or you ride a bus, but somebody else is always driving. I didn't know my way around the mine and I wanted to learn how to run the manbus myself, so I could get out of the mine if I had to. No one ever bothered to teach me, even though the track and the manbuses have been underground for five years, so I finally just taught myself. But the boss, and I mean the general mine foreman, took time out to teach a young lady—of course she was white. He says to her, "Come here, let me show you how to run this manbus... ya'll." We were working overtime through vacation and he was pulling her off her job and taking time out to teach her how to run a manbus!

I've experienced a lot of stuff like that. It makes you angry. A lot of the foremen are so used to doing this stuff, I don't know if they really think twice about it. But any person is not totally ignorant about right and wrong. Anybody in their right mind knows this is discrimination. I think they must know that what they do is wrong. What really irks me is those reformed Christians down there. There's this one foreman who calls himself a devout Christian and he goes around singing that song and doggin' us black folks at the same time. I want to say something to him, but I'm not as vocal as I should be. When that happens, then I argue with myself, "You dummy, you should've said something. You should've spoken up." But I think, inside, I'm a very strong person because I keep trying.

Nina Saltman • Carpenter Foreman

No girl born in the fifties was born to be a carpenter. Just ask anybody. Carpenters are boys; born with tools in their hands, digits exactly one inch long and the uncanny ability to see level at twenty yards. How then, could I, a midwestern Jewish girl born in 1950, end up as a carpenter? I certainly wasn't told by my high school counselor to "try a hand" at the trades. Not by a long shot. I was a typical female student at a public high school. I took sewing and cooking, as was required for girls, due to our obvious genetic qualities that facilitate our usage of ladles instead of levels. I was on a college-bound track with an emphasis on English, drama and art. I loved art, and if the truth be known, I loved sewing. (I still do, although now, I never seem to get past mending my coveralls.) So where was the transition? What was the impetus for a career outside my track?

It must have been something to do with my Great-Uncle Borach who was a carpenter in Lithuania. I guess the genes got passed down to me instead of my brothers. Perhaps the fact that I find great similarities between building and sewing and art has had an effect on my career decisions. Or, maybe, it's my love of seeing something created out of nothing, and made beautifully and skillfully. I have always loved working with my hands. It gives me a sense of accomplishment to create a thing of beauty, be it a work of art or a well-hung door.

As typical as my schooling was, my work history has not been. After graduating college with a BA in English Lit and a minor in Drama, as well as a teaching credential for secondary education (good in thirty states I'd never consider for residence), I left the States and traveled to Europe. I lived in Amsterdam for a year working as a leather crafts artisan in a snazzy, hip leather boutique on the shopping street, the Nieuwendijk. I remember my dirty hands and the feeling of creativity. I was also the shop "go-fer," and often had to carry heavy leather skins back to the shop on the streetcar. My first effort at physical labor, and I loved it. I also loved the way people would look at me carrying these heavy items... what a woman....

After two and a half years of living and working abroad, I came back to the States and moved to California. It was 1974 and I was ready to try anything. I took a number of odd jobs from housepainting to more leather work. While housepainting, I met a couple of friends of friends who were working at a cooperative food warehouse. The slogan was "Food for People, Not for Profit." I liked that a lot. I also liked the fact that the warehouse was relatively new at that time, and the business was just starting to blossom. I ended up working there fulltime and becoming a member of the collective. As the warehouse grew, our collective consciousness changed. We had lengthy discussions about workers versus management, worker control, trade unions and general organization, as well as how to run our business. So, in addition to building myself up physically by doing manual labor forty hours a week, I learned, ironically enough, management skills, group organization and general business skills. By the end of four years I could lift and heave one-hundred pound sacks with the best of them. I also learned how to operate a forklift and qualified for a Class II license by driving a ten-wheeler truck. I was, however, tiring of the long hours of political discussion while the business failed... I was ready for a new job. Oh, and did I mention the salary??

I quit the warehouse and took a vacation. When I returned,

I went to the Women in Apprenticeship Program (WAP) office in San Francisco. I was interested in getting into the ILWU or the Teamsters, preferably as a warehouser, but I was open to anything. After a few weeks, I received a call from WAP that Union Carbide in South San Francisco was looking for a woman in their industrial gas plant. Union Carbide had federal contracts to honor, and was being pressured to comply with affirmative action requirements. There was a woman working there, but she was leaving. They needed to fill her spot. I went down and had an interview. I was asked to demonstrate that I could handle a hand truck and was physically able. I started as a Teamster for twice what I had been making at the warehouse. During my time at U.C. I learned how to deal with a lot of insults, smutty pictures and imbecilic behavior, as well as a somewhat boring job.

After about a year, it was time to move on. I knew a couple of other women who had started apprenticeships in various trades and had talked to them about the work, the atmosphere and the men. Although I knew I would have to put up with the same childish behavior from my co-workers that I experienced at U.C., I also had confidence that I would end up with a marketable skill and a stimulating job.

I approached the trades using what I now refer to as the "blitz" method: sign up for all tests and all trades, and whichever pans out first gets the prize: me. I had taken one test for operating engineers and signed up for the electrical and sheet metal tests when I started to look for carpentry jobs. Carpentry had always been my first choice. The idea of building buildings and being able to work on my own place had definite appeal. I started looking into the cabinet shops in the area. I went to about fifteen with no luck whatsoever... they were, in fact, a big turn off. The shops were nearly all white and completely male. They didn't want to have anything to do with me. By the time I had visited most of the shops, I felt the same way about them. I was undaunted, though, and my search continued.

I started visiting big construction sites in the city. It was rainy season and many of the jobs were muddy holes in the ground. When I visited a Dinwiddie Construction site downtown (now Saks Fifth Avenue), Dean, the general foreman, looked at me, looked at the muddy hole in the ground, and asked, "Would you be able to handle working in this?" "Sure, why not?" I said... and he told me who to call. I set up an "interview" for the next day with a superintendent of another jobsite. When I got there the next day, instead of an interview, I got a little speech that was becoming all too familiar.

"Well, uh, er, we have had other girls work here before. (PUFF, PUFF on the cigar.) And, uh, er, they just haven't been able to handle the work."

TRANSLATION: We don't really want you broads here, but we're being forced to hire you. The other women couldn't take the abuse... will you?

"One girl missed a lot of time, and another didn't want to do the heavy work."

TRANSLATION: Your period is no excuse... and you're gonna get the shittiest, dirtiest jobs we've got. You're gonna have to work twice as hard as the men if you want to stick around.

The "Everywoman" speech. Ah, yes, I'd heard it before. Did all these guys get together and practice it? I had heard it at Union Carbide, at the Sheet Metal union office, and from some of the cabinet makers. I was hearing it from Dinwiddie, and would later hear it from others. I wondered how many men ever got these "interviews." My answer to their speech was sort of pat, by now, too. "Try me out, and judge me on my own merits," or words to that effect. What I shoulda said was, "!@#$%&*()!!!°°!" Anyway, I got hired and started my apprenticeship.

I worked for Dinwiddie for the next two years, went to apprenticeship school in the evenings and started to feel like a real carpenter. I was fairly active in my union and also got involved with the local women carpenters' committee, meeting many wonderful and able women carpenters. It was unusual to be steadily employed, and I felt very fortunate. I also realized this reality: that I am white, heterosexual, well-educated, physically fit and very mouthy. Unfortunately, most employers are not known for their efforts to combat racism and sexism, not to mention homophobia in their hiring practices. In addition, I was in the right place at the right time. There had been a couple of other women that had worked for Dinwiddie, so I wasn't the first woman that most of these men had seen in a tool belt. I don't want to minimize the fact that I busted my butt. I worked very hard, was never late, and rarely missed a day of work. I fell in love with the trade and had an intense desire to be a proficient craftsperson.

After two years of building concrete forms for high-rise construction with Dinwiddie, I decided I needed to expand my knowledge of the trade and work for another contractor. I quit Dinwiddie, took a vacation and came back to town ready to work for someone else. That's one of construction's best perks: the opportunity to take long vacations between jobs. With the help of a friend, I got hired by an extremely reputable remodeling contractor, Plant Builders. They needed women on a redevelopment job, so, after an interview, and an "Everywoman" speech, I started to work for Plant.

The new work was varied, and I was finally doing something besides concrete. The men I was working with seemed decent and friendly. Once again, I had the advantage of a woman predecessor. As in my jobs at U.C. and at Dinwiddie, there had been women working with the crew before my arrival. They had, in each of their ways, broken in the crew for me, to the extent that I had it better than the women before me (but not so good as those who followed). The one other woman working for Plant at that time was a very good carpenter that all the men respected. Besides this woman carpenter, there were (are) rarely other women on my jobs. Despite this fact, I kept fairly content at my new job. I learned a lot, and Plant was training well. Unlike a lot of other women apprentices, I was being given some responsibility at work. For the most part the men were willing to share their expertise without any apparent prejudice. I had to put up with occasional badgering not only because I was a woman and therefore an easy mark, but also because I was an apprentice.

After two years of working for Plant, as I approached the end of my apprenticeship, I started to get a little apprehensive. I knew that I would be expected to know everything the day after I "turned out." Magically one goes from apprentice to journey status in one day. Once one is paid the same as other journeylevel workers, one is expected to produce the same, even though, clearly, the experience is NOT the same. Fortunately, because I'd been working for the same company for awhile, they were aware of my capabilities. I probably felt more pressure from myself than from bosses or co-workers to perform better or faster. To this day, I am probably my own worst critic.

After a few months of work as a journeywoman, I started working on what was referred to as the Service Truck. Plant had and still has a lot of clients who require follow-up work, or pick-up work at the end of jobs. I had a company truck, a beeper and a purchase book. My partner on the truck was one of my favorite carpenters in the company, and he broke me in to the ins and outs of service calls. It seemed clear to me that this position was a training ground for future foremen or women, as the case may be. I had to fill out time cards, daily reports and lumber lists, as well as plan small projects and deal with clients.

After six months on the truck, I worked on a couple of different projects as a regular carpenter, and was then given my first job as a fore...woman. I was flattered, but also worried. What if I screwed up? Was this a set-up? I had never really wanted to run work. Remember? I was the one who worked in a collective, with no bosses. Now, I was gonna be a boss? Oh, irony of ironies!

The job was a relatively easy one to run. There were no plans and only a couple of subcontractors. Plus, the real clincher was that my immediate boss was the owner of the company, Mr. Plant, himself. Hmmm, was he just checking me out? Or what? Or, maybe, they didn't think I could handle it, so they made sure that I couldn't screw it up too much. The thoughts that went through my head.... Needless to say, though, the job went off without a hitch.

The ribbing I got from some of my co-workers was incessant. "Hey Saltman. I thought you didn't want to be a foreman! Hah! ForePERSON Nina... Hey Boss...." Then, of course, there were a few people who probably had a lot to say behind my back... oh, to be that fly on the wall.

I think that the nature of this particular company has had a positive effect on my success in the trade. Plant hires carpenters from the union or the field, and if they work out, they keep on working. If they continue to work and can take on added responsibility, they start to run work. I feel fortunate to be a "company person"—Plant has treated me fairly and generously and I doubt that I would be running work were it not for the fact that I work for them. As far as I know, I am the only woman who has run a job in the capacity of superintendent the size of my most recent one. I marvel at the speed with which I have been given this amount of responsibility. After all, I've been in the trade less than ten years. Still, when people ask me what I do, I sometimes hesitate, and say, "I'm working as a carpenter." Not that I am a carpenter, for I don't always feel like I am. After all, I wasn't born with tools in my hand. Sometimes I feel like an impostor. "Who is this person wearing these coveralls?" I ask myself.

Since my first job as fore...MAN ("forewoman" isn't a recognized term—yet), I've run four other jobs of some magnitude. Two of them were twelve-week jobs, and one was a nine-week butt-kicker. Sometimes the shorter the job, the more hectic the pace. The first two jobs were finished on time and within budget. The third job was not so smooth, and the fourth was a whole novel in and of itself.

All four of these jobs were in historical landmarks of one kind or another. The first one was at the only Frank Lloyd Wright building in San Francisco. I found out during the job that part of the reason that I had been given the job was because, being a woman, they thought that I would take care of the building, and make sure that nothing happened to it that wasn't supposed to. A woman's touch.... This is, I think, part of the rationale when I have been chosen to do a particular project. Women are more careful than men... Nina is a women, therefore she will take better care of this building! In some cases this may be a warranted consideration, but definitely not always. I did respect the Wright building, no question about it; the job went well and I have felt close to Frank Lloyd ever since.

After that job I had nine months or so of working on a crew again. This was fine with me, as I felt (and still do) that there is a lot for me to learn. I arrived on one jobsite and found a crew composed of some old and new faces. After a coffee break, one of my buddies, Uncle Harry, as he is affectionately called, came over to me and started to laugh.

"Nina, you see that guy over there? (Points to a carpenter I'd never met before.) He asked me if you were a journeyman or an apprentice. I told him, 'Yeah, she's a journeyman all right... In fact she's a foreman!' The guy looked at me in shock, 'You mean she's a foreman?!' Yeah, he just couldn't believe it. I thought you'd get a kick out of that, so I wanted to tell you."

I sure did.

I like the fact that some carpenters (men) don't quite know how to relate to me. I like the feeling I get when a tradesperson comes on to my jobsite and asks who is in charge, and I can say, "Me!" There are also some aspects of being a foreman that have their drawbacks. When I'm on another person's job, and I make a mistake, the response is usually, "I thought you were a foreman." Or, now that I'm a little more experienced at running work, invariably, during the course of the job, I'm bound to hear, "Is this your first job?" at least a few times. I don't know if this is because of something missing from my performance or if it is just so unusual to see a woman in charge.

After a summer project at an all-girls school, I ran the nine week butt-kicker. It was a tenant-improvement job with a high pressure schedule and an unrealistic budget. I was doomed before I started. The owner's agent was an ex-marine sergeant, a woman with no sense of humor and a penchant for putting the blame on somebody. I'm sure she saw me as a likely scapegoat. I had a number of exercises in personal diplomacy. I really learned what it meant to literally bite your tongue. I must say that this aspect of running work—the politics of being a foreman—is one of a number of things that I don't like. I am in between a rock and a hard place, namely the workers and the management. My attitude is not necessarily supportive of management all the time. I don't like being put in the position of having to defend an unrealistic schedule, for example, or a decision on the work that may lack integrity. I don't see the point of lying about the work. This can cause conflict, needless to say, when the project manager has a different agenda.

That job was the only one, so far, where I had a real blowout with a subcontractor. The aforementioned project manager was pushing the schedule hard, which meant pushing me to push the subs. One of the subs was responding in a very lackadaisical fashion and was not responding to my daily barrage of phone calls, so the project manager sent him a telegram. For some reason the subs hate this, and it never fails to get them pissed off. On the other hand, it does usually produce results.

It certainly did in this case. The two workers for this sub were working overtime to compensate us, and they and I had worked out a plan for them to proceed. Their boss came onto the job, obviously very uptight, and started barking orders to them, contrary to what we had just worked out. He then came over to me, all red in the face, and got right up in my face, and says, "You send me a telegram that I have to have such and such done and you're not even ready for us and how can you do this and you better have A B and C ready in five minutes or BLAH BLAH BLAH...." It really shook me up; I knew he would never have related to a man like that. At that moment I really wished I had been six-foot-four and weighed two hundred and sixty pounds. I walked away from him, so furious that I started to cry.

This same jerk came over to me about fifteen minutes later and asked me if I would accept an apology. He told me that his crew explained that we had already worked everything out.

Reluctantly, I said I would consider accepting the apology. Grrrrr.... It was at the end of this job that I really started to evaluate how I felt about running work. It is definitely different from being a regular carpenter. There are endless challenges and it's become clear that the skills needed to run work are not always the same ones needed to be a good carpenter.

Aside from the stress factor, which is my number one complaint about the position of foreman, there are a lot of things that I *do* like about running work. My day is scheduled by me. I decide when and how to get my daily work done, as well as everybody else's work. Despite the fact that I have a project manager, who is, officially, my boss, I have a lot of autonomy on the job.

Though very active, it is not as physically demanding as the trade itself. Rarely will I have to do physical labor. After all, I am the boss. I can get someone else to do the grunt work. What I do do, though, is run around a lot: checking everybody's work, answering the phone, answering billions of questions like "How do you want this done?" trying to mediate differences between the subs, ordering materials, scheduling people in and out of the job in the proper sequence, and dealing with all the personalities from architects to cops. The trade has been, in general, a stimulating test of my will and endurance. Being a foreman has heightened the challenge of the test, and it can be an exhilarating feeling to meet it head on.

Meeting the challenge on my most recent job was much more than I bargained for. The building was the first high-rise built on the West Coast (1897). The first three floors of exterior facade were to be stripped off, and new facade was to be engineered and re-attached. The new look would be 1980s Art Deco. It was an extremely interesting project, with every known building material in the world on the new facade, and I learned a tremendous amount. Not only did I learn a lot about construction, but about people, too, myself included.

The job was started by another foreman, a friend of mine. After about a month on the job, he and the project manager, a guy who I had worked with before, were not getting along and my friend was ready to quit. I was working on another job, happy as a clam to be using my tools again, when I got a phone call from this project manager asking me to take over the job. I called my friend to check out what the deal was. He explained that the job was a tough one: the client was difficult (a woman, of course), the estimates had been all wrong so there was no money in the job, the schedule was a mess, the plans were incomplete because the architects were inexperienced, and he thought that the project manager was a horse's ass.

Needless to say I was not anxious to get involved. It meant working with a difficult project manager, which I wasn't looking forward to. It also meant taking on a very large, long-term (seven months), already confused job. All this equaled a lot of overtime, and a *lot* of stress. For the extra dollar-fifty an hour foreman's pay, it didn't seem worth it. However, after a conversation with Mr. Plant I was convinced (coerced?) to help out and take the job.

It was everything I had expected and more. There were more than fourteen subcontractors on the job, each with three to twelve people on a crew, as well as our own crew of carpenters and laborers. From the second I hit the jobsite in the morning until I left, which was rarely a mere eight hours, I was on the go. There were a number of days when I literally did not have time to pee. The jobsite was large and it was difficult to keep track of what everyone was doing at all times.

Like, for instance, the time that the ironworkers were up on the second floor putting in their structural steel. Apparently they had to keep stepping over this phone line. Little did they realize that the travel agent next door was connected to that line. The effort to step over this wire must have simply seemed too much of a burden, so they just took their snips and... snipped it! All hell broke loose. I was summoned to the office of the owner and scolded. After all, I was responsible, because the ironworkers were a subcontractor of the general contractor on the job. I was also responsible, of course, when these same ironworkers were using the women's restroom on one of the occupied floors. Oh those ironworkers....

Some of the moments of frustration were offset by funnier ones. There was this young guy who came to the jobsite looking for work. He must have talked to someone in another part of the site and then came in to the area of my job shack. He approached me and asked, or so I thought, "Where's the chick?"

I flew out of my office in a rage, and said, "If you're looking for a job here, you better think twice about referring to me as a chick. I am not a chick. I am a woman, and I am also the foreman here... so you better ask again."

The guy was flabbergasted. "I thought your name was 'Chick.' One of the guys over there told me I should go to the office and ask for Chick. I'm really sorry... I would never... if I had known...."

The fire department must have shown up at this job at least four different times because tenants in the building would smell smoke from our welding or burning and think we were all on fire. Each time I would have to apologize to the chief and show him what we were doing, and then have to deal with the owner, tenants and my project manager. One morning, after I had worked until 11:30 the night before, I walked onto the job, dealt with a couple of problems a sub was having and heard the fire trucks pull up. I went around the corner, and there were two trucks with their lights flashing and sirens going. My project manager pulled up to the job just at that same moment.... We both walked over to the fire trucks and the fire chief says, "Who's in charge here?"

At the same moment we both started to say "I am." I looked at the project manager like, "Who the hell do you think you are?" and he says to the chief, "She is."

Through all the stress and tension, and all the years leading up to it, I have neglected to say how big a role the support of friends and family has been. Without that support and positive feedback, I doubt I would have had the singular strength to survive. My companion James, for example, has been great about being a friend and listener when I've had a rough day. He says, "I don't have a choice!" Of course, he benefits—I do a lot of carpentry work around the house. My family has also been very supportive. I think that they get a kick out of the fact that their sister/daughter is a tradeswoman. How unique! Of course, they *also* like it when I come to visit and fix a few things around the house. My mom recently commented that she thought my four years of apprenticeship were at least as difficult as the medical school my brother has gone through. Many friends gave me the encouragement to go on. And the fact is that some of my co-workers have also given me a lot of encouragement, telling me that I was all right and as good as the next person... and not to be afraid to "turn out" or run work.

Having a network of tradeswomen is also invaluable. Any woman involved in a trade or occupation where she is isolated can benefit from the camaraderie and strength of networking with other women in their field.

I don't know when or if I will be running another job. I will undoubtedly accept the new job, if and when it's offered. I plan to try to expand my expertise in carpentry no matter what my position. I really love the craft and the trade. The seemingly impenetrable old-boy network has, at least, been punctured, if not thoroughly pierced. I have no illusion that I have made it in their world. Rather, I have met my own challenge and thereby weakened their hold, just a bit. Little by little each one of us must make our mark, meet our respective challenges and take charge of our lives. With time it will make a difference.

Photographs by Sandy Thacker

Laborer

Ironworker

Above: Painter

Right: Telephone Cable Splicer

Above: Electrical Winders

Right: Welder

Above: Oil Refinery Worker

Right: Pipefitter

Railroad Worker

Ironworker

Top: Electrician
Left: Machinist
Above: Carpenter

Carpenters

Vicki Smith • Sprinkler Fitter

This scheme of mine to become a skilled craft union apprentice never included getting up at 5:30 A.M. and driving fifty-five miles to work. If in 1977 someone had told me that ten years later I would be rising before dawn and working only with men, I surely would have thought that they had me mixed up with some other woman. I had sawed my first piece of wood only three years before. Had anyone told me I could make thirty dollars an hour for blue-collar trades work, again I would have been sure they were mistaken. Until I moved to San Francisco in 1981, I was not aware that skilled, blue-collar, unionized workers were some of the highest paid workers in the world. (Neither was I aware that the life-threatening dangers of construction work are second only to those of mining.)

In 1977 I was coming out as a lesbian, living in Vermont with a four-year old son, collecting welfare and working in a collective daycare center, where I made three-forty-five an hour. Three years later my mother died. I was thirty-two years old, both my parents dead, my only family my son. I had no money and few skills. I no longer felt that I had to stay in New England: I wanted to escape the cold, get training in a job that paid real money, and embrace the cultural diversity of California and the safety of a large gay/lesbian community. I had read in an East Coast women's paper about the union apprenticeship programs—and the strength of the trade unions—

in San Francisco. Women were starting to get into the programs there. In Vermont I had worked on a few construction projects as a carpenter's helper and as a laborer and had really enjoyed the work. I decided that moving to California and getting a union apprenticeship job would be my late-in-life attempt to start a focused career.

The apprenticeship program with Local 483 Sprinkler Fitters opened in 1983. Over 1300 people applied for the 175 apprenticeship positions that opened up over the next five years. Federal and state affirmative action guidelines required that women make up twenty percent of each new class. However, many of the women who entered did not complete the program and today, out of approximately 750 sprinkler fitters in the Bay Area's Local 483, only eighteen are women. When I entered the program in 1984, at thirty-five I was the oldest apprentice in my class. I was one of five women in a class of thirty. Four years later, in May 1988, I am a journeywoman sprinkler fitter, often running the jobs I work on.

I went into this trade having only a vague idea of what I might be doing. Let me tell you what it is that sprinkler fitters do. We install the overhead piping systems that automatically put out fires in both commercial and, increasingly, in residential buildings. When an area of a building gets too hot, a thin metal disk melts inside a sprinkler, allowing the water just behind to spray the area. This is certainly a worthwhile job, and I feel pride in my work. Automatic fire control systems will hopefully be a requirement one day in all housing, hotels, schools and hospitals—wherever there is the possibility of loss of life from fire, and that is almost anywhere.

Sprinkler fitting involves running up and down ladders or using lifts to raise pipe to ceiling height. We then hang the steel, copper or plastic pipes, attaching them to the wooden or steel frame of the building by drilling or shooting metal hangers into concrete or steel. Next we use ten-inch to thirty-six-inch wrenches to "make-up" the threaded ends into the fitting ends of the previously placed pipe. Every day we use various tools: drills for working on wood, concrete and metal, pipe wrenches, torches and pipe-threading machines. It is often very strenuous work, involving the lifting of heavy pipes or machinery. We also need to be able to read blueprints and to place the pipe accurately in the building. On each job, a control area, including automatic control valves, drains, alarms and water pressure gauges, must be set in place. We then tie-in the whole system of pipes into a city water supply—this often means working in ditches as well as dealing with city water department officials. Once we make the water tie-in, and all piping is placed, the system must be filled and pressure-tested, and finally approved by fire department officials.

It has been very satisfying to see my progress in accurately measuring and cutting pipes. My mechanical understanding of piping systems and water pressure has steadily improved with classroom instruction and on-the-job training. I no longer "space out" or "fog up" when presented with a complicated layout or blueprint of a piping system, like a pump room that raises huge columns of water up thirty stories or more in a high-rise building.

Some people ask me if this work is too heavy or physically difficult for a woman. It became very apparent early on that I had to teach myself the proper way to lift heavy objects, so I joined a gym and have worked out regularly with weights ever since. I'm seldom called upon to do anything at work that is beyond my strength—there is usually a way to get wheels or ropes to do work that would be too heavy for me, or for anyone else for that matter.

Sometimes I do wonder whether I want to keep exposing myself to the sexism and racism on the job, or to the dangers to my body from physical stress and possible accidents. (As a white woman I don't bear the brunt of other workers' racism directly, but each time someone makes a racist comment I have to make a decision about whether or how to challenge them about it.)

But many other jobs have these same shortcomings without all the benefits I enjoy: the chance to work with my hands and to learn a skilled trade; a feeling of pride in the trade and in my individual work; the knowledge that I have proven to myself, friends and co-workers, the construction industry and the world that I and other women can do this work—and do it well. Other very tangible benefits include a wage of nearly thirty dollars an hour, ninety percent medical and dental coverage for myself and my son, a pension plan for when I retire—in addition to a supplemental retirement account in which I receive four dollars for every hour I work—and accident and death benefits.

I need to emphasize that these kinds of financial benefits exist only because of years of union organizing and the struggles of union workers to win them. Unions also fight to make sure their members have job security and high safety standards at work. In addition, construction unions are beginning to address basic issues about worker control of construction projects.

Unfortunately, many women who enter my apprenticeship program never get to enjoy these benefits because they leave the trade. Some leave because of the nature of the work, the heavy lifting, working at extreme heights, exposure to hazardous substances, the dirtiness. But for many I am sure the main reason is the men. If I end up leaving myself it will be because I have not been able to break through their resistance to my presence. It is hard to go to work day after day, always feeling different, like an outsider, always watched a little more closely.

Let me mention a few of examples of this sexism. Women are often not allowed to do the most prestigious aspects of the work, but we are always allowed to clean up—in fact are often expected to do so for as many as twenty to thirty male co-workers. (Of course, apprentices are also often expected to clean up on a job. Sometimes it was hard to sort out which work was assigned to me because I was an apprentice and which because I am a woman.) Women are often not taken seriously; our solutions to mechanical problems are passed over, ignored or even ridiculed.

Perhaps the most frustrating aspect of sexism in tradeswork is not getting equal training. I experienced this firsthand in my training. At the start of my third year I came onto a job where there were two lower-period apprentices, men who had less time in the trade than myself. We were putting in piping, starting on the second floor and going up to the seventeenth. One of the two apprentices had arrived on the job the day before me. After a couple of days doing "go-fer" work for them, cutting pipe and doing general clean up, I decided I didn't want to get locked into this pattern, so I took a risk and complained. I started with the journeyman who was working with us, but his reaction was very condescending. I went on to the foreman, who reacted by stepping up my cleanup time. At this point I called our apprentice coordinator, who asked if I wanted to be moved to another company or to file a grievance. I didn't really want to do either, so I next approached the superintendent of the company. He ended up writing a bad six-month character report on me over the incident. I also received serious bad vibes from most of the guys on the job. Looking back, I think I should have filed the grievance, but at the time I didn't think I could face living with the backlash the rest of my fitting career. I was afraid I would develop a reputation as a major bitch.

In spite of these problems, I respect the men I work with—and it *is* men I work with. Usually I am the only woman on a job site. In four years, I've only worked with another woman once, for a three-month period. My male co-workers are truly amazing mechanics and very hard workers. Their years of experience in the fire protection industry, their skill and their seemingly inexhaustible knowledge deserve a great deal of respect.

A few weeks after I started this work, I spent about three straight days in a six-foot ditch full of water. My foreman and I were attaching to a pipe an eight-inch fitting that weighed about eighty pounds. We had to bolt it to the pipe under the water, using three-quarter-inch bolts and a ratchet wrench. We were soaked and freezing. I cannot remember ever being so physically tired before or since. I told the foreman I had gained a new respect for all the men I had seen in ditches before those three days. He knew I meant it. He told me later that he had gained a lot of respect for me during those days, too. He even bragged about me to the company superintendent and other workers afterward.

Many of the men I work with are not from California. Affirmative action requirements have brought minority men into the trade, and this has increased my exposure to black men, Asian men, Native American men and Chicano men, whose acquaintance it would have been more difficult for me to make otherwise. The regional, racial or cultural stereotypes I brought to the trade have definitely been challenged, and I am enjoying this opportunity to meet people with backgrounds different from my own. I've found that minority men more often understand the sexism affecting me on the job and that they will comment to me that they see the unfairness.

Some of the men I work with are not high school educated, yet this says absolutely nothing about their intelligence. I can't say how important a process it has been for me, a working-class woman, first in my family to have either a high school or a college education, to challenge the class bigotry of our society, which would have us believe that uneducated people are both stupid and crass. Some of the men I've worked with are miracle workers with their minds and hands. Taking huge pipes and miles of small pipe and filling an empty space with a functioning fire extinguishing system is a wondrous task. The engineers who draw the plans can't foresee the problems encountered by the installers, but these workers always find the solution on the jobsite.

Many of the men I work with fill break times with Depression anecdotes, union organizing and fighting stories that make me glad to be a part of this work and history. At the same time, some of them can be extraordinarily narrow-minded and bigoted. I was laid off from one job the day after confronting my foreman about his calling blacks "porch monkeys"—an expression found in Ku Klux Klan literature. Lunchtime talk has also often left me feeling coldly aware of myself as a woman alone in a misogynist world.

Clearly I feel a certain amount of alienation on the job: as a lesbian, a never-married mother, and a woman who has worked for years for progressive and radical social change. I spend much of my free non-working time fundraising for groups fighting U.S. intervention in Central America, for AIDS support groups and for groups working for women's rights. I never know at work when my co-workers might start haranguing about queers, dykes, wetbacks, commies, Sandinistas, welfare recipients, blacks, whores, their wives. All of this grates on me, rattles my cage. When I speak up I never know how long they will make me suffer for it. Sometimes I shut up and fume. Sometimes I think, "I won't take this for one more day." And then I think, "They will not force me to leave this career, this security, this pay. I'm here to stay."

Lucy Lim • Utility Switch Operator
Interview by Shelley D. Coleman

I've worked in the trades since 1977. My first nontraditional job was in an open-pit copper mine in Arizona. I started there in an entry-level position as a laborer on a labor gang of ten or twelve people. Two of the others were women. The company was pushing affirmative action, because it had a class-action suit brought against it by a group of women in the mines in 1973. I was hired four years after the suit was filed, but even then, there were only a few women working for the company.

Being one of the first women was hard, and I didn't always have a comeback for every put down. But I held my own. I remember an incident involving a real macho guy on the labor gang who was hired around the same time I was. We were in the lunch room, and a discussion started up about whether women belonged in the mines or not. This guy believed women had no business in the mines, that it was a man's job. I said to him, "Hey, Sanders, what's your problem? I'm five-foot-two and 120 pounds. We're doing the same job shoveling and sweeping dirt and rock. Our shovels are the same size, and you can only put so much dirt in it. Just because you're bigger doesn't mean you can put more dirt on your shovel. They don't make bigger shovels for bigger guys." As I looked at his mouth hanging open, I thought, "Hey, yeah, this feels good. You macho guys may be bigger, but your brain is so much smaller that I can outthink you." A person my size has them so threatened. I used to tell them, "You guys go home to your wives and tell them about all the hard work you've done to maintain that macho myth about miners having to be six-foot-four and 250 pounds." It is pretty physical work, but you're not limited by your size. I worked there for five years, until the mine shut down. I'd still be there if it hadn't.

I grew up in an interracial marriage; my father is Chinese and my mother is Mexican. I have an older brother and a younger sister. I had a happy childhood, and I have fond memories of growing up in Arizona. My mom and dad ran a small corner grocery store, and we lived in the back. I went to school, came home, and there they were, every day. The store was open nine to nine. My dad was very Chinese in that he was a strict disciplinarian and really emphasized the importance of education. He had come here as an immigrant at age fifteen. He tried to go to school in Arizona but he was placed in a class with six- and seven-year-olds and felt so uncomfortable that he couldn't continue. My mother only went to ninth grade, so she agreed with my father about the emphasis on education. I knew at a young age that my brother, sister and I were going to college in order to get good jobs.

I was pretty assertive as a child. My brother and I used to box together. I used to do a lot of rough playing—the kind that usually just boys were allowed to do. My brother never had a problem with me being a girl. He used to be a leader in the neighborhood; he was always team captain and would pick me to be on his teams—football, baseball, basketball. He has the same respect for me now as an adult.

After college, I worked as a retail clerk. Then I decided to get a job in the mines. My dad couldn't understand why I left a well-paying job at six dollars an hour as a retail clerk to go work in the copper mine for a quarter more an hour. I felt there were more promotion possibilities in the mines, and I also wanted to work outside and be more physical. I was twenty-seven and married at the time. The guys at the mine would complain, "Why don't you stay at home and take care of your husband?

Your husband works, so you're taking someone else's job." I'd tell them, "I have a right to a job, regardless of my marital status. Also, I can't depend on my husband being there all the time. What if I wasn't married at all?" My co-workers and I had a number of verbal battles.

Now I work in San Francisco for Pacific Gas and Electric (PG&E), a private utility company. For the past four and a half years, I've been a systems operator, or switch operator. We work in the electrical substations, where we do high voltage electrical switching and operate circuit breaker disconnects. Not all substations are automatic, so when PG&E electrical maintenance crews need to work on equipment, our job is to clear breakers or sections of line. To do this, we have to write a procedure tag to physically clear switching, so the crew can work on the de-energized line. We sometimes have to de-energize a whole neighborhood or even large areas of the city.

My union affiliation is International Brotherhood of Electrical Workers (IBEW) Local 1245. My starting wage as a trainee was ten dollars an hour. Hourly wages for journeylevel craft workers vary according to the shift, but they are basically in the range of twenty dollars, plus we get a twenty-five percent discount on our utility bill and good benefits.

There are a few other women working in other stations in the city. The first woman switch operator in San Francisco has been promoted to a prestigious job in PG&E. After working for the company for ten years, she's now assistant dispatcher and works in the company's brain center. Some of the guys said the reason she was up there was because she could type superfast. There have been several men who've gone up to the top and then down in a few months. The pressure is tremendous. It makes me laugh to think of them rationalizing away her intelligence.

I really enjoy my job. You never know what you're in for when you arrive at work. Once on the graveyard shift, when I was a few months into the job, I got an alarm from another substation in the field. All I knew from the alarm was that there was something wrong. It could have been anything from a false alarm to fire. I got into my truck, and off I went. On my way to the substation I heard on the truck radio that there had been an explosion in a manhole and an operator was on the way. That operator was me! When I got there, I ran into the control room and saw that the enunciator alarm lights were flashing all over the place. I turned off the alarm and checked the panel lights. Then I had to figure out what had happened. The explosion should have opened up a circuit breaker in the substation, clearing the fault. Instead, the 34,000-volt breaker failed and caused other breakers to open. It took my entire shift, till six in the morning, to bring it back to normal. Luckily it happened at a time when no one was out in the field.

I have a lot of responsibility in this job. You really need to be careful not to turn a switch the wrong way or you can energize a line when someone is working on it. A worker once closed a ground switch on an energized line instead of opening it, which caused an explosion. Opening up circuit breakers can cause a huge power outage and damage to equipment. We're talking about 230,000 volts. The breakers themselves weigh hundreds of pounds. Some are huge—six to eight feet square, others are the size of a kitchen stove.

From doing nontraditional work, I've definitely become more confident—partly because I've topped out; I'm now journeylevel. I feel like I've really achieved something. What I'd like to do now is to gain more knowledge about my job. I feel fortunate to be working with a great group of guys now. Maybe it's just the times. It's the way it should be, that women are now less a novelty. But it hasn't always been easy dealing with the men.

I do have a support group, Blue Collar Asian Women, which feels real good. It's fun to share our stories and see how similar they are, to talk about how to survive on our jobs, trade comebacks to sexist and racist comments. It helps us feel like we belong. Wherever I go, I endure racism. Just one look at me and you surely see I'm not WASP. I hear a lot of racist ethnic jokes and I never let the jokes slide. For example, when I worked in Shreveport, Louisiana, in an oil refinery, there were about twenty-five women out of three hundred workers. I worked with a wonderful black woman named Viola. She was telling a joke which involved a Chinese male cook. I let Viola tell her joke, all along thinking, "What am I going to do?" And the thing was, it did have a funny punchline. So afterwards I told her, "That was a pretty funny joke, but it would be better if you didn't use the word 'Chinaman.' That's derogatory, like using the word 'nigger.' Could you use 'Chinese cook,' or whatever; you could even forget about the idea of using a *Chinese* cook. Why not just say 'cook'?" Viola apologized and said she had never thought about that before.

My dad taught me to be independent, because he wasn't going to be around to take care of me forever. And he gave me strong cultural messages: "Have a lot of pride that you are Chinese, that you are Mexican, that you are both." He encouraged my self-esteem and confidence. He always stressed being happy in your work and being very good at it, no matter what you chose to do. My parents had a hard time with racism. They weren't allowed to get married in the state of Arizona in the 1940s, because there were laws banning interracial marriages. It wasn't because my mother was Mexican—because Mexicans were considered white—but because my father was Chinese. So they got married in Mexico. The schools I went to reinforced cultural stereotypes: Chinese kids were supposed to be submissive and well-behaved, smart, cute. I've seen the stereotypes work in other ways: for example, if a black woman and an Asian woman apply for the same physical labor job, the black woman often gets hired over the Asian woman because the Asian woman is supposed to be passive and weak, and the black woman aggressive and tough. These stereotypes are damaging to everyone.

Sometimes I wonder how I have survived working with men. On a one-to-one basis, it's okay, but when they're in a pack, watch out. Some of them tell me that I was hired because of affirmative action, that I am a token. I just say I don't care, it has to start somewhere, and there are going to be lots of other women after me! For all of us who are breaking ground for women to follow, we feel we have something to prove; it's a lot of pressure to bear. Sometimes I think we underestimate ourselves, but unfortunately we become Everywoman. We're no longer individuals; we represent the entire sex.

My attitude is important to my survival on the job. I'm happy about eighty percent of the time. I have no regrets. The ideal I strive for is not to subdue my aspirations, but to incorporate emotional freedom and creativity and be more of myself at work.

Terese M. Floren • Firefighter

When I keep my mouth closed, I seem to belong there. At a fire, that's pretty easy, because we all look alike. Properly dressed, anyone would. In full gear we are identical forms in dirty yellow, padded to bulk by triple-layered thermal protection, trudging like snowsuited toddlers. We are distinguishable one from another somewhat by size, and definitively only by a name in Reflexite lettering on the back of the coat. For a woman, only speech is the giveaway.

In the firehouse, out of the turnout gear, it should be a little easier to tell the difference. But since, like the men, I am white, and my hair is cut short, and since even off the fireground I wear the same uniform as the men, I am frequently mistaken for one.

Such misjudgements are a reliable source of amusement for the men I work with. Firefighters love fires, food and laughter, and while uneasiness came readily enough to the men of the Miamisburg Fire Department when I was first hired, it wasn't worth missing a good joke over. The reaction of an unsuspecting citizen who realizes, several minutes on, that one of the firemen they've been talking with is a woman, is always a good joke. If the individual has been swearing or otherwise speaking unguardedly, it's usually considered a good enough joke to repeat later to others. The more hilarious forms of firefighter humor are usually at someone else's expense.

Possessing a sense of humor of my own—who could survive here without one?—I've developed a knack for the quick comeback. Only a few months ago, a man came to the station selling tickets to a dance. Firefighters, a captive audience bound by unwritten code and their public employee status to be polite to all, have many opportunities to buy dance tickets, raffle tickets, pancake dinner tickets, Girl Scout cookies, and all the other petty extravagances basic to grassroots fundraising. The man, a garden-variety Ohio good old boy in his sixties, spotted his targets as we sat talking in the kitchen. He went into his spiel. Only ten dollars, take your wife to the Lions' Club May Dance. Noncommittal silence and tactfully averted eyes were the response. He shifted to the one-on-one offense and asked each man in turn. Casually, politely, each declined the honor. I was last in his clockwise sweep.

"How about you? Wouldn't you like to take your girlfriend to the dance?"

Four sets of ears were suddenly, imperceptibly, attentive.

"I don't have a girlfriend right now."

The ticket seller did the expected double take. "Are—are you a girl?" The guys blew snot. Blowing snot is a firehouse term for the snorts that keep you from laughing out loud. I confirmed the seller's belated observation. Hiding any embarrassment, he left in search of brighter prospects. Laughter erupted as the door swung shut.

The really funny part was that I was serious. But the guys didn't know that, and such a couple would not likely have found themselves welcome at the Lions' Club May Dance.

Anyway, when I'm not talking, I can seem to belong there.

I was hired as a career firefighter in 1975, becoming only the third or fourth woman in the country to do so. I was twenty-two years old with a background as a volunteer firefighter, a degree in history from Antioch, and an interest in doing things that were unusual. Getting the job wasn't part of a careful career plan. My intention was to try it for five years and then see if I still liked it enough to stay. I did expect to like it, since I knew from my volunteer time that I was capable of fighting fires and very much enjoyed it.

I knew, of course, that it was just about unheard of for a woman to go through the testing process. And I knew that the physical test would be difficult, that I would have to work out in order to prepare for it. What I didn't know was how nervous my application made people within the City of Fairborn's administration. Probably even now I know only a fraction of the whole story. I did push-ups and pull-ups to get ready, improving my strength as much as I could in the short time available, and went to take the test. My written score had placed me second on the hiring list; all I had to do was pass the physical agility test and I would be virtually assured of being hired.

The agility test was held in a school gymnasium. Events were set up at various stations around the room and outside, things like push-ups, pull-ups, a shuttle run, grip strength measurement, etc. All of the applicants, about seventy white men and me, were lined up along one wall of the gym, which meant that the first candidates to go through were under the scrutiny of the competition. Of course, I was one of the first. It sticks in my mind that only the men's restroom had been opened, and monitors were running around fretting over where I would change my clothes. They were much relieved to find that I had worn my sweats from home and would not need to change. I don't know now if that's exactly the way it happened, but it would be a good example of how things were for me on that job in general: them nervous, and me adapting to unequal conditions, amused by their anxiety.

One of the first events of the agility test was push-ups. I had been working hard on my push-ups and was sure I could do the minimum fifteen that were required. Candidates were allowed to do up to thirty-five for extra credit that somehow either compensated for deficiencies in other scores or could bump one up higher on the list. My concern was just in getting to fifteen. As I prepared to start, the monitor stepped in and asked if I knew how to do women's push-ups. (Actually, he probably called them girls' push-ups.) I stared at him and said yes. He told me that those were the push-ups I was to do. I figured out later that they thought they would be sued if I were forced to do men's push-ups.

I could hardly believe it. So-called girls' push-ups are done with the knees on the floor, rather than using the toes as a fulcrum. They are immeasurably easier, requiring and developing much less upper body strength. A mere applicant, I was in no position to quarrel with the authorities who had it in their power to bestow on me this $10,000-a-year job, but I looked again at the monitor and asked, "Are you sure?" He was sure. I went to the floor and did thirty-five women's push-ups. Knowing I could have done the others, it was annoying to have all the male candidates watching me get this unfair advantage. I was comforted to find out later that they had also noted my questioning of the monitor and my surprise at his directions.

No gender-based variations were offered or ordered in the remainder of the test. The only break I got was that the chin-up bar at the school was too low for adults to use, so the chin-ups were eliminated from the test. That had been my only other weak area. I breezed through the remaining events, meeting many of the maxima. Possibly these helped me compensate for the grip strength test, in which I can't have done very well. I do know that the agility test was completely redesigned a few months later to include more fire-related activities, such as a six-foot wall obstacle and an aerial ladder climb. Whether this was in hopes of keeping other women off the department, or simply because they realized how irrelevant their shuttle-run-and-standing-broad-jump test was, I never knew.

My three years on the Fairborn Fire Department could be characterized as "successful under the circumstances." It never became the home to me that firehouses often are for male firefighters, but neither did I encounter overt hostility or harassment. I loved being a firefighter, and that helped me close my eyes to the incompleteness of my acceptance there.

My first days on the job were just that—days. As with many departments, new recruits in Fairborn work forty-hour weeks at first, in order to meet and work briefly with everyone on all three shifts. This is known as being on days, as opposed to being on shift, which is much preferred. It helps orient the new employee to procedures, equipment, and facilities. I met the troops: thirty-five men ranging in age from twenty-five to fifty and, with one exception, ranging in color from white to redneck. They greeted me cordially, without malice, without welcome.

Like most people who enjoy their work, they were willing to show me things: how the hose was loaded, how to fill air bottles, how to drive the engines. It helped me that I was already an EMT (emergency medical technician), as I could thus immediately take a place on the ambulance, an unpopular assignment. My volunteer time gave me no credentials in a professional department, but it gave me a private confidence in my abilities that I was badly to need once I realized how much doubt others had on that score.

In the fire service, social and domestic issues are a factor on the job to a much greater extent than in most other careers. The twenty-four-hour work shift means that not only do crews make ambulance calls and fight fires together, but they also cook, clean, watch television, and spend the night together. The first woman to enter the environment of a particular firehouse, whether in 1975 or now, is faced with skepticism over her ability to do the job. She must also deal with questions about whether she'll be able to fit in.

When it came to spending the night, Fairborn dealt with my presence in the station about as awkwardly as it is possible to do. At first they came up with what they must have thought was the perfect solution. Though most small towns use police dispatchers to handle fire and emergency medical calls, Fairborn had its own fire dispatcher. She was the department's secretary, who worked weekdays from eight to four and dispatched calls in addition to her other tasks. At night and on weekends, a firefighter had to be assigned to dispatch. He slept in the alarm office and remained in the station when everyone else went on calls.

In management's eyes, this was the ideal spot for the female firefighter. She could go on calls during the day, and then have her "own bunkroom" at night. I'm not sure if the total inequity of this failed to strike me, or if I simply assumed the situation would be temporary. In any case, I was quickly trained in the dispatch procedures.

Dispatch was about the stupidest place to put a rookie, especially one who wasn't from the area and didn't know the streets. I once sent fire equipment to a fully involved house fire at "3 Galewood." A few minutes after the engines left, people were calling me back wondering why they had heard sirens but not seen engines. The fire was at 3 Dellwood, and between the incoherent shouting of the phoner, who was calling from inside her burning home, and her to-me-unfamiliar Appalachian accent, I had mistaken the name of the street. Had I been familiar with the town, I would have known that there could be no number 3 on Galewood, but I wasn't. I was not reprimanded or disciplined over the incident—a review of the tape showed I had repeated "3 Galewood?" back to the excited caller for confirmation—but neither did anyone decide at that point that I shouldn't be running the radio.

Dispatching was the most undesirable task in the fire department. Only a few of the men did it by choice, and then only in the hot summer months or in the coldest part of the winter. Although everyone hated ambulance calls, missing out on fires was a drag, and it was a real pain to have to be awake every time a piece of equipment went out. Waking up to answer the phone was difficult and stressful, and for me there was the additional annoyance of having people not believe that this was indeed the fire department, convinced that, at night, a female voice meant a wrong number.

I finally let the chief know I felt it was unfair for me to be spending every night dispatching, when it was a rotated position on other shifts, as it had been on mine before I was hired. He agreed; probably he had known all along that he would have to do something when I finally complained. His solution was to order the purchase of a rollaway bed. I could have the bed as my bunk, and set it up in the TV room after everyone else had gone to bed.

In retrospect, it is either appalling or funny what contortions they went through to avoid having to put me in the bunkroom. The rollaway bed was, once again, an improvement over the previous arrangement, but it was not without its problems, as conflicts inevitably arose when someone wanted to watch television late at night. I was never allowed to go to bed until after the eleven o'clock news, and I'm sure some of the men felt constrained from watching late movies. It was a situation hardly designed to breed good feelings between the men and me.

Stations Three and Four, under construction when I was hired, were completed within my first year. I was not permitted to work at either of them. As the stations were new and attractive, remote from the chief's office, and didn't involve any dispatching, being assigned there was highly desirable. I complained about being restricted to Station One, but it did me little good. The captain told me, "The citizens of this town simply won't tolerate having a female firefighter sleeping in the same bunkroom as the men." I personally doubted that the citizens of the town knew that much about their fire department, since when we went on calls they were always shocked to see a woman on the engine or ambulance. The citizens the captain had in mind were probably the ones who happened to have seats on the city council.

I can't remember why simply moving the rollaway bed to one of the other stations was deemed unacceptable, but clearly the chief wanted me where he or the lieutenant could keep his eye on what was going on, not that anything was or would have been. It was not until my third year on the job, after the fire chief moved on and a new one was hired, that I was permitted a rotation at Station Four.

My three months there were like a different job, and not just because I was finally in the bunkroom. (No citizen protests came to my attention.) The attitude was freer and life was more enjoyable. In general, things had loosened up considerably with the hiring of fourteen new firefighters in the year after I came on, substantially lowering the average age of the department and eventually bringing a change in the atmosphere in all of the stations.

After my rotation at Four's ended, I was sent back downtown. Without hesitation, and without asking anyone's permission, I chose a bed in the bunkroom and put my sheets on it. The lieutenant walked in and asked what I was doing.

"Making my bed," I said firmly.

"Oh." If I wasn't worried about it, neither was Jake. He watched me for a moment, then shrugged and wandered off. That was the end of it.

I'm now the president of my union local, IAFF No. 3115, and I've been on the negotiating team for the past three contracts. Maybe having to deal with the bunkroom issue in Fairborn gave me a shove in that direction. It let me know up front that fire department management and city administrations work in strange and predictable ways that may or may not have anything to do with fairness.

I don't much enjoy fighting with the city. Negotiations end up being protracted battles that leave hard feelings on both sides, and somehow even simple grievances have a way of getting people into a snit. But while I don't enjoy conflict, I feel I'm a good president and not a bad negotiator. It's reassuring to know the guys I work with think so, too. They don't concern themselves with gender issues; they want someone who'll stand up for the union.

Back in Fairborn in 1975, a lot more was going on besides hassling over bunkrooms. We had fires and cardiac arrests and traffic accidents, the tragedies and catastrophes of people's lives that are the routine of a firefighter's day. We had water fights in which we dragged hose lines up to the kitchen. We had a food fight that was interrupted by an ambulance call. A patient healthy enough to care that Al Eider had meringue in his hair or pieces of potato down his collar probably wasn't sick enough to need us anyway.

Much of a firefighter's work is hurry up and wait. The blast of a buzzer, toot of a tone, or jangle of a bell, and you're shifting into high, onto the equipment, out the door, down the street startling traffic with your sudden flash of color, noise and light. Sometimes the hustle is rewarded by a job to do. More often the problem is minor or non-existent: a malfunctioning alarm system, a hot electrical odor from an overheated light ballast, a car fire out on arrival. You hurry up to get there; then, if there's no emergency, you wait. Wait while the officer finds the maintenance person. Wait for the power and light truck. Wait while the report is taken.

One day not long after I had come to work in Fairborn, we were waiting. Bill Soders and I and someone else, probably Minnow Malloy, were hanging around the tailboard. An Indian tank was sitting on the tailboard, too. An Indian tank is a water extinguisher with shoulder straps, with a pump nozzle on a two-foot hose. You wear it on your back to put out small grass fires, and to give yourself a backache, since it weights over forty pounds when full and the metal rim digs into your hips. Its design criteria were not done by Kelty or Gregory.

I slid the tip of the nozzle into the opening of Soders' folded-down boot. He didn't notice. I squirted a stream of water into his boot. He jumped.

"Son of a... "

Minnow was amused. Soders was, too, despite his wet foot. Practical jokes are another mainstay of the firefighter's existence, and this was a standard-format firehouse prank. The problem was that it wasn't going to work for me.

By unwritten law, Soders owed me. He was entitled to get me back, and I was entitled to live in apprehension until he did. But Soders didn't feel free to get me back. You don't hit a girl. And you don't accept an outsider into your circle as readily as I had assumed. I got away with it.

I didn't want to get away with it. I wanted to be part of the group bound by the rule that says paybacks are hell. Instead of demonstrating my membership in the group by inviting him to play a trick on me, I had demonstrated—at least to Bill Soders—that I would take unfair advantage of my protected status.

Seeing my humor backfire was frustrating, since it was one of my few survival mechanisms. Usually it worked, even though it meant buying into a lot of their assumptions. When I told Minnow that I'd bought a living bra but it died of starvation, he thought I was an okay gal.

Although I didn't know it until much later, legends about me came out of a fire in 1977 at Wright Patterson Air Force Base. Many women firefighters get undeservedly bad rumors going around about them: "She's scared of heights," "She can't start the generator," etc. I was lucky to get undeservedly good ones.

At the time, the fire was notable to me for another reason. Along with being the biggest fire I'd been to, it was where I learned that while you get a lot of prestige and glory out of being at a major fire, the work isn't any harder than that of fighting an average house fire. Often, it's actually much easier. Though there's more work, many more people are on hand to do it, and usually there's very little interior attack. You just sit outside and throw water until the fire goes out or the thing burns down.

I also started to understand the irony of publicity over large fires. A firefighter has a funny relationship with fire. Fighting fires is exciting and fun. It's what your training focuses on, and younger firefighters in particular are eager for the challenge. But a fire, in reality, is a failure of the fire department's most important job, which is, or should be, fire prevention. So it's ironic that you get all sorts of glory for your work at a house fire in which the whole building is lost. The real story is that the fire prevention people failed to prevent the fire; the suppression or detection systems were nonexistent, inadequate or malfunctioning; fireground command was unable or incompetent to make an aggressive attack; and the firefighters all sat around holding down master streams for six hours while the fire made a half-acre parking lot out of a three-story building. But the television stations got a lot of good footage because the flames were huge and dramatic and they kept burning long enough for the cameras to get there.

When one of the big office buildings at Wright Pat—next to their fire station, which is always an embarrassment—caught fire, it was a "y'all come." Fairborn, adjacent to the base, responded quickly.

Fire was raging in the north end of the building but had not yet spread to the south. The lieutenant and Minnow and I took a line up the south stairway. It got very hot as we approached the second floor. Minnow was ahead of me, so going up the stairs he was several feet higher. His facepiece started to get sticky. He warned the lieutenant that he felt it was far too hot for us to be in there, so we backed out, taking our line with us. A few minutes later, fire rolled down the hallway. It might have flashed over; I didn't see it. I do remember seeing flames coming out the window here we'd been, but I didn't know at the time whether to be glad we'd gotten out safely, or embarrassed that we'd failed to stop the fire.

The rumor that spread, I heard many months later, was that I had been blown down the stairs and out the door by the flashover. I had then, according to the story, picked myself up, dusted myself off, and gone back in to continue fighting the fire. It wasn't a bad image to have.

One thing that makes emergency work different from most other jobs is that you have to be ready to handle things you will probably, in fact, never encounter. This makes training for them feel like a waste of time. For other people, learning CPR or knowing how to use a fire extinguisher or practicing home exit drills are examples of the same principle. They're vitally important if you ever need them, but since underneath you don't really expect to, it's hard to motivate yourself in that direction.

Most firefighters never have an opportunity to perform a rescue in their entire career. That reality clashes with our public image. Reporters doing stories on women firefighters sometimes ask how many rescues you've made, and you sound like a weenie, or a token, when you say, "None." If they asked most of the men, they'd get the same answer, but they don't ask.

Still, you have to be ready. And you have to be trained for occurrences even rarer than rescues: tornadoes, hospital fires, hazardous materials incidents. The shocker is when you find out that they really can happen to you.

One hot, sticky summer afternoon eight years after I'd begun working for the Miamisburg Fire Department, it happened to us. Several cars of a freight train decided to jump the tracks on the west edge of town. One of the cars was full of phosphorus. Another one held sulphur. The result was the disruption of the lives of thousands of people for more than four days, and the full-scale takeover of the lives of area firefighters for a week and more.

Phosphorus has some interesting properties. It is a toxic substance that, burning, produces slightly less toxic smoke. It is pyrophoric, which means it will ignite all by itself, as long as its temperature is above 86°F. Phosphorus is what's on the head of a match: the friction heat from striking causes it to ignite. The amount of phosphorus on the head of a wooden kitchen match can be measured in milligrams. We had 12,000 gallons of it, and it was beginning to burn.

Within a half hour, the wreckage of the phosphorus tank car was at the center of a fireball bigger than anyone had ever seen. The sulphur tank was also involved, feeding the combustion. The flames were fifty feet high, a beautiful pale shade of apricot, glowing intensely. The plume of white smoke—phosphorus is one of only a few substances that burns with white smoke—billowed high into the air and drifted on the wind towards Dayton.

I had come off duty that morning and was home, just getting ready to go to the gym. My pager went off, advising off-duty units of "an unknown-type chemical spill resulting from a derailment." I hesitated. I was training to lift at the Gay Games, and I grumbled at the prospect of missing a workout only a month before the competition. Even leaving the house I wasn't sure where I was going; I took both my gym bag and my uniform. I turned towards Miamisburg, but then had a change of heart. It was too hot and miserable an afternoon to spend slogging about in acid suits. Near my house, on Salem Avenue, there is a traffic light that's usually red for cars coming off Wabash. I decided if I hit a red light, I'd turn right and go to the gym. Green, and I'd go to Miamisburg. The odds were at least ten to one that it would be red. It was green. I went to work.

On the freeway south, I punched on the AM radio to see if this spill had made it into the evening news or traffic watches. It had, and that was how I learned there was also a fire. Then I saw the smoke, a white column of biblical proportions. The adrenalin kicked in, and my grumpy rather-be-at-the-gym attitude ran off and hid.

For nine days, I was part of the biggest incident I ever expect to see. We were the lead story on the national news, not that any of us had time to watch it. I've never worked as hard as I did on some of those hot afternoons, pulling hose lines around in the mud and rocks. I've never gone so long on so little sleep, or lived on fast food for over a week straight. I only got back to my house three times, and then just long enough to check the mail, take a shower and tumble into bed. If all of this sounds negative, it's not. Events that demand everything you can give leave you with an unconquerable feeling of exuberance that lasts well beyond the fatigue. Given a choice, there was no place in the world I would rather have been.

The fire department in Miamisburg consists of twenty-three full-time people protecting a population of 16,000. We did have the derailment, but it's a small town and we normally aren't a busy department. We do a good job of fire prevention, or so we say, and working fires are few and far between. Occasionally when I'm lying in my bunk at night, I worry a bit about getting rusty. Are the old skills still keen when I haven't been on a hose line in months?

But not too long ago, we got a long-overdue working fire in a two-story frame house. I was the driver of the second-in engine; the temperature was in the teens, and an inch of snow had recently fallen. We responded to the scene and set about our job. During the course of the activities, a new thought popped into my head: that it was nice to know this stuff so well that I didn't have to worry about it. I was doing it by heart.

What had happened to bring about this moment of confidence? It was more than just having known where the address was—Third Street is, after all, pretty easy to find between Fourth and Second—or having driven the slick roads safely. It was the cumulative effect of a series of minor tasks that I could have done wrong, but didn't.

For example, we dropped a firefighter off at the hydrant to pull the end of the hose off, in order to lay a supply line to the attack engine. I saw him wave to signal me to move out, but I also noticed that he had only pulled the hose from the bed. He was standing with the end of the hose in his arms; he hadn't wrapped it around the hydrant. Okay, big guy, I thought; you're the fifteen-year veteran. I pulled away, but glanced back in my sideview mirror after a few seconds. I saw what I expected. Mike was running down the street after the engine, minus the hose. It had pulled out of his arms, not the hose bed. I stopped again to let him catch up and yank out the length of hose he needed, then drove on, chuckling, to the fire.

The captain had already gotten off to help with the initial attack, so I pulled up to the other engine by myself. Without even looking, I thought: when you're using hundred-foot sections of hose, you're always x-hundred, plus ten, feet from the hydrant. Sure enough, a coupling connecting two sections lay ten feet behind the engine. I pulled hose from the bed until the next coupling finally appeared, broke it, handed the end to the pump operator, and walked back to flake the excess hose along the curb so that it wouldn't kink and so that the truck and air unit could get by.

I returned to my engine and pulled up to a spot that was out of the way but still close enough for fetching any needed equipment. I put the pump in gear to keep it from freezing up, then got into the rest of my turnouts, grabbed an air pack, and headed for the fire. It was during that brief walk that I had the thought about knowing what I was doing. Working alone, without anyone to supervise me or remind me or help me, I had done all of these things without even consciously thinking about them.

And it wasn't that they were such remarkable or brilliant things to have done. It was that I hadn't had to tell myself, "Don't forget to put the pump in gear," or "Get an air pack off your own engine." If I hadn't had a feeling about the hydrant not being wrapped and been alert enough to glance back, I'd have been at the fire before someone called me on the radio to let me know the supply line hadn't been laid. What I felt was that it was just plain nice to have the very basics—the unremarkable things—down to where they were truly unremarkable.

Of course, after eleven years on the job, I *should* have this stuff down. Maybe the real point is that this learning comes through experience, and the little things can each be a hard lesson. They are learned through head-thumping and through having done them all wrong many times before: having parked the engine in the wrong place, having been yelled at about the pump freezing up. Hardest of all in the learning process is living in the fear that one will forget such little things at the crucial moment. Undoubtedly, that was why doing things right felt so pleasant. The pain and embarrassment and worry pay off, and they also wear off.

We're never home free in a job with so many variables and so many new situations. Tomorrow night, I may leave Mike at the hydrant without a hose, or park the engine where it blocks the ladder truck. But what I'm finding, overall, is that I'm doing more things right, and being less mortified by my mistakes. I'm becoming skilled at my job because I'm learning it by heart.

Naomi Friedman • Plumbing Contractor
Interview by Nancy Powell

I'm a plumbing contractor in Oakland, California. I got into plumbing because I wanted to make my fortune and be my own boss. I was working as a clerk making a dollar-eighty an hour, which was barely living money—and that was in 1973. It was very frustrating and boring. I knew the only reason I stayed there was that I had no skill to sell in the job market. You just go door to door praying someone will hire you for a lousy bit of money at a lousy job—I was really tired of that. So, I sat down to think about it one day and I said, "Who makes a lot of money? Boy, plumbers make a lot of money—I think I'll be a plumber!" And that was how I started. The more people said to me, "Oh no, you can't be a plumber," the more I was intrigued by why I couldn't. That gave me the impetus to become one—just to show everyone that in fact I *could* do it.

The first thing I did was contact Advocates for Women in Hayward, California. They did everything they could to help me get into the plumbers union, which in Alameda County wasn't very easy to do. I went in to take the test and I was the only woman out of three hundred people. That was a weird experience—to walk into a room of three hundred men and have them all turn to look at me. One man even came up to me and said, "Not only do I have to compete against all these guys, I have to compete against you, too." I wondered what difference it could possibly make—*one* woman! I was able to survive their arithmetic test which wasn't that complicated, then they gave us a little five question questionnaire, which really didn't ask anything to do with plumbing and was a poor way to evaluate us. I ended up on the list ranked fifty-two and they were taking the top ten. I didn't think that was very satisfactory, so, through Advocates for Women, I went back and appealed to the school board. They basically told me to go away. So I went away—telling them that they hadn't seen the last of me.

I spent a year going around to different plumbers looking for someone who would teach me the trade. Most of the time I'd go into plumbing companies and the receptionist would laugh at me—I'd never get beyond her. Other times I'd meet the plumbers on the job. I'd see some work going on and I'd stop and find the plumber and talk to him about it. Finally, I met a woman who knew a plumber in Berkeley and she convinced me to go and see him. I talked to him and ran through my little spiel complete with pauses for laughs, and in my pauses he didn't laugh. From then on I started working with him. I still had another job at that time to pay my bills. For a month I worked for him on the one day off I had during the week. Then I quit my job and went to work for him full-time. The deal we had was that he was going to teach me plumbing and I was going to work for free—because he was teaching me something that no one else had been willing to give me any access to. I was very glad and I'm still not sorry that I worked for free. After working for him for nine months, I decided I had enough skills to go out on my own.

Thank god for the East Bay Women's Yellow Pages because that's how I got my real start as an independent plumber. The women's community was just crying for women plumbers. I got a lot of work and I'm very grateful to those first women customers for allowing me to learn on the job. Some of the them are still my customers many years later and that's very satisfying for me.

I kept going this way until I had enough nerve to apply for a contractor's license. You're supposed to have four years of journeylevel experience. I just told them I had four years of self-employment experience and they bought it. I don't know if they would still go for that, but at that time, which was 1978, they did. All I wanted was for them to give me a chance to take the test. When I passed it they were glad to accept my money. It was a wonderful boon to have a license, it really legitimized my existence.

I started out doing repair. That's when people really need a plumber, when the toilet is overflowing or the water won't shut off. One reason I chose plumbing is because everybody's got it and it's always going to break or need to be moved. That's a real advantage—there'll always be work even if there aren't any new houses built for the next ten years. Every now and then I'd take a stab at doing remodel work, but I'd usually get burned. I didn't really know what I was doing, so I'd bid a job and say it would cost three hundred dollars and I'd end up working for three extra weeks for free just to finish. Learning was really tough, but now that I have more experience I can do more accurate estimates.

Finally, I hooked into a couple of big projects—new jobs, and those are definitely my favorite. They're so straightforward and you're not dealing with somebody else's mickey mouse, screwed-up plumbing. I like remodel work better than repair because you usually work at least a week at a time on one job, and I like that better than going to ten or fifteen jobs in a week.

People have the impression that to be a plumber you really need a lot more strength than to be a carpenter, which isn't true. A lot of things can be done in plumbing if you just know leverage. If something doesn't work with your ten-inch pipe wrench, you get your eighteen-inch pipe wrench. When I started plumbing I had no more strength than the average twenty-two-year-old woman. I've developed big shoulders and big arms from the work that I do, but I didn't start out that way, and I've never lifted weights to prepare myself for the work. The heaviest thing you could possibly lift would be a cast-iron bathtub or a concrete sink, and they weigh about four hundred pounds. There's no way that any human being is going to lift a four-hundred-pound bathtub alone—even a big gorilla man (although some of them will talk like they do—plumbers are great bullshitters!). So you get four women to help and then you can easily lift the tub wherever it needs to be moved. I've done it many times and I'm only five-foot-two and weigh one hundred and twenty pounds, so I'm no Amazon.

You do need a strong stomach to be a plumber because you're dealing with shit—literally! You can't be afraid of tools, or you at least need to learn not to be afraid of them. You use mostly hand tools—the only power tools I really use are a drill and a reciprocating saw. You need a certain amount of manual dexterity. You spend a lot of time crawling under houses, so you can't be afraid of the dark or spiders! You get very dirty. Crawling around under houses is the worst—sometimes you have to pull yourself along on your elbows while you're laying on your stomach because the space is so tight. You have to have kind of a hard head because you can bang it a lot on the joists and other pipes that are down there! Most jobs are in basements or under cabinets and other awkward spaces where there's not much room. I just worked in a cabinet where I strained three muscles I didn't even know I owned. You've got to fit yourself and your tools and your head in so you can see. That's usually the key problem—you can get everything in there but your head!—so you've got to learn how to do a lot of things by feeling your way.

I don't know of that many women who want to be plumbers. I always wonder why more women don't go into the trade. I guess it's because it's dirty and because plumbers work with metal. I happen to like working with metal, but I think more women can relate to wood. But there's good money to be made and we sure could use more women plumbers—ten times more than we've got now. I would love to have enough women plumbers so that when I couldn't get to a job, I'd know another woman who could. As it is, I have to recommend men.

I've faced lots of obstacles, but overall I've really been treated pretty well. Before I was licensed, I was more apt to run into men who simply wouldn't believe I was a plumber. It helps if you can talk their language. For example, if you can go into a supply house and rattle off the right names for fittings, they'll respect you for knowing at least that much. You may not know what to do with a part once you get it, but as least you know what to call it! I actually have more problems in supply houses than I have with people on the job. When you're called in on a job you're usually the only plumber they've got, and since most people have only a rudimentary knowledge of plumbing, they assume if you call yourself a plumber then you must know what you're doing. Also, if someone calls me, they know they're going to get a woman—you can't call "Naomi Friedman Plumbing" and not expect to get Naomi Friedman! Even if all they want to do is hire a woman because they think she's cheap, they at least know they're hiring a woman. My latest problem has been with some inspectors who haven't heard that there are women plumbers out there. One guy made me show him my license three different times; I think he thought I was using someone else's license and he could catch me when I didn't have it. Once they see my work though, they realize that I know what I'm doing.

I enjoy my job—I've been doing it now for fourteen years. I like being able to solve problems. If someone calls and says, "There's this horrible banging in my pipes every time I turn on the hot water," I love to go and be able to fix that problem for them. When I'm doing new work I enjoy doing the layout—figuring out how the system is going to go in, how to use the least number of fittings to be most efficient. I also like it to look good—it's an artistic thing, although there isn't a lot of "art" involved. I like the satisfaction of having produced something tangible at the end of the day. I try to bring a lot of enthusiasm to my work. There's no way I would stay with it if I didn't. This year it was time for me to renew my contractor's license, so it would have been easy to put my license on the inactive list and go do something else. But I'm not going to give it up now. The work is interesting, satisfying and challenging—and I'll tell you, I've paid my dues to do it!

Gigi Marino • Merchant Sailor

In grade school, when all the other kids talked about their dads working in the coal mines, I boasted that my father, an able-bodied seaman, had sailed around the world at least four times. For "Show and Tell," I showed conch shells, abalone and dried starfish, while the other kids brought in anthracite, fossils and slate. In the fourth grade, when girls my age played with Barbie dolls at recess, I preferred my Japanese dolls with their delicately painted faces and ornate kimonos.

By the age of twelve, I reveled in my father's notoriety—he held the distinction of being the only sailor in our small, landlocked coal-mining town in western Pennsylvania. He spent many holidays sailing on a ship in foreign lands, but every time he returned from sea, he brought gifts. His homecomings surpassed Christmas celebrations. He also displayed a few eccentricities, such as shaving his head bald twice a year (kept him cooler under the ferocious sun, he said); staying awake all night long in an insomniac trance, staring straight ahead of him, smoking cigarettes, not talking (said his body spent too much time on the twelve to four watch); and painting continuously, everything in sight. Not only did my father paint our house deck green so that it resembled an oil tanker, but one weekend, when my mother was away, he painted her beautiful oak cupboards the same color. The same weekend, my father intervened while I mopped the kitchen floor. He wanted to show me the proper way to "swab a deck." I watched in horror while he threw an entire bucket of water on the floor, which drained onto the living room carpet.

I used to spy on my father when he'd sit alone in the kitchen eating breakfast. I'd observe him from the living room, admiring his tanned, olive skin, his Roman nose and jet-black hair. But his eyes intrigued me the most. He'd stare out the kitchen window at the hillside, but I knew he wasn't seeing the hillside. A tranquil ocean, I wondered, or a flashback of a sinking ship in World War II? Whatever he saw, the faraway look in his eyes helped me see a new possibility. The possibility that many worlds existed beyond my strip-mined hillsides, and that someday, I, too, would find them.

Several years later, after I'd followed my father's footsteps to sea and achieved equal status with him, I wondered, now what? The old-timers, the tatooed men with leathery faces who'd shipped for thirty or more years, told me to get out of shipping. "You get addicted to it," they warned me, "The salt water gets in your blood. Pretty soon, you're in a rut and can't do anything else." They didn't realize that the salt water had gotten in my blood long before I ever set foot on a ship.

As a college freshman, eighteen years old and idealistic, I wrote to my father, saying that college bored me. I wanted to travel, to get out of Pennsylvania, go to sea. In his reply, he wrote, "I was like you at your age, always looking for that rainbow. I'd travel to Boston, Buffalo, Baltimore; get bored. Move again, always moving, sometimes running. I never could find that rainbow." But he didn't discourage me. Together, we traveled to the nearest Coast Guard office and filed the necessary papers to get my Merchant Mariner's Document. I applied to Exxon for a job onboard oil tankers and waited.

A year and a half later, in 1981, Exxon called and asked if I could join a ship before noon of the next day. They needed an emergency replacement for a woman who'd walked off the ship. I jumped at the chance. After two years at Penn State, I rejoiced in leaving pasty-faced professors and introductory courses behind me. I dashed to the drugstore and bought lotions, shampoo, a two-month supply of tampons; then I dashed back home, called everyone that I worked for and canceled the nine part-time jobs I'd just lined up for the summer.

My father drove me to Bayonne, New Jersey, the next day, where I joined my first ship. As we drove through the refinery to get to the ship, mazes of pipeline networks, huge holding tanks and fat, steaming smokestacks loomed around us. The alien refinery scene, reminiscent of 1950s science fiction movies, intimidated me then, but during the next five years, such scenes began to be familiar and commonplace.

We drove on a rutted road, past derelict warehouses, rusted railroad tracks. Broken glass and tin cans littered the roadside, not even weeds grew in this no-man's land. At the end of the road floated my new home, the *Exxon Bangor*, an old, rusty, two-housed* dinosaur of a tanker (the company scrapped her a year later), held to the dock by thick, greasy, wire mooring cables. My father walked ahead of me, carrying my bags onboard, as I stood on the dock contemplating the skeletal-looking gangway, which descended from the ship at sixty-degree angle. I could die doing this, I told myself, but if I wanted to be a sailor, I'd have to bite the bullet. Timidly, I advanced up the gangway, clinging to the manilla rope rails and not daring to imitate the long steps of my father, whose motion and weight caused the gangway to sway from side to side.

When I stepped on the main deck, I saw several gruffy, unshaven men hustling, looking down tank tops, turning valves, talking on hand-held radios. They looked like they'd been awake most of the night (and had been). Their faces registering no emotion, they looked me over and said nothing. Barely able to control my excitement, I blurted out overzealous hellos and smiled. At the dangerously naive age of twenty, I made my first mistake of my shipping experience: attempting to be friends with everyone on the ship.

My father gave me one piece of advice: Don't go to any-

---

*Superstructures containing living quarters are called houses; all modern tankers are built with only one house.

one's room, and don't let anyone come to your room. My father innocently believed that the guys on the ship would treat me like a daughter. But the reality was that most of the men who shipped out wouldn't *allow* their daughters to go to sea. They didn't view me as someone's daughter, but as fair game. Most of the men saw women on ships as loose and lascivious creatures, their most commonly asked questions about women didn't concern their competence, but who they slept with. I cringed with embarrassment when a shipmate on my first voyage confided in me that the crew discussed my breast size at coffee time.

Within my first week of work, a middle-aged officer propositioned me. Upset and flustered, I consulted the chief engineer, a lanky, gray-haired, contemplative man who wore a baseball cap cocked to one side and spoke with a slow Texas drawl. He consoled me by saying that if he were a female on a ship and didn't get propositioned, then he'd start worrying.

During my first year and a half at sea, I worked in the entry-level position of a utility. I described my job to friends at home as a glorified maid's position. I swabbed the decks, cleaned heads (toilets), made officer's beds. I hated it, but I loved the idea of going to sea, so I stuck with it, hoping another position would open up, preferably in the deck department. I had wanted to work on deck (just like Dad) ever since I first watched a deck gang bring the gangway in. They rigged a block and tackle first and hoisted the gangway on the ship. Then they broke into two groups, each group lifting one side of the gangway and carrying it to the midship house. From that scene I formed my initial image of a deck crew—everyone working in unison.

My father encouraged me to stay in the steward's department and try for a cook's job. I sailed as a cook for one trip (two months) and discovered that I hated the subservient position of waiting on men worse than cleaning up after them. Also, cooking for me, represents a labor of love. I couldn't cook loveless food, nor could I cook for loveless men.

While I debated whether to be a cook or to defy my father

and become an O.S., or ordinary seaman (O.S. is the low deck rating; an able-bodied seaman, or A.B., is the Coast Guard-qualified position), my favorite captain, Howard McCartney, tried to persuade me to attend an academy instead. He repeatedly told me that deck work was hard and dirty. Nevertheless, I decided that working on deck, under the sun, with sea spray and wind blowing in my face, suited me better than staying inside, scrubbing pots till my fingernails turned translucent.

I wrote a letter to the company, requesting to transfer departments, and asked Captain McCartney to sign it. Captain McCartney, a no-nonsense man with a dry, New England sense of humor, signed my letter with a snort, then added, "This isn't going to be as much fun as you think. Just wait till you're covered from head to toe with shit from cleaning cargo tanks." I retorted, "It'll be a damn sight better than changing nasty sheets and cleaning piss off the bulkhead." Captain Mac's spectacles slid down his nose as he raised his eyebrows. He looked me square in the eye and said, "I think I can see what you mean."

Captain Mac's admonishment challenged me. What could be worse than cleaning up after sailors who tracked oil, grease and paint throughout the house, who didn't always flush the toilet, who ground cigarette butts onto my clean decks? Just to work outside with the men, instead of for them, I'd put up with the wind, snow, rain and sleet.

The first thing that I learned on deck was the origin of my father's painting obsession. Fighting the never-ending battle against rust consumes a great deal of the deck department's hours. This involves chipping rust, applying acid, priming and painting—over and over. People either love it or hate it. My father loved it so much that he carried on during his vacations.

On my first deck job, the chief mate instructed me to apply acid to the side of a pump house and then wash it down. I covered the pump house, but when I tried to wash it down, the alleged acid repelled water. Instead of acid, I had grabbed a bucket of lube oil that someone had put in an acid container.

My blunder earned me the title of the Lube Oil Queen for a few weeks. Of all the menial jobs I was assigned to, I preferred chipping. Even though I had to cover every inch of my body to prevent paint and rust chips from sticking in my hair, bra, underwear, socks and shoes, the tinkling sound of the needle gun was so loud that no one bothered me. I'd put on my goggles, particle mask and earplugs and slip into my own little world for several hours. However, if I chipped all day long (eight hours) my hands and forearms sometimes went numb from the constant vibration.

On days when my body ached and my head buzzed (usually after working eight hours on deck and four hours overtime in the engine room), I retreated into the comfort of my room and fell into a deep, exhausted sleep. My stark and simple quarters on the ship provided me with everything I needed—a bunk, desk, reclining chair, wash basin and a shower and head, which I sometimes had to share with the person next door. This utilitarian setting provoked monkish thoughts in me; I realized how little humans truly need for survival.

My quarters never appeared plain, though. I always decorated the walls with pictures of friends, bright posters and cards. My seabag contained several items that my male counterparts' didn't: pillowcases that I had used as a twelve-year-old (that I carried from ship to ship for five years), a box of toys (magic markers, glitter, glue, colored paper) that I brought out when boredom struck, at least a dozen books and my teddy bear. I also lugged my typewriter from ship to ship, even though it weighed twenty-five pounds. Leaving my typewriter at home was worse than forgetting my Buck knife.

One of the most attractive aspects of the seagoing life is the solitude. If I didn't work overtime at night, entire evenings belonged to me to read alone in my room, gaze at the moon or compose poems. The work also provided me with autonomy when I vacationed. When I came home, I could travel as I pleased and a paycheck still arrived in the mail every two weeks.

The solitude, autonomy, financial security and the beauty

of the ocean itself are the things I miss the most now that I have left the trade. I don't miss the dinner conversations, which ranged from dull to duller; being tossed out of bed on nights when the ship rolled; being summoned from a warm bed at 2:00 a.m. to dock or undock in freezing temperatures; and cleaning tanks. Nothing, not even Captain Mac, prepared me for the tank cleaning experience, or "mucking," as we called it.

The first time that I left the bright world of sunshine and fresh air to descend sixty feet into a cargo tank, grasping oil-slick ladders, I couldn't believe that human beings actually cleaned these things. Nothing I know compares to the inside of a cargo tank. The cavernous, steel-partitioned structure creates an eerie feeling and the slightest sound echoes in several directions. Visible, noxious fumes linger in the heavy air. The tanks are dark—the only light filters through the tank top or a butterworth hole (a fourteen-inch opening in the deck used only for tank cleaning). For time-and-a-half pay, those of us assigned to the job of mucking climb over seven-foot-high steel beams and maneuver like moles with our flimsy flashlights.

Mucking involves scraping, shovelling, and scooping muck out of the tank into heavy, black rubber buckets (which look like industrialized versions of a child's sand bucket), and sending the buckets topside on a hook that is attached to the wire of a winch positioned over a butterworth opening. Crew members topside then dump the muck into a fifty-five gallon barrel and send the empty buckets back into the tank. From the bottom of the tank, the buckets look like they're floating back into the tank of their own volition.

Muck comes in various forms. The grimiest muck, found in black oil tanks, is like asphalt mixed with hunks of rust. Ballast tanks contain a different kind of muck, since these tanks hold salt water rather than crude oil. This muck, a more organic sort (it's basically mud: thick, gooey, green-brown) smells as ancient as the musk of a heavily wooded forest. I always preferred mud to muck as it reminded me of primordial origins.

Staying clean within the tank requires Herculean effort. Oil coats everything. Whenever I emerged from a tank, I looked like I had rolled in the stuff. If I brushed my hair back, oil smeared across my face and in my hair (I often had to put "Spray 'n Wash" in my hair to cut the oil.) The oil taste stayed in my mouth for days afterwards. The muck penetrated my coveralls, the clothes underneath, even my skin. Several showers couldn't wash away the thin layer of oil that eventually covered my body. After tank cleaning, I didn't feel clean until the second week of my vacation home.

Tank cleaning ranked as my most-hated job; Captain Mac was right after all. After I passed my Coast Guard exam and received my able-bodied seaman's endorsement, certifying me as an A.B., I expected a reprieve from the dirty work. I did gain some new responsibilities and problems, but I still dirtied my coveralls most days. My new responsibilities included steering the ship and operating the deck machinery (winches, cranes and anchor windlasses) as well as retaining a working knowledge of marlinspike seamanship (splicing line and tying knots). Steering the ship thrilled me, especially one memorable trip on the Mississippi River, where I had to fight the strong currents to say on course. Whenever I stood at the helm, I felt like an extension of the ship.

My problems came not from the work, but from the men, especially after I gained equal or higher status with some of my shipmates. On my last ship, I worked with two ordinary seamen who would ignore me or turn and walk away when I spoke to them. The majority of men who work on deck express sentiments that women don't belong there. I've been disappointed numerous times when I've formed a friendship with a male shipmate, only to hear him tell me later, "God created women to make babies. It ain't natural for you to be here." Another shipmate told me that I had no respect for the male ego. "How do you think it makes us feel," he asked, "to have you go out and do the same job as us?"

Other strong, independent and supportive women whom I met and formed lasting friendships with supplied me with doses of strength to continue doing my job. I often sailed as the only woman on a ship in a crew of thirty, but once I sailed with six other women. We stuck together and felt the freedom to be ourselves; we could discuss clothes and exercise instead of World War II stories.

When I first sailed A.B., nothing I did could please the captain. For the first few weeks, he wouldn't "let" me steer (even though it was my job) until I practiced every night and convinced him of my ability. Every day he criticized me for some petty reason: I walked onto the bridge from the wrong door, I drank coffee on the bridge, I used the wrong binoculars, I wore a hat when I steered the ship, I believed in Darwinism. Ridiculous as his actions were, I had to tolerate it; he was the captain. And in the ship world, the captain sits next to God. Not being able to get away isolates the ship world from the "real" world.

Fortunately, I was lucky to have Beth Fisher, a feisty woman who had built her own sailboat and worked in the industry for twelve years, sail on that ship with me. I'd grown tired of the uphill struggle of having to "prove myself" daily to men who didn't matter to me, and without Beth's support I would have walked off. She reassured me that I wasn't imagining the ridiculousness of the situation. She'd experienced similar trials; on one ship, she learned that the engine room men had heard she was a feminist and had set out as a group to "bring her down to earth" before they even met her.

My father never empathized with the problems that I experienced as a female sailor. During the five years that I spent at sea, I began seeing him, and ultimately myself, in a different light. When I first set out to sea, I idolized my father; I saw him as a hero. But the more competent and knowledgeable I became, the more my father looked like a normal man.

When I made plans to leave shipping I felt immediate relief from a number of responsibilities I had wearied of, one of the worst being tending lines. This task produced more stomach knots and nervous flutters than all other jobs combined. Tending lines simply means keeping the ship flush with the dock by heaving in on, or slacking off the mooring lines (thick, eight-strand wire cables attached to winch drums and poly lines), depending on whether the ship is being loaded or discharged. The ship either moves up or down. The tide change, wind direction and traffic in the ship channel also affect the ship's upward or downward motion, as well as which tanks are moving cargo. The bow could rise as the stern sinks. I tended lines for a year and never figured out a method that didn't keep me from running from the stern to the bow the whole time. Several of my shipmates tended lines without breaking into a cold sweat, but for me, the idea of keeping a nine-hundred foot tanker next to the dock seemed like an awesome responsibility.

I left shipping last year because I wanted to see the seasons change, to graduate finally from college. But I can't deny the salt water that still runs through my blood, and restless energy fills me at odd times. While studying for tests, I'd fantasize about dropping out of school and signing on a ship that travels around the world. (Exxon didn't sail foreign; Panama and Alaska filled the bill for my exotic adventures.) But I also realized that shipping out translated into a socially acceptable form of running away for me. As long as I continued hopping onto another ship every few months, I copped the perfect excuse not to make commitments to people, to myself, to my writing.

I fell in love with the ocean instantly and missed her more than anything. I missed the days when I'd watch foamy whitecaps ride on purple-blue waves, making me feel like I was inside of a vibrant painting. On misty mornings, I'd look out of my window and remember the low, melancholy cry of a fog horn. I'd remember full moon nights of standing lookout on the bow, silver reflections floating on the water as porpoises swam with the ship, emitting phosphorescent tails, jumping and suddenly twirling. I'd think of sitting alone on the poop deck, drinking coffee, watching the day emerge from the ocean, understanding exactly what Homer meant by "rosy fingered dawn."

I wrote a poem a few years ago for a soon-to-be-married shipmate. The last stanza read:

> *Sailor, set your course*
> *Homeward-bound, to the*
> *Heart of all things.*

I followed my own words home.

Juanita Sanchez • Machinist

Maybe it's because I'm a woman that I'm so often asked how I became interested in being a machinist. Most of the time, I begin my reply to this question by saying that I must have been insane at the time. I tell about going to vocational school to become an auto mechanic. I had *really* wanted to work as an auto mechanic specializing in auto machining, which is quite different from precision machining. Then I detail my hard times learning the basics of machining and how I promised myself that I would never end up inside a precision machine shop, so help me "pagan spirits," but I did anyway!

I had been giving presentations through the Women's Trade Center about women in blue-collar work to various women's groups and high school students. The Women's Trade Center was designed and developed to recruit women into the skilled trades by providing them with information on apprenticeship and other training programs. The director of the Trade Center gave me a pamphlet on a machinist apprenticeship opening at a national laboratory in my hometown. The women at the Trade Center were actively seeking women to apply for the program, but it was the director herself who really wanted me to apply. I resisted. I was reluctant to accept the idea of becoming a machinist. I wanted to be an auto mechanic. I had taken a course in machining and I could not develop a liking for it. Machining can be stressful, especially since it takes so much time to learn (four to five years) and is highly technical, requiring not only manual dexterity and coordination but mathematical skills and mental concentration as well.

After much debate with myself, I finally decided to apply, but with the attitude that the company would have to pass *my* standards. I would interview *them* as well. I asked to meet with a journeylevel machinist and an apprentice who were women. I even asked for a guided tour through the facilities, which was probably a lot to ask since the laboratory is situated inside a military installation with very limited access to outsiders. As a matter of fact, all employees must undergo intensive investigation to obtain a government clearance.

The time was ripe for hiring; a woman was needed and I was the right woman for the job. After a few interviews and a few tests, I found myself working in a weapons laboratory. Like Alice through the Looking Glass, suddenly there I was trying to make sense of it all.

After five years, I graduated from the machinist apprentice program. However, after four years, I was recognized as a journey"man" machinist by the International Association of Machinists (IAM). Being in the apprenticeship program was a period of high anxiety for me because there were many times when I thought, as did others in the program, that I just wasn't going to make it. The program wasn't really difficult. What made it hard was not getting exactly the same type of training that the men received. I'm sure, in retrospect, that my male trainers didn't know how to cope or work with a woman apprentice. Consequently, the jobs given to me were not as challenging as the jobs given to the male apprentices.

I didn't think they had much confidence that I could do the job, and even at the very end of my training, I was told that I might be kept in the apprentice program longer because my supervisor and lead man both felt I wasn't progressing. I was devastated and vowed to fight that action any way that I could, including consulting a labor relations lawyer.

In the last year of my formal training, the apprentice shop

supervisor brought in a new lead man. He was a soft-spoken, gentle man who seemed sure of himself and had no problem dealing with women in the machine shop setting. I asked him for more challenging jobs that would give me more exposure to the computer-assisted machines. He immediately trusted me, gave me more complex jobs, and allowed me to operate the computer-assisted mill. I excelled and graduated. I think many of the members of my apprenticeship class thought I wouldn't "stick it out" and I think I gained their respect when they saw that I was competent.

Today I don't pretend to be a crackerjack machinist, but I hold my own as a respectable one. However, most of my supervisors still tend to keep the more complicated jobs and machines out of my hands. It's frustrating to know that I can do the job but I am not trusted enough with either the more complex parts or machinery, and that my requests for such work fall on deaf ears.

A few of the supervisors have given me demanding work but, since I am rotated periodically within the department, I very often have to begin at the beginning to try to convince my supervisor of my abilities. Strangely enough, most of the older male machinists have been the most supportive, trusting and helpful.

So here I am "sticking it out." If it were not for the job itself, I would have left a long time ago. The relationship between the machinist and the machine can feel mystical. Sometimes I feel as if I am a musician conducting a sophisticated orchestra. The parts I make are my children and it's hard for me to see them get into the hands of the engineers or consultants. I have made parts that are as tall as my bedroom ceiling and parts so small that I need a microscope just to see what I am cutting. I make parts from almost every material imaginable, from the hardest—for which special cutting tools are necessary—to the softest—fragile as soap. I've also worked on material where a special type of extinguisher is required because the material becomes highly flammable during cutting. I have made pieces for use in a museum as well as pieces that are demolished in testing. My work is not classified as production (many pieces of one thing), but prototype (one of a kind). I have made many pieces of one type of part, though usually there are no more than thirty. The tolerances are tight. We have to be accurate with dimension sizes as small as two ten-thousandths of an inch. This is the equivalent of splitting a hair three times, then splitting one of the pieces ten times. In some cases, tolerances are even tighter. The tools are expensive, as is the training, and I've grown to love the trade. The work I do is satisfying but is not without its problems.

The biggest problem I have, besides the usual problems of working with men, is working in a weapons research and development laboratory. Working at the laboratory contradicts my ideals and philosophies. It is difficult for me to reconcile making bombs while I speak out against weapons development and escalation. It gets especially difficult when I am participating in a function sponsored by a peace group and I am asked by some of its members about where I work. I receive responses such as, "Oh, the enemy," or "You know you should find yourself another place to work." When this happens, I lose a sense of myself and become very anxious. I feel guilty and I internalize the criticism. I begin to hate myself for not having the courage to leave my place of work, but where would I go with my training?

I suppose I could move out of the state or I could change careers. I love New Mexico and I love the trade. All around me I am seeing more and more employees wrestling with the same conflicts I have. I get the most support from my Chicana/Indian sisters, who know poverty, racism and just how second-class we are treated in this society. High-paying jobs in my home state are not plentiful for anyone, much less Chicana/Indian women. We have few choices about where we can work while we are being trained and making a living wage. So, while my Chicana/Indian sisters don't praise weapons work, they don't admonish me or react punitively to me when I say what I do or where I work. We understand the basis of the conflict and we know our own people's struggle to survive.

I've examined my soul and studied my options. I've decided to stay here at my job until I find what I want and where I belong in the world. For now, I am at peace with my decision. I accept what I am: a Chicana/Indian deeply involved in her roots.

As a curandera (healer), I decided that I had to heal myself of the pain from working in a weapons research and development laboratory. I needed to resolve the conflict I had with myself and I did so with a ritual I performed about two years ago.

I thought about performing the ritual after I had been working closely with an engineer on a special weapons project. I had fabricated some parts for the project and, after completion and in gratitude, he gave me an eight-by-ten color photograph of the weapons system that was going to be tested. When I looked at the picture, my heart sank. The photograph was of a missile to be test fired. I couldn't believe that I had participated in building such a monstrous device that could be used against men, women, children and other forms of life sharing this world. I knew I had to do something symbolic to affirm myself as a curandera who is concerned with the future of the world.

I went to Chaco Canyon, where the ruins of the ancient Anasazi Indians rest. The ruins are magnificently spread throughout the desert canyon, which contains dramatic mesas contrasted with deep arroyos. I needed to call upon the ancient spirits to help me accept the part of me that is creative and good. I came with friends to help me with the ritual. I had brought the picture of the missile with me. As I walked along one of the canyon's trails I looked for the spot that would talk to me and tell me it was right for the brief ceremony. We hid behind a large rock. I pulled out my medicine bag (given to me by another curandera sister), took out some sweet grass and root, lit it and let the women who were with me inhale the richness of the smoke. Then, with my hands, I dug a small hole, took the picture of the missile and lit it with a match. I placed the burning photo into the shallow grave and covered it with the sands of the Chaco desert. I then placed a shard of Chaco pottery over the small mound. I called upon the grandmothers of the ancients to destroy this deadly weapon. I called upon them to soften the hearts of the men and women who develop these weapons without conscience. I called upon them to destroy the banners of hate that are waved from the hands of hateful people.

I didn't want to carry away negative feelings from the ritual. So I ended it not by asking that men and women of the weapons facility lose their jobs, but by asking that they become aware of what they are doing in a world that increases in danger every day.

With these thoughts and emotions, I left the Chaco. I returned to the machinery and the metal of a male-dominated trade, a trade I love but one which I know I will eventually leave. I have been described as a pioneer woman, having been one of the few (certainly not the first) women who dared break the male barrier to join the ranks as a bona fide journeylevel machinist.

Currently, I am working part-time on a master's degree in Human Resources Development with a special interest in labor relations. This is due in part to my recent election as a union steward.

Perhaps it will be in union participation that I can work toward improving working conditions, especially for women and minorities. But I also want to work for the general tradesperson of any background and ideology. While I am a poet who happens to fantasize about Utopia, I am firmly grounded in reality and can face a challenge.

If I remain a machinist, I will continue to search for an alternative to weapons-creating machining. For now, the pain I feel from fabricating parts for weapons development will never go away. Though I live a life full of contradictions, I try to maintain a balance by looking for options that will lead me out of the weapons industry and out of the painful conflicts I experience in affirming myself as a curandera—working as a machinist in a weapons facility.

Marian Swerdlow • Subway Conductor

In the late 1970s, the New York City Transit Authority opened the titles of motorman and conductor to female applicants. By the time I became a conductor in 1982, there were still very few women working in these titles. We remained oddities, pioneers.

Most people on the subway trains don't really have much of an idea what the motorman or the conductor does. The motorman works in the front of the train and drives it. The conductor works at or near the middle of the train, operates the doors and makes most of the announcements.

A lot of people think the subway conductor and motorman job must be easy or even fun to do. That wasn't my experience. The high noise level and the vibration are nerve-wracking. It's against the rules to use earplugs, though that never stopped me from protecting my hearing that way. The air is full of steel dust which gets in your eyes and your nose and gives your uniform a silvery sheen that the oldtimers call "silver dust." The trains are often brutally cold in the winter and hot as hell in the summer. The work is fairly dangerous: each employee averages one lost time accident a year and about one motorman or conductor out of a total six thousand dies in a work accident each year.

By the time you get off your train after a trip of around two hours, you are ready for a break. But usually you get less than ten minutes in the crewroom. At lunch, you might, if lucky, get thirty minutes. Even then, the crew room is pretty grim, dirty and noisy. Not exactly climate-controlled, either. The ones underground are the worst. The toilet facilities are unreliable, often smelly and sometimes flooded, and you can practically never get soap or towels. To make matters worse, most terminals do not have separate facilities for men and women, but more of that later.

All too quickly you are back "on the road." For a conductor, this is time to play "duck the rider." When I was working the Number 4 line, I was the target of an average of two attempted physical assaults a week. When I tell people this, they usually assume I must have done something to provoke my assailants—they just can't imagine that human beings would attack someone completely innocent. Well, guess again. The assaults were mostly from children! The conductor has to observe the train for three car lengths as it pulls out of each station. That means we have to have our heads out of the window of the cab as the train pulls out, until it moves 150 feet. The kids know this. They wait there on the platform, getting ready to spit, hit or throw something as the conductor passes. They get a kick out of hitting someone who can't do anything back. Some of these kids look as young as seven or eight. Usually the injury is more psychological than physical, but not always.

As you can imagine, after eight hours of this, a conductor is dying to go home, unless he or she has a crying need for "soap," as overtime is called. But the average shift has been growing longer and it's now about nine hours. And, if anything goes wrong on the road, you can end up working many more hours without any choice or advance notice. So on my last return trip I'd always have my heart in my mouth, afraid of getting "turned," that is, being forced to make an extra trip.

Since the subways run seven days a week, and days off are picked according to seniority, it takes at least five years for a conductor to get even part of the weekend off. Hours are also picked by seniority. My first year, I was forced to work evenings and nights. For motormen on some lines, it can take years to get onto days.

This is the job, whether you are male or female, but as women, especially "pioneers," we faced some extra problems.

There was only one other woman in my conductor's class, Helena.* When we came out on the road we were bombarded with attention from our co-workers, who mostly wanted to know: "What does you husband think about you doing this?" This was a way of finding out whether we did have a lord-and-master, or were unattached. The first few months, I got propositioned so consistently that I finally joked about giving a civil service exam for the position, with a filing fee and a physical (which is what you have to do to become a conductor). I was relieved that no one took rejection personally—they were like someone who routinely looks in the coin return of pay phones to see if there's a quarter there, with the hope that you never know, you just might get lucky.

In some ways the men were happy to see us. We were a distraction, something different. But we were also a threat. Not to their jobs—the union and management had had a no layoff policy for years—but to their self-image. They saw themselves as doing a man's job. They had a big stake in believing they were doing a job only the superior sex could handle emotionally as well as physically. They really didn't believe that we could handle it, that we could have the presence of mind, the courage, the cool. But here we were.

Ironically, one of the results of their skepticism was that, as individuals, we got a lot of praise. It really knocked their socks off when we handled a violent rider, or a door problem, or even just did our job competently. It didn't take much for a motorman to come into the crewroom telling all the others what a great conductor I was.

But even as each motorman or conductor thought his work partner was the glowing exception to general female helplessness, he was hungrily listening to, and repeating, tales which reinforced the old stereotypes. Every time a woman made a mistake it was endlessly repeated, and embroidered, and

---

*All names in this story are pseudonyms.

repeated, in crewrooms throughout the system.

Donna March was one of the first women to "go to the motors" (become a motorman). She was legendary for her knowledge of trains, her vulgar mouth and her sexual appetite. All of this made her particularly threatening to the men on the job. Then one day she took the wrong "line-up" (track) heading for the wrong terminal. She tried to get back to the right track by backing up the train, which is absolutely forbidden, and she got caught. She was busted back to conductor. Now, plenty of men have backed up trains, and plenty of men have been caught and busted. It gets discussed in their terminal a few days and then it is dropped. But when Donna screwed up, it was talked about all over the IRT for years. After Donna got her handles back (was restored to motorman) the guys in the crewroom started talking about it all over again!

When I first came out to the road, I was assigned to midnights. My very first night on the road, I was sent out of my usual line, to the Number 1 line. On my second trip, two of the riders shot each other right outside of my cab. That kind of thing never happened again on my train, but it happened my first night when I was brand new. Well, I was not delighted, but I never thought of quitting. The next night I was back on my usual Number 4 line. About a year later, I worked on the 1 again and all the guys said to me: "What are you doing here? You quit when you had the shooting!" That was their image of women: the job was too rough, what we'd see would be too much for our maidenly delicacy. That image was much more convenient than the facts.

But as more and more of us came on, did the job, didn't scream and faint when the riders shot each other, when the cabs blew up (as mine did once), when people fell between the cars, or when riders threatened us with mayhem, it became obvious that, yes, we really could do the job.

The men never stopped believing that we were given extra privileges—privileges they as men did not receive. For example, they believed "all the women conductors go down to Jay Street." Jay Street is the Transit Authority headquarters in

Brooklyn. There are a few clerical positions there reserved for conductors. It *is* possible that a lot of the first women to get called for conductor ended up there, which might have had as much to do with the Transit Authority not wanting women on the road as with what the women themselves wanted. But as far as some of our male co-workers were concerned, that's where all the women went—straight to those cushy desk jobs, while they slaved on the road. A friend of mine once met a conductor at a bar, who gave her a song-and-dance about the women all going to Jay Street. My friend quickly referred to me as evidence against this. "Oh sure," he responded, "I know Marian. Tell her Redford says hi." Almost immediately after that I had to visit headquarters for some reason, probably unpleasant, and who do I find there, working a cushy desk job, but Conductor Redford.

Another legend had it that women never worked terminals or hours they did not want. I sure didn't know that when I spent six months working nights on the 2 line, which was nicknamed "the Beast." Helena didn't know that when she got stuck working with the farebox on the 5 line. The box weighs at least thirty-five pounds and she, just like the men, had to carry it on and off the trains, and up and down steps, several times in an evening. One night, lifting it, Helena felt a sharp twinge. She'd gotten a hernia. She was out for a total of almost two years. The Transit Authority disputed her worker's comp claim, too, ludicrously claiming that she came on the job with the hernia. That's the special way the Transit Authority treated women.

There was also the tale that the signal system was changed to accommodate women motormen. In the early 1980s, some signals were changed to make it easier to bypass them if they malfunctioned. The old way, the motorman had to fasten down a heavy trip arm next to the tracks; the new way, he or she could just insert a key in the signal. Well, the guys all said it was because women weren't strong enough to fasten down the trip arm. The change might have had more to do with a fatality in the summer of 1980. A motorman was killed when he accidentally touched the third rail while fastening down a trip arm (the third rail carries 600 volts of direct current). And he wasn't a woman.

Management's main policy towards the women on the job could be summed up as "malign neglect." They refused to recognize we'd arrived. We wore uniforms designed for men, which meant they fit terribly. They felt awful and looked worse. More problematic was the absence of separate toilet facilities for women and men at most terminals.

The trouble of sharing with our male co-workers was exacerbated when the toilet cubicles lacked latches and sometimes even doors. Outside the cubicles were the urinals, which meant that even when locks were put on the cubicles, it wouldn't necessarily spare you and your male co-worker an embarrassing encounter as you stepped out of your cubicle.

The big Transit Authority innovation was to put latches on the doors of the restroom itself. But this meant that one solitary woman in the restroom, if she locked the restroom door to keep men from using the urinals and risking that oh-so-embarrassing encounter, could effectively prevent anyone else in the terminal, male or female, from entering to urinate, wash their hands, or get water for the kettle. With lunches and breaks inhumanly short, this created tensions between the men and the women. When I started a petition for a separate women's toilet at the Number 4 line terminal, Woodlawn, there wasn't a man who wouldn't sign it. The sheets I posted on the walls quickly filled up with signatures. Unfortunately, management was much less cooperative than our male co-workers.

One of the times I faced disciplinary charges arose out of the unisex toilet situation. About a year after I came on the job, I one day ate or drank something that did not agree with me. I was working out of a terminal in which there was no lock on the restroom, and no doors on the toilet cubicles. I just could not bring myself to use the toilet.

I tried to book sick. I was told I could either go to a hospital or face immediate suspension. I decided to continue working. I fainted at Times Square at the height of the rush hour. After I revived, I had to talk to the bigshot at headquarters, the desk trainmaster, for this infraction of passing out. He wasn't satisfied when I explained what had made me sick and told me that I faced disciplinary charges. I said: "I think this is the Transit Authority's fault for not having separate facilities for women." He said: "Next you'll want powder rooms." This guy is now the chief of the subway command center.

The union presides over all this misery. Local 100 of the Transport Workers Union (AFL-CIO) has been so unresponsive that most motormen and conductors see it as a company union. No copy of any contract was available to the members the whole time I worked as a conductor. (One was given out in late 1987, after a ten-year wait.) There are no elected shop stewards, and there was no shop steward training from 1981 to 1986. Union officers blame their own members for the worsening conditions of work, tell the membership, "You're lucky to have jobs," and generally justify management policies.

The union officers were pretty much indifferent to whatever special problems we faced as women. One such issue was maternity leave. Boda Trinshaw was probably the first female operative to become pregnant. When I tried to get information from the union regarding maternity leave I was given an elaborate runaround, probably because no one knew, and no one wanted to take the trouble to find out, our rights. One union officer I spoke with angrily accused Boda of "stirring up" all the women operatives. Another officer confided in me that his brother officers' attitude was basically, "Why didn't she keep her legs together?" This comment was made even though her husband was also a conductor and a union member.

I was very interested in being active in rank-and-file efforts to democratize and revitalize the local. At the beginning, I tried to work with the experienced union dissidents who had been influential in the late seventies. Their strength culminated in the 1980 New York transit strike, which was won on the picket line by the workers and lost at the bargaining table by union leaders who wanted to discourage future militance.

These "old" dissidents were not much better than the union leaders in many ways, including their attitudes towards women. They were suspicious of the early attempt of women on the job to organize the "Lady Motormen's Association" (bad name, good idea). And in the summer of 1984, the old dissidents tried to exclude Donna March from their slate for convention delegate because of what they considered her reputation for promiscuity!

I was very fortunate, though, because I found other rank-and-filers I could work with, who generally had better attitudes about women and women's issues, on and off the job. We founded a rank-and-file newsletter, *Hell on Wheels*. Working on that rag was by far the best part of the transit job for me.

The four years I worked as a conductor, more and more women came on the job. Almost all of them were black. Women enter this field because, compared to the jobs in the pink-collar ghetto, transit offers better pay, better benefits and better opportunities for promotion. Working as a conductor is difficult for women because of the intense contact with the public, though it's hard to know whether women get more physical or verbal abuse than men.

Motors is a step up from conductor and gets you away from the public. But it also requires strength and more physical confidence than I, for one, had. A motorman can expect to spend a lot of time on the tracks, both in the hole (the tunnels) and on the structure (the elevated tracks). I was, to be quite honest, afraid of this work. Afraid of the third rail, the "shoes" protruding from the train which were also electrified, the trains speeding by, and, on the structure, the huge gaps between the ties you had to jump across. I didn't feel I could refuse an order, no matter how dangerous I thought it was, because it would just fuel the crewroom scuttlebutt that women couldn't do the job. And if, god forbid, I were clumsy or unlucky enough to get myself badly hurt, it would cast doubts on any woman's ability to do the job and survive. So I stayed in my conductor blues (this refers to the uniform, but for me it got to be a state of mind). But plenty of women went to motors, plenty more are going, and my hat's off to them.

I left transit in the summer of 1986. Today, there are many more women operating on the subways than when I came on. They are no longer oddities, no longer pioneers. But working conditions are still worsening for transit workers, and the special problems faced by women in these jobs are still not recognized.

Laura Deane Mason • Rural Contractor
Interview by Elizabeth D. Ross

I am the eldest of six kids. My father was in the Texas Major Leagues Triple A Baseball, which meant he wasn't around much. So whenever anything needed to get done, I was usually the one who did it. My parents were originally from San Jose, California, and we moved back there when I was nine. Eventually my father became a firefighter. He also worked for a construction firm, and I helped him with different home projects: converting our garage into a bedroom, roofing and painting the house. When my grandfather moved in with us, he and I putzed around and fixed things together.

After college I got a teaching credential. Until I landed a teaching position I worked at a variety of odd jobs—as a change counter in a hardware supply store, as a substitute teacher and as a recreation instructor teaching tumbling to four- and five-year-old kids. Finally I was hired to teach junior high school. I taught math and physical education for three years, until my partner's mother had a heart attack and we moved to Los Angeles to be near her. I wasn't able to find another teaching position so once again, I did odd jobs, trying to keep the money coming in.

A friend suggested I go down to the carpenters union and look into construction jobs. I took a test and spent the next four months trying to find work. Finally I contacted a group which helped Mexican-American men and women and other disenfranchised people get into construction work. They agreed to send somebody to go around to jobsites with me. Eventually one of the companies we talked to told me to come back the next day, which I did. After I had been working for them for about four hours, they still hadn't signed my indenture papers, so I said, "Well, are you going to sign or not? If you're not, then I'm leaving." They signed, and I got hired on.

I was one of two women in the Orange County carpenter apprenticeship program. I was with that particular company for eleven months. Once when I was working on a second floor of a condominium, I saw another tradeswoman outside the window. It's amazing how you can spot each other like radar. I'm not sure exactly what trade she was in, but she saw me and we gave each other the thumbs up signal. It was a great feeling seeing another tradeswoman on the job. We never spoke but I felt a tremendous connection. I wasn't alone.

I did my second and third years of my carpentry apprenticeship in San Jose with another company. It took awhile for them to let me stack roofs (putting up the ridges and rafters of the roof) because they didn't want their only "girl carpenter" falling and getting hurt. I learned a little bit of everything, and found out about the rigid hierarchy in the apprenticeship program—the "I had to do shit therefore you have to do shit" pecking order. As an apprentice you have to survive the age-old ritual of doing grunt work for four years and dealing with power trips from people one rung above you. I was able to survive by being big physically—five-foot-eight and a half—and being good with verbal volleyball. A quick comeback saved me many a time. I'd practice on the way to work or driving home: I'd try to think of any potentially troublesome situation I might find myself in and think of a one-line comeback. It was amazing how I could defend myself without having to pause and think about it—I became a quick draw, a verbal slinger.

Eventually we moved to Healdsburg in Sonoma County. My next jobs were pretty far away, two hours or more each way. After that I made the decision to stay within Sonoma County as much as possible, and things were pretty lean. I did a lot of banging on doors, trying to get work here in town. I got a job with a local union contractor. I did interior trim, the cabinets that have contact veneer—the same knothole every four inches. Tacky tract. It did make me feel good though, because I could lift an entire upper cabinet by myself. I had to install a door in fifteen minutes, just using finish nails: tack it and put the jamb on quick, because that holds on the door! Hardware, shelves, closet poles and window sills, I did that for about six months. That was one time I worked with another woman. That boss hired women; I suppose he thought they did a better job on interior trim. It was great working with another woman. She was a friend of mine and we would have lunch together and talk about everything, especially about how it was being in the trades.

I participated in the carpenters union apprenticeship contest in 1981. There were three women in my graduating class that year, myself included, and we had a really good instructor who worked with us every Saturday before the contest. Viarra and I were entered in the competition and Lesta was chosen as an alternate. The contest was held at the Napa County Fairgrounds. My mother, my sisters, my grandmother "Mum," my niece and my partner came to watch—all the women in my family. It was also a 4-H day at the Fairgrounds and there were lots of kids. In the morning everyone laid out their tools to be checked, then we had to build a bus stop structure, on which we were timed. I was building the bus stop in sections on the ground and the others were building theirs upright. So when I put the walls up and the roof on, I was one of the first ones finished. The judges tabulated their scores and began to make the awards. They started at third place—which Viarra won. Then second. Then first place. The guy wasn't saying anything, just stuttering and mumbling. Then finally he admitted it; I had won first place! I got a check for one hundred dollars and a tool box and some tools.

From there we went to the Northern California contest. I

was very nervous. At the get-together the night before the contest, one of the judges came up to me and said, "Over my dead body will a woman place." That's the thing about construction, they'll say it right to your face! I just laughed. The atmosphere at this competition was very different; almost all of the competitors were men and there was a lot of hostility towards me. This is when I coined the term "the sound of penises shriveling"—a dry leaf kind of sound I heard all day long. Fortunately I had some good support: my father and lots of women from Sonoma County came to watch me and my mother went with me to the banquet. But when I took fifth place and beat the guy from my local, I was glad to get out of there with my skin.

At the apprenticeship graduation ceremonies—for all the apprentices turning out in all the union locals in Sonoma County—Viarra, Lesta and I were all there with our significant others. We sat together with the teacher who had helped us in the Napa Fairground contest. You could feel the hatred in the room towards us, three sets of couples—all women. A woman from the State Division of Apprenticeship Standards stood up and pronounced us journey*men*. Viarra, who was commended for winning third place in the competition, went up and told her it should be journey*level*. When the woman said that the term journey*men* was generic, Viarra answered that she didn't have those kind of generics. Then they handed out the Clyde Vogel Award for the Outstanding Apprentice of 1981, and I won that.

After I turned out as a journeywoman, I worked up at the Geysers, a geothermal plant for generating electricity. At the geysers we built cooling towers to turn the earth's steam into energy. I learned a lot about "help." Guys come up and want to give you a hand—if you accept it that guy will go and tell everybody that he *had* to help you. At that job a guy told me not to push it so hard. This was a commercial job so it was a slower pace than residential tracts where it's assholes and elbows (that's all the foreman wants to see). We got a new foreman on the job, and because he was new at it he couldn't keep us busy. There was a woman apprentice laid off the week before I was.

When I was laid off I went and talked to the superintendent, who was a small man with a small man power problem. We exchanged a few words. I was still laid off, but I felt better. Later, I found out they were fishing through the union pool. They would call up about fifteen people, then lay off fourteen in order to get the one they wanted. You can't constantly request from the union, so this is the way around that. I've found this is a common practice although it may not be legal.

In 1982 I started working for the County of Sonoma. The county hadn't hired too many women up to that time, but there was a woman on the grounds crew. She filed a grievance over pornographic magazines left out at one of the facilities by male co-workers. I checked it out myself and it was true. I went out to one of the facilities, and there was all this pornography—not even the stuff you see in the stores, but the worst, most violent stuff—the sleaze of the sleaze. I talked to the superintendent and the magazines disappeared for a while, but then they reappeared. So one time when I was working there by myself, I took all the magazines and cut them up with the tablesaw into two-inch squares, then put them back in the drawer. They never appeared again—at least not while I worked there.

Being employed by the county was definitely *work* in the boring sense of the word, so it was a relief to leave after two years. I did a variety of jobs and then got hired doing bridge construction. The company that hired me advertised for a "female-type" carpenter. So I went to the foreman and introduced myself as "the token." He laughed and things were fine from then on.

I worked with good people and my partner was great. One day when we were down in the bottom of one of the form holes he started talking about how it reminded him of Mother Teresa going down into the mines to talk to the workers in Calcutta. This was a surprise—that he even knew who she was. The creek we were working on was dammed upstream with a giant culvert running downstream through another dam. It took all the clean water upstream so the bridge-building wouldn't pollute the creek, since it was a spawning area for salmon. This bridge was finished in December and we had to take the pieces of forty-eight-inch diameter pipe out. There we were with our waders on, taking the couplers off, water pouring inside our waders. We're slipping and sliding and it's freezing. It was hard, messy and fun. It was also the first time I had been around really heavy, loud and dangerous machinery. You had to be alert.

People get killed doing bridgework and I could see why. On one bridge, we put up iron I-beams across the creek, two hundred feet, that we would then walk across. The drop was thirty to forty feet and the beams were six inches wide and several feet apart. That wasn't too bad, but then we had to put what are called cambers on top of the beams to create the curve on the top of the bridge. The cambers were only about an inch wide, and we had to go down the beams and strap them on with metal strapping tape. That narrow, rounded surface was what we had to walk on until we put on the plywood and poured the concrete. There were also huge support timbers all around the bridge forms until after the concrete was poured. Then they were sent crashing down, which was very dangerous if not done properly.

I also worked on a bridge in which they brought in seven prestressed concrete girders. These were each one hundred feet long and weighed forty-seven tons apiece. Once the girders were in place, we had to go in and form in between and up inside them and put in the diaphram, which connects all the girders together. Well, to do this work you're out there hanging over nothing—you have what looks like big swings and you push them out over the creek and then put a plank down. I loved the work, not only learning about form design, but being outside, listening to the sound of flowing water and seeing the wildlife—mink, herons, and egrets. And building.

I worked on the bridges until January of 1987. In 1987 I started my own business, Alchemy Construction, with Pamela Miller, a journeylevel carpenter. One thing that's nice about working for myself is that I don't have to protect myself so much. I don't have people attacking me verbally, trying to tell me I'm fucking up all over the place when I'm doing just fine. Women could get a lot more done on the job if they could just go and do their work and not have to fend off the constant verbal abuse, the sexual hostility. Women in any job, whether in officework or in the trades, have to put out so much energy just to make it safe enough to work.

When I worked for a foundation company I wanted to belong. But when I was put in the position of leading work and running a job, I found myself having to tell the guys what to do. They started potshotting and sniping at me and I felt hurt. I didn't belong anymore. Then I realized I didn't necessarily *want* to belong. Since I'm never really going to be accepted because I'm a woman, I might as well be in a position of power. It's very important to hold onto your self-esteem as much as possible and move forward. I don't need to put up with a lot of crap; I can say, instead, "Hey, I have a trade—I can take it and use it someplace else!" Throughout my career in the trades I've been fortunate to have had a supportive family and partner, who've seen me through the bad days as well as the good. And, most essentially, I love carpentry.

Working in the trades is like taking a journey into a foreign land. I read a book that talked about women and minorities checking out the white boys' system in order to survive, because we have to know how it works, how we can fit in when we need to. The white boys, they don't have to mess with doing this; they *are* the system. I once considered becoming an anthropologist. I picture myself as one, checking them out, finding different signs of how they live. When I go out on a job, I view it as alien territory—male territory. I make friendly gestures so they don't get frightened. I do a lot of observing. Sometimes I participate by being rowdy. Sometimes I start swearing like crazy, which shocks them, and the next day I act like a nun. Men see you either as a nun, a whore or a crazy woman. I've always opted to be the crazy woman, because then they can't pigeonhole you as easily.

A lot of guys don't understand why I would give up a nice, clean, dry job like teaching to come outside and work in the mud. Most of them got into the trades because they got married out of high school, had kids right away and needed to make money. So when their Uncle So and So said, "You can come frame," they went to work and got stuck. They don't see why women would choose to go into the trades and stay in. But it's a good way to make a decent buck and a lot of women are supporting families on their own these days. On the other hand, we also have to love the work enough to put up with all the crap.

Sometimes I say that I haven't had it too hard. I haven't been physically assaulted or had someone come up and threaten me. But then I think the damage that is done is all relative. There's all the subtle shit that happens: the racist jokes I hear, the sexist comments. It eats away at me.

I also worry about the physical aspects of the work. As I get closer to forty and fifty I know my body is not going to last. Much as I try to take care of it, I have to look ahead to other things I can do in the field, but not necessarily out there raising walls. A lot of guys ask me, "Whaterya gonna do when you're fifty?" Well, I'm going to do what all the old farts do, I'll do the gravy jobs. I'll go put on doorknobs and I'll put in trim, I'll do customer service. There are places in the trades for everybody. None of the women I went through training with are still doing carpentry, although one is a drafter. They feel bad, they wonder if they've sold out because they didn't stay in the trades. But the fact is a lot of men come through and use the trades to make some money and then go back to school or do whatever it is they want to do. Women need to be able to come through and get the skills, and not stay in if they don't want to in order just to prove a point.

For the last three summers I've run a rural retreat called Women Empowering Women with two other women, which serves as an introduction to construction. Women come from all over the country to learn basic tool use and building skills. The idea for the retreat came from a woman named Mary Gaddis, a union journeylevel steamfitter. She and I actually graduated from the same high school, but it took fifteen years for us to meet up again. We decided to start Women Empowering Women to encourage women to get into the trades, because we were tired of being the only women on a job. We also wanted to get women in and *keep* them in. A lot of women leave the trades because they get fed up, not necessarily because they want to do something else. We thought if we prepared women better for what was ahead, like a pre-apprenticeship program, they might stand more of a chance. We tell every horror story we've every heard. We tell them about the pin-ups, the stuff that's on the walls of the shitters... and little things like when you go in and your last tampax falls on the floor of the shitter. We let women know what they're in for.

We ran the first session of Women Empowering Women (also known as WE Women) in 1985. Twelve women came, mostly from the San Francisco Bay Area. We began building a women's retreat center in the mountains of Humboldt County, California, a project still underway. We use mistakes for education because we want everyone to learn; we make it a safe and supportive environment. We teach women how to use power tools and basic building skills: raising walls, mixing concrete, siding, and so on.

We've had students, business professionals, RNs, teachers, therapists, women in the helping professions who were burned-out. Women who just needed to see something concrete that they built, something completed and substantial.

Since 1985 we've had a wide variety of women from all over the United States participate in WE Women. The oldest was sixty-one, the youngest eighteen. They've come from all walks of life, from all classes and backgrounds. They've had one thing in common: they came together to build. One year we had a pacifist and a military lifer, and I thought, "Oh no, this is going to be it." But they agreed not to talk politics—not to talk military—just talk construction. Whatever their differences, the women come together here.

I think being in a rural environment is essential to WE Women; we're temporarily away from the world and all its distractions, all the sexism. We've had women who've never really seen the stars, people who've never camped. The stars up there are incredible. One woman told us it was cloudy one night and we said, "No, that's the Milky Way!" She kept swearing it was clouds. There's also lots of wildlife to see—deer, redtail hawks, raccoons, possums, bear and mountain lion tracks, fox, owls, and much more.

At WE Women we also try to show the wide variety of trades in construction and how they are integrated. The first time I ever got on a jobsite I was amazed how many different trades went into building a house. There's the electrician, the plumber and the carpenter, and then there's also the insulator, the sheet rocker, the taper, the sheet metal worker, the landscaper... I think the project has been successful as a solid and encouraging introduction to trades work. Ten percent of the women who've come through WE Women have become union apprentices. Not just apprentices, but *union* apprentices. That's a very good percentage.

As I look back on my career in the trades, I have a deep appreciation for all the women who have gone before me. Not only the tradeswomen, but also the women who worked in construction offices because that was the only construction work open to women at the time. To an extent, their presence helped make it possible for other women to enter the trades.

Women who have gone on before have paved my path, making it easier for me to reach my goal. Now I can help build the bridge for all those who will follow.

Cassandra Miller • Electronics Inspector

I am a quality control tester and inspector for an electronics company in Reston, Virginia. My job is to inspect circuit boards and completed instruments to make sure that there are no pieces of solder touching each other, and that there are no missing parts. If pieces of solder are touching each other, the instrument will short out. My eye is pretty trained by now; I inspect the boards visually and it takes me a few seconds. When I first started, it took me several minutes to do each one.

Whatever the customer orders, it's my job to make sure that the instrument is built specifically to their orders. I check the calibration of each instrument to make sure it has not drifted. Since I'm the final inspector, I've got to make sure that everything is perfect before an instrument goes out of the plant.

I've been in the electronics field for fifteen years. Growing up, I always tinkered with fixing TVs and radios. If something happened to the TV, I had my little screwdriver going in the back. I never knew what I was doing; I just did it. When the repairmen came to fix the TV, I watched so I could learn something for next time. Electronics came naturally to me, but I never thought it would be my career. My mind was geared in another direction. I wanted to be a career military person.

I went into the service when I was eighteen. I had hoped to become an air traffic controller, but at that time it was very hard for females to get clearance for those positions. So I took my second choice—clerk typist. From that job I learned one thing—that I definitely didn't like working in an office, pushing paper.

After leaving the service, I got a job in the telephone company. Basically, I was in the right place at the right time. I'm a veteran, I'm a woman, and I'm *black*. I was hired as an assembler, but I ended up testing and repairing telephones as well. Instead of giving a broken piece to the quality control tester, I'd troubleshoot with my screwdriver and fix it myself. The only time I'd turn it over to someone else was when I'd exhausted my own knowledge.

Sometimes I get in trouble because of my independence. I'll ask for help, but I like to try to do something myself first. At the phone company, some of the technicians seemed to be afraid that females would take over. I used to tell the male technicians that one day I would have their job. They wanted you to stay in your place and they felt more secure when you brought them boards to fix. I'm the kind of person that just shrugged those attitudes off. I liked to get my job done. If I had to take a board to a technician, I'd watch and figure out what he did to repair it. When I ran into the same problem the next time, I wouldn't have to bother him again.

Women basically worked as assemblers at the phone company. The doors weren't open, as they are now, for a female to do installation. There were only two to three women installers in the area where I worked. Even today, the typical female job is assembler—just putting things together. That's not for me. I want to use my mind.

When I left that job and moved from Florida to Washington, D.C., I had a hard time finding work. Then I learned about Wider Opportunities for Women (WOW) and their training program in electromechanics. This gave me a chance to get some of the book-knowledge that I never had. In the program, we studied Ohm's law, Kirschoff's law and other formulas. We learned to read meters and use calipers. I think I was one of the top ten in the class. But even though I always had the right answer, I could never really explain how I got that answer—I just seemed to have a natural aptitude for electronics. In the training program I also learned job search and marketing skills, which helped me get my next job.

After graduating from WOW, I landed a job at the Bendix Corporation. With my schooling and experience, I didn't have to go through their training. They started me right off on the job. But the job ended up being just running a machine. I manually inserted components into boards, and the machine did all the rest.

I soon decided it was time to move on. I went to Eurotherm, the company where I work now. My first job title was assembler, but again I was doing basically repair and touch up. I would also fill any special orders, building custom-made circuit boards. Eventually, I got a promotion to supervisor. Actually, the work was the same old thing I had been doing all along, but now I had the proper title.

The company's vice-president of manufacturing eventually became aware of how I really worked with the assemblers to show them their mistakes and help them learn. He was impressed and asked me to transfer to work in quality control. That's what I do now, and I love the challenge. I can really use my mind and it's closer than ever to being a technician.

My plan is to become a technician in five years and I'm now getting ready to start electronics school. That will become a stepping stone to so much more. My long-range goal is to work in satellite communications, and then, who knows. The field is wide open and you can grab as much as you want. It takes a lot of hard work, but then you have to work hard for anything you really want.

Some women think that if they do nontraditional work, if they go out and repair something, they'll lose their femininity. That's one of the biggest difficulties in getting women into non-traditional work. For instance, some women are afraid to really get into stripping a copy machine down, to get their hands dirty. Of course, in my job, I can't work with nail polish. But I've never been concerned about losing my femininity.

When some people find out what kind of work I do, they ask, "Oh, how could you do that all day long, down in the dirt and the dust?" But it doesn't bother me. I've always been a tomboy. I've always done things differently from other people.

I am definitely glad I've chosen a non-traditional career. The work is challenging and that I get to solve new problems every day. For someone like me, who's independent and likes to learn new things, this is the perfect place to be.

Susan Eisenberg • Electrician

Being an electrician has become just another part of who I am—shaping the strengths and weaknesses of my body, the ways I express myself and solve problems, and what I notice. After ten years, both the honeymoon bliss and those first rude shock waves of reality are only strong memories. I find myself both looking back at my decision to become a union electrician without regrets and looking ahead to a life in the trades with a good deal of ambivalence.

Like many of the first women in their locals I've met across the country, I started in 1978, when affirmative action guidelines were mandated. I graduated four years later in the first apprenticeship class of IBEW Local 103 (Boston), to include women. Of the six women who started together, five of us graduated, a higher percentage than the men in our class. We owed that largely to the support, information-sharing and prodding we gave each other. Four of us carpooled together to our two-nights-a-week of school for four years. Our carpool conversations made up somewhat for the isolation of usually being the only woman—of any trade—on our jobs. As more women entered, we formed a group, meeting together for personal support and to identify and address the common problems we faced as women in our union.

Entering construction in the late 1970s was a little like falling in love with someone you weren't supposed to. The initial honeymoon was powerful. Enormous pride as I gained agility with tools I hadn't even known the names of when I began. Amazement as I watched new muscles pop out in the mirror almost daily. Fierce loyalty toward the older mechanics who took me under their wing and taught me their special techniques. Everywhere I would go—movies, airports, restaurants—immediately, I would notice the wiring: where fixtures were placed and how they were fed; whether receptacles were two-prong or three-; suddenly imagining what was behind ceilings and walls.

I remember, particularly in those first years, the enormous encouragement I felt from women on the outside, as though I represented them as well. Not only friends, but strangers, too. Women driving past my jobsite who would notice me and honk and give me a raised fist. The neighbor who rode to work on the same early morning bus and always cheered me on. The older black woman I met once in the bathroom of a remodel job, who had noticed my tool pouch on the sink and told me about her own unfulfilled ambitions of a jobs in the skilled trades, and how she had taught herself radio electronics from books. I felt indebted and privileged that I was able to live out a dream of generations of women who had been locked out. This magnified each success and failure, and kept me from following the urge I sometimes had to just walk away.

My initial experience in union construction was my worst. In the first shop that I worked for the journeymen were extremely hostile and unwilling to train me. There was even a foreman I worked under who tried to get me injured. Fortunately, I was laid off, and went to work for another shop where my experience was just the opposite. I was able to work on small jobs with some good mechanics who took me seriously and gave me a chance to learn the trade. They taught me how to mount boxes, pull and connect wires, and lay out the circuitry from a panel in an electric closet to the receptacles and lights in a room. After a lot of insisting, I got a chance to do the bigger and heavier work: wiring motors; cutting, threading and bending pipe; mounting equipment. I learned how to climb and carry ladders, use power tools, and maneuver myself around the debris and dangers on a construction site.

Even though the work and its newness were exhilarating, I also found myself often overcome with anger, depression or the feeling that I was in over my head. Working outside in a New England winter, or even by the water in the fall, is *cold*. And there were a lot of times I just had to grit my teeth and plunge across fear to do what I was asked: climb a crane, walk across a beam, work on scaffolding.

The hardest part of the job for me to get used to, though, was the talk on a construction site. Not the swearing—which guys often apologized for when I hadn't even noticed it—but jokes about beating up wives, racist and anti-Semitic slurs, degrading remarks about each other's girlfriends or some woman who happened to pass by, and comments about each others' personal lives that I found incredibly cruel. Sometimes I was grateful to be an apprentice, the one designated to go for coffee, so I could have the chance to walk outside and cry without being seen. On one remodel job, a residence for elders, one of the electricians joked about pulling the fire alarm and raping all the women residents—mostly in their eighties and nineties, many of whom I had gotten to know in the months working there. When I tried to say why a comment like that wasn't funny, he suggested that I could rape all the men. It was the casualness of the conversation for him, the assumptions underneath, and everyone else's silence that broke right through my armor. Conversations like that would eat away at me for weeks. I had to learn to harden myself, to expect little support from co-workers in group conversations, and to be selective about who and what was worth responding to. It quickly became clear that responding to all the comments I found offensive would guarantee not being heard. It would also mean being set up for entertainment, like anyone on a construction job who is too predictable—that is, things would be said just to get a rise out of you. So, I learned to let most offensive remarks pass by unchallenged, except in one-on-one situations, and often wondered whether or not I had made the right choice.

I had both my children after I became a journeywoman. As the second woman in my local to give birth, I found I had to do a lot of ground-breaking. Our union's disability and health and welfare policies were written only for the pregnancies of a member's wife. A group of women in the local met for several months, doing research and asking a lot of questions, and then wrote a pamphlet explaining how these benefits applied to a pregnant union member. Unfortunately, like many of the changes women have brought to the union, the pamphlet was only in circulation as long as the women members passed it around themselves.

I worked into the sixth month of my first pregnancy without telling anyone except the general foreman and a woman elevator installer that I was pregnant. I told most people on the day I stopped working. Even my foreman and partner only thought I had gained a little weight (thirty pounds!).

To my friends who saw me after work in maternity clothes, it seemed inconceivable that my pregnancy was anything but obvious. But since I wore baggy clothes to work (what I called my maternity overalls) and since no one *expected* to see a pregnant woman on a construction sight—they didn't. I presented myself as I always had—as an electrician there to work and earn a paycheck.

For me, deciding whether, when and whom to tell I was pregnant raised issues of privacy, safety, emotional vulnerability and confidence as a mechanic. I handled the choice differently in two pregnancies that followed, but for my first pregnancy, not telling felt like the right choice for several reasons:

Safety. During the first trimester, when danger to the fetus from chemical hazards is greatest, I was—by good luck—on a job where there were none. It was the finish stage of a new hotel and there were—a pregnant woman's dream!—twenty-eight new bathrooms on each floor. If safety had been an issue, I probably would have made a different choice.

Insecurity as a mechanic. I was a new journeywoman, out of my time (finished with my apprenticeship) only a year. As one of the first women to graduate in our local, my work performance had always been scrutinized closely. I felt I had worked very hard for years, proving I could do the job. I didn't want to call attention to what had become harder and more tiring.

Gaging limits. Pregnancy lasts a while, and it's not something you can un-tell someone. I wanted to come to my own decisions (from talking with my doctor, reading the little I could find, and listening to my body) about what I could and could not do as a pregnant electrician. I didn't want to have to deal with everyone else's perceptions of my capabilities or their reactions, which I suspected would be overprotecting, followed by resentment.

Gossip, jokes, careless talk. When I am feeling emotionally raw and vulnerable, a construction site is never where I want to be. Pregnant, I felt very raw. Knowing there is a big risk of miscarriage, particularly in the first trimester (one out of five pregnancies ends in miscarriage)—I did not want that to be everybody's business. But even in the second trimester, I found that I wanted the pregnancy to be quietly personal, that I didn't want to risk being the object of crude remarks. Pregnancy was new for me and for the local: I was the second member, the first journeywoman, to be pregnant. It represented big changes in my homelife and in my relationship with my partner. There *were* men on the job who were friends, whom I would have liked to tell, but it was a very big job (fifty electricians), and there were a number of guys who were pretty hostile toward me. It didn't feel possible to tell a few people without everyone knowing fairly quickly.

Not talking about my pregnancy exaggerated the feeling I often have in construction of feeling split in two. At coffee break, I would be intently aware of the kicking in my womb while having a conversation about the Red Sox. It also meant making a clear pact with myself to ask for help when I needed it or refuse to do things I felt I shouldn't do—that I *would* put health and safety ahead of ego.

My second pregnancy—on another job, with another company—began to miscarry on the job. I began bleeding, called my doctor, who told me to come in immediately, and then told my foreman that I was leaving. When he asked why, I just said, "I have to leave." A few days later I did miscarry. When I called to say I would be out another day, the foreman again said he was concerned, did I need help, what was wrong. At that point, I told him what had happened. He said the other guys on the crew were concerned, too, and asked if he could tell them. He said it wouldn't go beyond the electricians (we were a crew of about six). I said that was fine, and I was very impressed and moved to find that that really was what happened. Aside from one bad joke, the crew was incredibly supportive and respectful.

My third pregnancy began a few months later on that same job. This time I decided to tell people once the first trimester was past. I had been out of my time for a few years and felt more confident. It was the same small crew that had been through the miscarriage with me, so I felt a certain level of safety and intimacy. People already saw me as a wife and mother, so this time around, being pregnant again was no big leap in how I was perceived. I had already had a baby and returned to work once. People expected that this is what I would do again (not, as I'd heard so often when I started: why waste this training on women when they'll only have families and quit). And I was more comfortable with being pregnant. I knew what would happen. I could predict what I could and could not do, how I would feel, making it easier to include other people without feeling like I was losing control.

Driving around Boston, I love pointing out to my daughter and son "the jobs we worked together." It brings back the times when I felt like I carried a delicious secret: lying on a plank across an open airshaft on the roof of a building, tying in a fan motor, talking to the baby-in-utero. It gave me a powerful appreciation for the changes we have brought about. "We built that, Susie?" my daughter asks as we drive by a big hotel. "You bet!" I tell her.

For me, one of the biggest rewards of a high-paying construction job has been to feel less trapped by traditional gender roles at home. My husband and I have been able to switch back and forth between being the primary income-earner and being the primary home- and child-care person. He was able to work part-time when I returned to work after our first child, and to take a break from work outside the home when I returned after our second. As I listen to my four-year-old daughter struggle with the differentiations of boys and girls, I am glad that she can try on my workboots as well as my jewelry.

When I'm feeling most positive about construction, it's because I really do enjoy the work, enjoy having a skill that's useful to people around the world, enjoy being able to use tools and think like a mechanic. The work is certainly not always interesting and challenging. Some days it's boring and repetitive: hanging fixtures, putting in receptacles. Some days—if the foreman hasn't ordered the stock or there's been a change and you have to re-do a job for the third time—it's incredibly frustrating. But change is a basic part of the business. Good and bad both pass, and I've been lucky to find enough encouragement around to carry me through the more difficult times.

I have continued to feel a lot of support from other women in the trades. Being a poet, I've had the chance to meet tradeswomen not only locally, but around the country. I've received notes, phone calls or poems from women who read my book* or saw a poem of mine in a magazine. I've met other tradeswomen when I've given poetry readings, and friendships have grown. It's been helpful to discover that women construction workers from different parts of the country share very similar feelings and problems. It has helped me to put my own issues into a larger context. Again and again, I find myself being glad to be part of what feels to me like a community of women who are pretty gutsy, hard-working and straightforward.

Black men were the first group to break through the barriers of the white, male, father/son tradition in the construction unions, with women gaining membership several years later. I've found a camaraderie and pretty consistent support and encouragement from the black men I've met in construction. They

---

It's a Good Thing I'm Not Macho, Boston: Whetstone Press, 1984

were the source of a lot of quick survival tips when I was starting out. My first month, I was carrying a heavy load on my shoulder, trying to get by a bunch of guys who weren't moving, even though I was politely saying, "Excuse me," over and over again. The laborer foreman on the job, a black man, amused by my predicament, called over to me, "You'll never make it that way. Just yell, 'Coming through!' and keep walking." I took his advice to heart.

During my apprenticeship, I felt very nourished, both by everything I was learning as a mechanic and by the progress I felt the union was making in recognizing its women members. Although I still learn new things at work, it's certainly not at the rate I did when starting out. What's been more difficult, though, has been my growing disillusionment with the union. After ten years, we still have to remind people, "Hey, we're here, too. Please don't send out literature addressed 'Dear Brother,' warning me that if prevailing wage guarantees are defeated, my wife will have to go out and work." Even though there are many more women in the trades now than when I began, the percentages are still ridiculously low (less than two percent). There is no commitment from the unions to change these percentages, nor any pressure on them from the outside that might make a change likely.

Sometimes I think my lows are just battle fatigue. Tiredness. Tired of the same jokes and comments. Tired of being expected to prove myself. Tired of racism, that, unlike sexism, I feel not much better at countering than when I started. I can't as easily challenge it by my example or by one of many acerbic anti-sexist comebacks in my repertoire. I find the constant racist jokes and comments and the difficulty of being heard when you speak against them very draining and discouraging.

The cultural life on jobs—how people talk to and treat each other, picking on someone just to watch them react—has changed little. The insecurities of the construction business, with layoffs a constant threat, make the kind of close relationships that can develop over time in other occupations more difficult. On top of which, friendships between women and men on a job tend to make people nervous.

I feel the pull of demands that offer more passion and intrinsic value. Building luxury hotels does not have built-in satisfaction for me. It's a paycheck. As I've become increasingly committed to developing myself as a writer and added the extra pulls of parenting, I find myself considering alternative work possibilities.

Whenever I have strong thoughts about giving up the work, though, I realize it is more than the high pay that keeps me there. There's something about the work and the culture that has crept into my bones.

Judith Foster • Truck Driver

Living in the Ozarks is a choice for me. I grew up in a city and after thirty-six years of it, I'd had enough. So in the autumn of 1977 I moved to Arkansas, rented a house in the country, and though I had to accustom myself to the occasional snake that crossed my path as I jogged the back roads and the spring peepers who sang to me from a nearby pond at night, it was certainly no sacrifice. I found it easy to trade carbon monoxide fumes and the sound of squealing automobile tires for soft country music.

In fact it all seemed pretty copacetic except for two things. Arkansas has a depressed economy and jobs for women interested in non-traditional areas are about as rare as hens' teeth. But the working-class women, lesbians and feminists in my new-found Arkansas met the challenge. They started their own trades companies and became electricians, stone masons, carpenters, house painters and more. The Ozark Womyn's Trucking Collective is but one of these stories.

It was August of 1980 when I learned that the collective was looking for a driver. Working exclusively with women was definitely my idea of a good job. Though I knew absolutely nothing about driving a truck, I decided to apply.

During the interview the collective explained that they were part of a natural foods cooperative system that extended nationwide. Their connection was through the Ozark Cooperative Warehouse, known then under the umbrella of the New Destiny Federation. The collective was in essence a private hauler for the cooperative. The first women had been taught to drive by the local truck leasing company. Now the collective members taught other women to drive.

At this point in the interview I flashed back to the grueling sessions I'd had with my father while I learned to drive the family car at sixteen. It's a wonder I ever got my license. In contrast, these women created an environment of support for each other so they could learn a male-dominated trade in a noncompetitive atmosphere. They were also dedicated to consciousness-raising; by working as an all-women collective they showed that women can run and are running their own businesses.

Although the collective started out paying low wages (two dollars an hour) and could only offer part-time work (one truck run a month), it eventually grew into a solid means of financial support for its members. The women not only learned to drive a truck but increased their public relations, accounting, coordinating and dispatch skills as well. Their enthusiasm was contagious. I knew I wanted to be a part of it.

At the end of the interview one of the drivers offered to take me on a run with her the following weekend. She said it would be a good way for me to find out if I was really interested in the job and for the collective to get a sense of my aptitude. I was assured there would be no obligation on my part. It occurred to me that I had no idea what I was getting myself into and that this woman knew it.

The collective had just leased a new diesel bob truck. This would be her maiden voyage, as well as mine. It had a twenty-six-foot box. That meant nothing to me except I knew it was longer than my living room.

I could hardly sleep the night before. I was excited and admittedly a little scared. The morning of the run I arrived at the warehouse at six a.m., as scheduled. When I saw the actual size of this ten-wheeler, my jaw went slack. Just climbing up in the cab was awkward. I wasn't sure which foot to put on what step of the accommodation ladder in order not to end up cross-legged in my seat. My co-driver smiled and assured me I would get used to it all. I repeatedly reminded myself that I dearly love a challenge and off we went.

At that time the cooperative covered a seven-state area with its delivery runs. To get in or out of any of those states you first had to get through the foothills of the Ozarks. No small feat in my book. For the first day I rode as a passenger. I asked dozens of questions, watched everything the driver did, and made copious notes in a journal I had brought along to log the details of what I hoped would be my new career. The woman beside me was not only extremely competent but patient as well. She explained about RPMs and split gears, about backing up using both side mirrors and flipping the courtesy lights to acknowledge other drivers on the road. But there was more to delivering food than just driving the truck, she added. We had to unload each item by hand and check it off the invoice. There were sales and credit slips to fill out, phone calls to make to our next customers and Department of Transportation regulations that had to be followed.

Finally, after a day and a half we ended up on Interstate 70 in Missouri. This was a flat stretch of highway, traffic was light, and my co-driver decided it was a good place for me to try my wings.

We sat on the side of the road and I repeatedly practiced all the gear positions. Finally she suggested I try the real thing and I realized she meant for me to actually take the truck out on the highway. My heart raced and my knees shook so much I wasn't sure I could engage the clutch as I watched the side mirror and waited for the traffic to wane. When there was absolutely nothing in sight behind me I eased forward, shifted into second gear and accelerated. I felt a surge of adrenalin. Then I went to third and picked up a little more speed. Then fourth gear. I raised the separator button from low to high gear and tried to shift to fifth. I couldn't find the gear and lost speed. My co-driver suggested I rev the engine a bit and try to get the rpm's back up. I pushed and shoved at every gear in my attempt to find one the transmission would accept and finally had to pull over to the shoulder. My co-driver said it had been a great first try. She explained what had happened and assured me that with practice I would be able to keep the truck on my side of the road and shift gears at the same time. I smiled weakly and hoped she was right. But the taste of what it was like to actually drive a truck on the highway—if only for fifty or so yards—was exhilarating. I wanted more.

Eventually I was able to get through all the gears without having to pull over. It was thrilling, and was made more so by the fact that the woman beside me was giving support and instructions with a gentle, calm voice. She clearly knew how to challenge me without exceeding my capabilities or putting us in any danger.

It took a couple more truck runs before I could downshift without grinding every gear, or check my passenger side mirror long enough to see if I could get back in the right-hand lane. Finally my co-driver suggested I was ready to get my certification. She was more sure of my abilities than I. But I agreed that when we returned home I would take the written and driving test. She was explaining the procedure of certification, assuring me I'd have no problems as we came out of Leslie, Arkansas, on our way to Mountain View. As I started up the mountain I tried to pick up speed but we had a load on and Highway 9 is steep. The engine began to lag and I tried to down shift to compensate. Still not proficient under these conditions, I couldn't find the right gear and had to come to a complete stop. And of course, the traffic behind me did too.

There was no shoulder this time, so I waited until the cars were able to pass and then looked at my co-driver for instructions. She suggested I try low gear. I had never used this gear before but first gear just wouldn't pull us up this hill, not initially anyway. I put the truck in low, pushed in the air brake and let out on the clutch. The truck moved forward. I knew by the whine of the engine that I needed to get into first again soon. I held my breath and shifted. In my eagerness to shift before I lost what little speed I had, I missed and went straight into reverse. There was a loud wrenching noise and the truck stalled then began to roll backwards. I nearly stood straight up on the foot brake to stop us. The knuckles on both my hands were white from gripping the steering wheel. My co-driver reached over and pulled on the air brakes. She told me to try low gear again but I think she already knew what had happened. I had broken the crankshaft. We were totally immobile. I was sure my short trucking career was over.

We quickly got out of the truck and put our safety triangles on the ground. I directed traffic around us—I didn't want to complicate my disaster with an accident. My co-driver said she would hike back to Leslie and call our lease company for a tow truck. I knew she would have to take the rap for what I'd done because I wasn't certified to drive the truck. It was a silent agreement between the local lease company and the collective that drivers were being trained. But it was also against our lease regulations to have a non-certified driver at the wheel. It was the only way collective members could teach other women and so they took this risk with all new drivers.

I stood on that tiny two-lane mountain road for what seemed like hours. I directed traffic to occupy my body but I felt wretched. It was hard to look my co-driver in the face when finally she came back up the mountain. But she smiled, suggested I eat one of the sandwiches she'd brought, and then took her turn directing traffic. There was nothing to do now but wait for the tow truck. It was a long afternoon.

When we got back home the women in the collective shared their own stories to let me know I was not alone in my experience, that in the learning process, no one can be expected to be perfect. As the years went by and I saw how many accidents on the road involved male drivers, I was quite happy with my one misadventure.

In the early days of the collective we went on the road as double drivers. This, of course, was costly and could only be continued until a driver was trained. We were eased into single driver status by sending lumpers, or what we called loaders, who helped us unload the food. This was mostly to take some of the workload off the driver until she built up her stamina for driving, unloading twenty thousand pounds of food and getting to the next stop on time. Eventually, it was necessary for me to go totally alone.

I was encouraged in this direction by the women of the collective and also by the fact that I would make more money when I was on my own. In the Ozarks in 1980, five dollars an hour seemed like a fortune. So, I started out on my first solo run. I was holding my own until about the middle of the week when I misjudged the time it would take me to travel from Tyler, Texas, to Paris, Texas. On the map it didn't look that far. But much of the road was two-lane and every few miles there was a small town where I had to reduce my speed. The Sesame Products plant where my pick-up was, closed at four and when there was no longer any chance I would make it on time, I stopped and called to ask if someone would wait for me. I was in luck—one of the workers would be there until five. But in my determination not to miss my pick-up, I had completely forgotten my three o'clock delivery.

I reached Paris at exactly five. While I was being loaded I ran to call one of the names listed on my manifest. After two no answers I finally got a buying club member. I apologized profusely and said I would be right over with the food. She told me that after two hours of waiting, everyone had gone home. There was no one left at the drop site to receive the food. She said she had to take her daughter to a school function but would come by and unlock the building for me. I agreed to unload the food by myself and put it inside. This, I thought, would get me back on schedule. What I didn't realize was that my pick-up was being loaded behind the buying club order and I would have to lift everything over the top of the waist-high stack of seeds, then carry the food to the back of the truck. I would then have to get out of the truck, lift the food down and carry it inside the building.

I had barely started before I was exhausted. I was about ready to kick a stack of forty-pound boxes of juice off the back of the truck and go home when suddenly the woman who had opened the building returned. She had come to help and brought two other women with her. I never forgot to call a customer after that.

The day did come when I was a competent driver. I was comfortable with my skills under all conditions, knew what was safe and what was risky. I was in charge. I loved the work, though it was probably the hardest physical work I had ever done in my life. Mostly women met the truck to unload but occasionally there were men too. When I would bring a fifty-pound bag of rice or flour to the back of the truck, if there was a man there, he would hurry to take it from the woman. He would usually say something like, "Here let me get that. It's too heavy for you." I would look at the woman and ask if she had any children. Then I would ask how much her child weighed. A smile of recognition would cross her face. I would tell her that if I put the bag on her shoulder it would be easier to carry. After that, the man would respectfully wait his turn to carry whatever was to be unloaded next.

I loved talking to women in buying clubs who met the truck, or those behind the counter at convenience stores where I sometimes stopped to make phone calls. "Do you really drive that big truck?" they would say. And often I'd hear them wish they could, too. I'd always encourage them. And there were women who didn't want to drive but who liked the idea that I was out there doing it. It gave them a sense of vicarious accomplishment.

After about a year and a half one of the collective members moved to another state and it was my turn to learn to drive the tractor trailer. I virtually had to start all over again. This time I was faced with eighteen wheels and two pieces of equipment instead of one. The trailer alone was forty-eight feet long.

We weren't big enough then to do deliveries on tractor trailers but we did bring back goods for our customers on our West Coast and Midwest runs. We all decided I could gain the most experience by doing the California run, as we called it.

Up to this point I had had limited experience with truck stops. They weren't readily available in most of the small towns where we delivered and so we stayed in motels and fueled at designated locations on our routes. Now I was traveling cross-country and sleeping in the bunk while my co-driver kept the truck moving, or vice versa. Truck stops were the major sources of accommodations for such a large vehicle on a cross-country run.

The first time we sat in the drivers' section at a truck stop restaurant, we were totally ignored. At that time some of the larger truck stops were beginning to get shower facilities for women because so many traveled with their spouses. But they still weren't acknowledging women drivers—alone or in pairs. Their attitude was: If you weren't a man, you didn't belong there. So when we tried to get service in the drivers' section we suddenly became invisible. Sometimes we were even asked to move to the public section of the restaurant until we identified ourselves. It was, at the very least, frustrating.

Backing up the tractor trailer was my biggest challenge. Because there are two pieces of equipment, the steering wheel has to turn in the opposite direction you want the trailer to go. It's a hard thing to remember when there are some half dozen male drivers watching your trailer zigzag across the parking lot. The Taurus in me stayed determined. The woman in me hated knowing my co-driver was standing on the dock being hassled while she tried to help me back into the bay. The little girl in me was embarrassed to tears. I had to remind myself that no one has ever died of embarrassment.

After several runs to California I got to know our route. We went as far south as Coachella for dates and as far north as Chico for Knudsen juice. It was grueling but the scenery was superb. Then it happened. My co-driver got so ill she was unable to get out of the sleeping bunk for two days. I was on my own. I did all the pick-ups and deliveries (including backing into whatever dock space the situation called for), all the paperwork and driving. I was over the hump.

At some point as a veteran driver it became my turn to help

train other women. This, I discovered, is a skill in itself. It's one thing to learn something new, it's quite another to share that skill with others. It is an act of faith that you will even like your co-driver, much less find the affinity you need to spend twenty-four hours a day in her presence for a solid week. Mostly I was lucky. But I now faced another kind of challenge—to let go of my need for control while someone else, less experienced than I, took the wheel.

The first woman I helped train must have been born with a steering wheel in her hand. We started out on the ten-wheeler. At times it seemed like I was on vacation and I felt a little guilty for earning money doing it. Then one night we were on our way back through Oklahoma when the truck started losing air pressure and our brakes began to intermittently lock up. We pulled to the side of the road several times and were able to get the truck moving again. At around eleven p.m. the problem became more serious and we pulled over in front of a house on a nearly deserted stretch of highway. We asked to use the phone and called our local lease shop. The mechanic I talked with suggested a couple of things we could try. He said if they didn't work to call back. We got our tools and the flashlight and worked for about an hour with no luck. But by the time we'd finished, the house where we'd used the phone was dark. Though we pounded relentlessly, no one would answer the door.

I could see a small light about a half mile up the road. As the truck was in a dangerous place on the shoulder, my co-driver stayed with it while I went in search of a phone. Either no one was there or they weren't answering the door at that late hour. The only option left was to hope for a passing motorist. Not a good prospect since we hadn't seen a car for hours.

It was nearly two a.m. when finally headlights appeared in the distance. We waved our flashlight as the car approached. It was a woman driver. She said she would take us to a phone.

We introduced ourselves and then there was a long silence. Finally the woman said, "I work on the night shift in a plant about fifty miles from here. I commute." There was another pause and with a nervous voice she continued. "You might not believe this but tonight I got an image of two women needing help on the road. It was so strong that I left work early." I looked at my co-driver as chills ran down my spine.

The next woman I helped train was as scared and unsure as I had been. She misjudged corners, backed into posts, and ground every gear to the point I feared the transmission would simply drop out on the highway. But I had to let her learn her own way with the truck. And in doing so I understood what other women had been willing to do for me. No one had yelled at me or told me I was stupid like my father had done when he tried to teach me to drive the family car. Instead, what I had gotten every step of the way was encouragement and support to learn not to be intimidated by big machinery. It's not something women usually get the chance to learn from other women. It makes a difference. A big difference.

Eventually the Ozark Womyn's Trucking Collective became an integrated part of Ozark Cooperative Warehouse and finally, because of discrimination laws, we had to be open to hiring men again. I became trucking coordinator and dispatcher and quit driving except for an occasional emergency. But the thing that remains dearest to my heart are the women who forged a place for those of us to learn a skill we would never have had the chance to learn if it weren't for their courage and daring. They are the women to whom we owe our gratitude, for without them some of us would never have had the courage to try.

These remembrances are lovingly dedicated to all the womyn, especially the mothers, of the Ozark Womyn's Trucking Collective.

Mary Baird • Phone Repair Technician

It's two-thirty—time for at least one more job. I pull up to 1225 E. 86th Street. Reviewing my trouble ticket, I note: No dialtone, all phones. Mechanized loop test indicates a break in the line 150 feet from the customer's phone, ninety-nine percent of the distance from the switching office to the phone. Hmmm... the break could be in the drop, the black wire from the pole to the house; or, it could be in the aerial cable, right at the pole.

Slipping a customer invoice into my pocket, I get out of my van and walk around to the back where I throw on my tool belt and grab my volt meter. I ring the doorbell, but find no one home. I go to the side of the house and connect the clips of my test phone (commonly called a butt set) to the pair of wires terminated on the protector (a fused connection block). No dialtone here. I turn and eyeball the drop. Sometimes you can see a rotten or corroded splice—an immediately visible source of trouble. Yep—there's a splice in this drop, out near the pole. It may or may not be the location of the break I'm looking for, but I'll have to replace the drop anyway—part of our preventive maintenance function.

To further isolate the trouble, I'll have to go up the pole behind the garage. I check it out and see that the way the pole is wedged between two garages, a fence and a row of thick lilac bushes, I'll need to get out my climbing hooks—can't maneuver my ladder back in there.

This is not my favorite part of the job, I'm thinking, as I get my hard hat, body belt and climbing gear out of the back of my truck. Like most of the guys, I've become pretty much of a ladder jockey—hooking poles only when absolutely necessary. Climbing school was actually fun. We'd practice four hours a day, at first ascending just a few feet and then working our way up to twenty-four feet where most telephone cables and terminals (work boxes) are comfortably within reach. They'd set fresh poles every couple of weeks—not like out here where the poles are cluttered with obstacles and hazzards, like metal plates and signs, rotten spots, flaking strips, and a myriad of drop wires and cable TV facilities to get tangled up in.

At least there won't be an audience here, I console myself, as I make my way through the underbrush behind the garage to the foot of the pole. I remember when I first started, working on pay phones, the poles were usually out in the open on busy street corners. I'd attract small crowds of kids and passersby. Pretty nerve-wracking, especially with my boss standing there barking me through the procedures. . . .

I'm all belted in now, having managed to hook the pole and reach my terminal. I have to remember to get comfortable, but not to bend the knee of my lower leg—that leg holds all your weight and keeps the barb on your climber locked into the pole. Thank goodness I've never cut out of a pole or had any serious falling accidents. I had just one scare when I cut out and immediately caught myself on a pole step with my armpit! That smarted all right, and I suffered several days of soreness—but no broken bones or nasty creosote soaked splinters. I've heard some pretty gory stories about having those dagger-sized splinters extracted from a guy's arms, chest and inner thighs. It's these images that add to my mild case of climbing phobia and my healthy fear of falling.

I take the rubber enclosure off this ready-access terminal, uncovering the usual snarl of color-coded wires and splicing connectors. I trace the drop wire from my customer's house and find its termination point. Plugging in with my butt set, I hear the dialtone. This means the break's in the drop. I'm going to replace it anyway, so I begin to unfasten the ends that are terminated. Oops—one of the ends breaks off the minute I touch it. Very corroded here, possibly the source of my trouble.

While completing the task of freeing my drop from the terminal, I plan the rest of the job. I'd already cut the drop at the house with my tree-trimmer and attached it to the reel of new wire. Now I begin pulling it up to me. I attached the new drop to the J-hook on the pole with a fresh clamp. Then I slit the wire on the end, skin back the insulation with my side-cutters, and attach it to the connecting block. Double-checking, I pick up the dialtone and verify my phone number.

I begin descending the pole. Slowly. Climbing down produces just as much anxiety for me as climbing up. I look at my feet, which would've caused my first boss to yell, "Look *up*, not down!" I remember one day I had to climb a pole behind a supermarket, with him shouting instructions to me at the top of his voice. A couple of beer truck drivers heard him and drove by yelling, "Why don't you shut up and climb the fucking pole yourself, you old fart!" That silenced him at least, and when I got down he insisted on using my hooks over his dress shoes to demonstrate his own method of climbing—about three feet up and back.

Back on the ground now, I roll up the old drop and take it, along with my climbing gear, back to my van. I get the ladder off the rack and clamp the new drop to the side of the house, just below the rain gutter. Then I bring it down to eye level, where I attach it to a new connector that joins the drop with the inside wiring.

Brrr! I hadn't noticed the cold until just now. Generally, the movement involved in pole and ladder work keeps me warm. But there are times when the sub-zero wind chill really gets to me fast, especially if I'm working up on a pole. When the wind blows, my eyes water and make it impossible to see what I'm doing, or the tears start freezing and burning my cheeks, or my glasses steam up. Now I remove my right-hand glove to finish up the wiring a bit faster. This is why I spend all winter nursing sore fingertip cracks. Of course, compared to the hell of the exceptionally cold winter the first year I came outside—they started me in January—this seems relatively mild. Besides, I probably do the operations about five times faster now!

Tying down the last piece of interior wire, I see the customer driving up. The whole family is climbing out of the car with grocery bags. I greet the driver, who's walking over to me. "Hi! You must be Mr. Brown. I'm just finishing up—your phone should be back on now. The break was near the pole, so I ran a whole new line for you."

"Great!" he exclaims. "That was fast service... Hey! *You* don't climb the poles, do you?" he asks, pointing to the pole in the back.

I wonder to myself just who he figures *did* climb the pole; or whether he thinks I levitated myself up instead of climbing. But, as always, I hold my inner sarcasm and deliver my usual line. "Yep, it's part of the job."

"Wow, I hear you!" he declares. I've learned just to accept those sorts of responses. Shock and surprise are nothing more than naive reactions to the unfamiliar.

"I didn't know they had *women* doing this," Mr. Brown continues, confirming my naiveté theory.

"Yes, but only a few of us. I'm the only female repair technician in this area." I let him know I'll be in to check the inside wiring and jacks just as soon as I put my ladder away.

◆

I guess I shocked my parents when I went to work for the phone company at the age of thirty-four. I could just hear them talking. "But her field is education—teaching and research!"

I had done some teaching and some research in the area of instructional methods of emotionally handicapped children. I'd also spent three summers waitressing between college years and had worked as a typist-receptionist in a college counseling center for a couple of years when teaching jobs were scarce. I'd never stayed in the same job longer than two years.

Despite my record of dabbling in a variety of jobs and still not having settled into a permanent career, going to work at Ma Bell, to my parents, seemed incongruous with my background. I suppose they figured I'd eventually settle down and become the professional I was trained to be. After all, my younger sister was in law school and my brother was several years into his career as a psychologist.

In the early 70s, along with a great many other people my age, I paid little attention to the social status of jobs and careers. White-collar, blue-collar, professional—who cared? I wanted something different, challenging, a job that paid well but didn't consume all of my time. I just hadn't found my niche in the world of work.

It was especially exciting to see women start to break into "men's jobs." And to me, the women pole climbers working for the phone company had a special appeal. An outdoor job. Drive your own truck. Exercise—I'd loved tree climbing as a kid! Work with tools. Meet people. Good pay. Benefits, job security. Union involvement—as an activist, I especially liked this aspect.

I don't remember whether the slick Bell System recruitment ads featured all of these benefits—certainly not the union activity. Nonetheless, these were the features that lured me to the job then and keep me there today.

My parents eventually came to accept my non-traditional line of work. Early on, when my mom saw how much money I was making and my satisfaction with the job, she decided I wasn't that far off. "After all," she said, "you've been a climber all your life!" She no doubt recalled the times she had had to coax me down from treetops, haylofts and rooftops in my childhood days.

As for my dad, who was somewhat more reserved in his acceptance, I was amused when, along with my sister "the attorney" and my brother "the psychologist," he introduced me to his pastor as the "labor activist." I was editor of my local union newspaper at the time and this was what my dad chose to emphasize about my career.

When I started at South Central Bell in Louisville in September of '75, I passed the written qualifying test, but the local quota for women in outside technical jobs was full. I therefore had to select an entry-level job until an opening was available. I chose the clerical position, as opposed to directory assistance operator, which I'd heard was nothing but mindless drudgery.

As it turned out, being a service order typist was no picnic either. Low pay, relative to craft (technical) jobs. Four walls. Repetitive, meaningless work—churning out as many as a hundred orders a day. Eyestrain from typing into video display terminals. After about two years of this, and following a transfer to Ohio Bell in Cleveland, I got promoted to customer service representative, which at least was an improvement in pay rate (though still lower than the "men's" jobs). I soon made myself into a troublemaker, becoming a union steward who consistently protested the rigid office policies and the stifling mode of supervision and monitoring of our work. After a year in this job, I developed stress-related migraines and was screaming daily, to no one in particular, "Get me *out* of here!"

In December of '78 my transfer request for an outside job was pulled and I went in for the recently developed Physical Abilities Test—an incredible three-part test of strength, balance and stamina. At the time, the P.A.T. was creating a backlog in the employment center. Several job requisitions from installation and repair had piled up because they were "down" one white female and, for several weeks, no one had been able to pass the test. The union objected to the test and even sent in men with fifteen years in the field who could not pass it. Nonetheless, having tottered miserably on the balancing beam for a grand total of .5 seconds, I somehow squeaked by. Or, who knows—maybe they fudged my score just to unblock the log jam.

Of the eight openings available, I chose pay phone installation, working out of a downtown garage. It just sounded more interesting than residential work. Besides, the other openings were in repair and the placement officer told me that the women "weren't making it" in repair—too much outside work, too cold in the winter.

Before reporting to my new job, I had to go for an interview with the manager in that department. He outlined the job requirements in very vague terms, answered a couple of my questions and took me on a tour through the garage. The place was empty except for one or two trucks. Then he pulled a fast one and pointed to the ladder on top of one of the vans: "Let me see you take that ladder down off the truck and carry it."

I had a hunch this was a trap, so I said, "Why don't you show me how—I've never had any ladder experience." I knew this was something they would teach you. A fortunate move on my part, because in demonstrating, the manager came close to dropping the ladder, nearly smashing a truck window. Later I learned that safety regulations prohibit handling ladders inside a garage, due to the slippery conditions of the smooth concrete floors.

I was now an installation technician, ready for my two-week stint at an OSHA-approved school, where I would learn pole climbing, ladder use, job safety procedures and the basics of installation. After I passed this course and survived six months of training and experience on the job, I officially made it through my probation period. I no longer could be sent back to my old job.

I worked on pay phones for about six years, learning the ins and outs of service connection as well as the basic carpentry skills needed to mount the various types of enclosures of the phones. There was also the challenge of locating and connecting lines that trailed through the maze of house cables and phone system equipment in warehouses, factories, shopping malls and steel mills—wherever the pay phones were located.

Shortly after I had been assigned to my new craft job, AT&T and the government came to an agreement that a systematic affirmative action plan with quotas was no longer necessary. This meant that efforts to recruit women for outside craft jobs came to a screeching halt. It also ended the policy of "seniority override," which had allowed me to transfer to my job ahead of men with more time. Combined with a very low hiring and attrition rate in the craft jobs, this meant that I would be forever frozen at the bottom of the seniority list, regardless of the location I might be assigned to. Lacking seniority, I'd have last pick of vacation time each year—a significant disadvantage. It's been ten years since I've had time off in July or August.

This lowly status also meant that I'd be the first to go in a layoff situation, which has not happened, or in an involuntary "force adjustment," which has. Five years into my career as an installer, a new contract agreement combined installation and repair into a single job title—services technician. This brought more efficiency to my department and before long, four of us pay phone services techs were declared "surplus" and bumped to other locations and job assignments. My only choice was whether to work primarily installation or repair. Both assignments were inner city garages and both involved mainly residential services. I figured I'd learn more in repair, and the little troubleshooting I'd done already seemed fairly interesting.

This is my current assignment—a good change for me as it turned out. I'd pretty much learned the ins and outs of working in the inner city, as my earliest job assignments had been in the most depressed areas. I suspect that this had been done to help me rethink my decision to take this new position. But residential work has been a little less hazardous than some of the poolhalls, barrooms and other public places in downtown Cleveland where I'd serviced pay phones—once I had to be escorted by a shotgun-wielding bar owner.

♦

As I'm hoisting my ladder to the rack on my truck, the familiar little white car with the blue and gold stripe pulls up. My boss gets out and I see he's holding the gas pliers I'd ordered—I'd dropped my others in a snowdrift somewhere. He always seems to have a concrete reason for coming out to the jobsite. He's not the sneaky type, like good old Fraye, who'd park a block away or around the corner and just watch—you never knew for how long.

"Hi, Mary, your pliers came in."

"Thanks, John. I just finished my outside work—still gotta check for a little bit of inside trouble." I feel I have to tell him what I'm doing and why, the urge to defend and justify being a hangover from the early days. Freddy, my first boss, was probably the worst. The minute he'd arrive he'd start his barking: "What've you been doing all this time? How many trips back and forth to your truck have you made? What time did you start? Why are you doing it so neatly—you're taking too long!" Sure am glad those days are long gone, or at least that John's pretty decent. He probably won't last long—seems every time I get a boss I can get along with, they ship him somewhere else.

Mr. Brown comes to the door—I introduce them. "This is my boss, John—Mr. Brown."

"Hi—I just brought Mary some supplies, so I thought I'd see what we have left to do here. Okay if we check some wiring in the basement?"

"Sure, but watch your step—it's pretty messy down there. I don't like to go down there much my own self!"

Lots of customers tell me that—basements being the areas of greatest neglect by slum landlords and where leaks, debris, crumbling cement, holes in the outer wall, broken windows, thick deposits of dirt and cobwebs all make for a wide assortment of job hazards. Unfortunately, most repair visits require a trip to the basement. To top it off, the worst basements have no lighting, so you end up fumbling around, working with one hand and holding a flashlight in the other.

I locate my ground wire where I'd stuffed the end through a crack beside the window casing. "Great—there's a conduit about a yard from the window." I attach a copper clamp to the pipe, connecting the wire and affixing a "Warning—DO NOT REMOVE" tag as well.

"You'd better strap up this loose bundle of wires," says John, pointing to a beam where the interior wires converge and have come loose over the years. I agree with him and, brushing away the dust and spider webs, tie off the bundle of wires with a plastic cable strap.

"I'm going upstairs to check the jacks—I read a light short circuit on my meter when I checked the inside wiring. Probably some corrosion," I tell him. "That's fine," John answers. "Everything's under control here—I'm going to move on. Good job." He yells farewell to the customer and takes off.

I collect my tools, shut off the basement light and move on upstairs. I wonder if the woman in the kitchen is Mrs. Brown, but don't make any assumptions. I introduce myself instead. "Hi—my name's Mary. How are you?"

"Hi. I'm Mary, too!" She smiles and puts away the cereal she was holding. "Hey—am I glad to see you. We women can do anything!" she exclaims—a common reaction I get from female customers.

Some of the women are a little less confident and make it a point to add that, although they admire *me*, they could never "climb those poles" or "handle that ladder." Or, they feel they're too old and say, "I wish I could've done that kind of work when *I* was young." When I tell them I'm forty-seven and started this job at thirty-seven, they are shocked—either because I look somewhat younger, or because of the false assumption that women have to be fresh out of high school to do a physically demanding job. But everyday we see any number of old white-haired *men* working on power lines, construction sites, road crews and garbage trucks!

"We sure can!" I return Mary's enthusiasm.

"See?" She nods to Mr. Brown who's just entering the kitchen. "We can do anything you men can do!"

He laughs, not particularly bothered by her comment. Some men get a little defensive. I remember one skeptical inquiry: "They have you working out there all by *yourself*?" The man's wife beat me to the punch and replied, "Sure! And she takes home her paycheck *all by herself*, too!"

I explain my next moves: "I'm looking for a jack or wiring somewhere that might be corroded or wet, causing a little trouble on your line."

"Mary, show her the jack in the kids' room—next to the window. It gets pretty damp there sometimes." I follow Mary upstairs to a bedroom at the end of the hall, where two little kids are munching pretzels and watching TV. The jack is down on the baseboard below the window.

The little girl, about four years old, runs over to Mary, staring at me wide-eyed: "Mommy! The phone man's a lady!" We laugh. Sometimes people don't notice my gender until they get a close-up look. One time a woman flirted with me from her bedroom window when I was working up on a pole—she quickly retreated when I turned around and answered back!

I clear out the toy boxes and hunker down to look at the jack. My knees *are* getting stiff. I remember one of the guys back in pay phones told me: "Years of squatting and kneeling will get to your knees, believe me!" I do now.

As soon as I remove the jack cover, I see the source of trouble—not only is the moisture evident, but a whole nest of cockroach eggs pops out. A house could be immaculate, but one roach in the area will be sure to locate its eggs in the nearest phone jack—a perfect dark, enclosed hideout. So I get out my handy little "roach brush" and clean off the connecting block and wires.

"Looks like we found it." I show Mary the corroded wires in the jack cover. She's somewhat aghast at the mess coming out of the jack. A couple of live baby roaches scurry across the floor. I let her know I'm not terribly alarmed or disgusted and while we're talking I replace and rewire the defective jack.

Yolanda, the little girl, is now gingerly examining and touching the tools in my pouch, quite fascinated by the whole operation. I ask if she'd like to use my butt set for awhile and hand it to her. She's thrilled, of course, and I show her how I use the alligator clips to plug into phone wires—I let her listen to the dialtone. Soon she manages to engage her younger brother in a somewhat primitive troubleshooting expedition. They wander off down the hall, after she equips him with a plastic spoon and a pencil for his "tools."

I test the line once more—one hundred percent clear of

trouble. So, I begin to gather up my equipment and we make our way back down to the kitchen. I fill out the invoice form—Mary signs it. We discuss a few aspects of billing since all the changes after AT&T's divestiture, and by now I'm waiting for a computer test and call-back. We close out every job with an M.A.—a maintenance administrator in the office where all the trouble reports are screened, analyzed and dispatched out one at a time using a computerized mapping system. Soon that job will be eliminated. We'll have small hand-held computers with display terminals to analyze, dispatch and close out our own trouble reports.

Makes me wonder when they'll replace *us* with remotely controlled robots. Somehow I just can't see little R2D2s hooking poles, climbing through debris-filled crawl spaces, exchanging pleasantries with customers... But then again, who knows. With the combination of deregulation, divestiture and new technology, the threat of job erosion always looms overhead. The pace of change over the past ten years serves as a constant reminder that we're no longer indispensable. For me, being at the bottom of the heap, the "first to go" phenomenon is an extra thorn in my psyche.

I'm on the line with the M.A. now—she's finished her testing. "Okay—everything looks good. I'll put you off the clock now—have a nice weekend!"

We hang up, I tear off the customer copy of the invoice for Mary, and as I leave, I say a special good-bye to Yolanda. "Bye now, you'll make a good repair technician someday!" She beams.

I feel good. Sometimes I have to chuckle at myself—I'm a bit evangelistic about my opportunities to shatter gender stereotypes and provide a role model for the kids I meet on the job.

I am abruptly returned to reality. On my way back to my truck, some guy across the street yells, "Hey baby, come climb *my* pole!" I almost let that sarcastic sneer in his voice get to me. I want to yell back, "Sorry, I only climb the *big* poles!" or "No, thanks—I'd probably fall off your pole!" Instead, I just laugh and wave, "No, thanks!" and go about my business. I throw my tools in the truck and drive off.

♦

It took me several years to reach the "comfort zone" on this job. Something's made me stick it out, something besides the job itself. Probably the challenge has kept me going. For a long time, I didn't feel any of the "freedom" I'd associated with this type of work—partially because I wasn't given any by my boss. Freddy was certain I wasn't cut out for the job. As he told me the first day: "I'm from the old school. Women shouldn't be doing this job. You have too many handicaps. You won't make it." This vote of confidence was overwhelming!

The first few months I nearly lost sight of the benefits of the job, because I was so preoccupied with the pressures I felt from being the only woman and therefore highly visible everywhere I went. These anxieties were magnified by being a rookie—a difficult position for anyone. I was the only rookie in my garage. The closest to me was a guy with about six years of experience on the job. Learning the ropes was rough when it all came at you at once: the intricacies of coding, time accounting and other paperwork, the various types of wiring, phone parts, tools, safety rules, along with the more technical aspects of locating and restoring dialtone. Not to mention the tendency for everyone to point out what you didn't know, what you did wrong, how easy it was for everyone else. One yelling match with Freddy went like this:

Freddy: "You're not progressing fast enough. You can't even remember the names of all your tools! I have the guys come out here for me to train—they know the tools, they've used a hammer drill before. You didn't even know what a Phillips screwdriver was!"

Me: "Well, I know now, don't I? I'm *using* all the tools, aren't I? I passed the test that said I had the aptitude to learn this job, didn't I?"

Freddy: "Yeah, but you're too slow. I have seventy-five orders backlogged on my desk—you're the only installer on my crew now!"

Me: "Freddy, none of that is my fault. It wasn't my fault that I wasn't allowed to take shop in junior high like the guys did. I *am* learning this job, and it's *your* job to keep training me!"

With the help of the guys I soon learned that Freddy's bark was worse than his bite and eventually found out that his biggest fear was that I'd get hurt on the job and he'd have to live with the blame and the guilt. I filed about three grievances during those early weeks—harassment, discriminatory treatment and public reprimands. It made me feel better and it let Freddy know I was there for the duration.

I learn new tricks and short-cuts on the job every time I get to team up with another technician. Despite learning the basics at school and from your training foreman, this is how you get down to the real nitty-gritty of the job. I found that the guys enjoy passing on their expertise—it's a reflection of pride in their work that would never be expressed directly in the group setting. There, it's important to have an "I don't give a shit" attitude and to trade masterfully embellished stories about crazy customers, filthy rat-infested basements, pit bulls on the loose or scantily clad women (and men) coming to the door!

Being the first and only woman on both crews I've worked on, I met with mixed reactions from my co-workers. Many treated me like they would any rookie, while a few ranged from openly hostile to blatantly sexist. The message was loud and clear at first: YOU DON'T BELONG HERE. The foreman who met me at the door that first morning took me into the meeting room where everyone gathers before starting time. "Meet the animals!" he said to me. And to them, "Meet Mary, the new installer."

"She ain't no installer yet!" snarled the friendly spokesman, followed by a chorus of concurring nods and guffaws. I was definitely on foreign turf—it would take me a long time to feel comfortable here.

"Okay, Beckley!" the foreman retorted, smirking. "Mary

will be riding with *you* today." Great. Now I'd become punishment for the guy who was brave enough to say what they all were thinking! Once we got off in the truck, this guy turned out to be pretty decent, despite letting me know right off the bat that I'd probably just become a permanent helper and get away with it because I was a woman. Beckley ended up helping more than most with the tricks of the trade as well as the strategies for coping with management and the intricacies of company policies.

As time went on, the game format became obvious: In the group environment I had to expect a lot of bravado, some snide or sexist comments here and there (not necessarily directed at me), and only minimal displays of genuine acceptance. The norms of a deeply ingrained macho workers' culture would tolerate little else, especially not in the beginning. I was an intruder and perceived as such. What a disruption I must've been. Now girly magazines had to be confined to their trucks, language had to be "toned down" and, even worse, they had to cope with the idea that perhaps even a female—who at five-foot-five and one hundred twenty pounds was clearly not an Amazon—could master *their* job.

Another introduction to the land of you-don't-belong-here came from a guy on my crew who told me what he thought of an article I'd written for the local union newsletter that discussed how both men and women might benefit from the ERA. His argument went like this: "You're taking a job away from a man who must provide for his wife and children—according to the Bible. The woman's sole function is to stay home and care for his children. If *you* are out here, especially as a married woman, taking a job that pays enough to support a family, then you're going against the whole thing."

Knowing that a full-blown rebuttal would be an exercise in futility, I simply said, "I see. But how am I supposed to support myself and my family when my husband's disabled and unemployed?" All he could reply was that he was sorry, he didn't know my husband was unemployed. . . .

Then there are the people on the street—the occasional

hostile reaction: "Hey, baby! You're the reason I ain't got a job!" Or the frowning customer. "You mean they sent a *woman*?" Even after I've worked on a job and restored the service, a customer might still refer to me as "the telephone operator." A woman just doesn't belong in the role of technician (a contemporary title for repair*man*.)

Although I came into my job armed with a healthy level of self-esteem and determination, I still needed the other resources that were available to me and, fortunately, I had enough sense to use them. I counted on the daily support of the people closest to me—the consistent encouragement of friends and my (ex)husband during the early months, and the understanding I get from the man I live with now (who's a phone company central office technician and really *knows* the social context of my job).

A real lifeline has been Hard-Hatted Women of Cleveland, a support group I helped to start a few months after I got my new job. Modeled after a group with the same name in Pittsburgh, the group has provided encouragement, information and resources for women in and seeking non-traditional jobs. Our meetings, workshops and retreats help us all deal with the ongoing issues we face at work and give us a chance to provide some pre-job training, so that newer women are a little better prepared for the pressures of entering a "man's job."

I also used the union and the grievance procedure from the outset, finding this the best method of defending myself while not further alienating myself from my co-workers. I eventually became a shop steward in my garage. Becoming accepted in that role, of course, presented another hurdle, but after organizing an effective walkout to defend one of the guys threatened with an unfair dismissal, I met with very little opposition.

I learned to replace my anxiety and my anger—that chronic undertow of disease that accompanied me to work for the first couple of years—with a healthy level of self-acceptance and a focus on the job itself, acquiring the skills and knowledge that bolstered my confidence. In a sense, by expanding and redefining the challenge of this job to include the unavoidable side effects of being a female minority of one, it's turned out to be a richer experience than I'd ever envisioned. Just noticing tiny changes, the small glimmers of new attitudes, all by virtue of nothing more than my presence—this keeps me going, helps to counter the flack, the bad days.

◆

It's four-fifteen—just time enough to get back to the garage, throw my garbage in the dumpster, fill in my timesheet and hang out a bit with the guys while we wait for quitting time. As I drive through the intersection at Euclid and E. 105th, I hear a voice from the midst of the road crew laying asphalt in the oncoming lane: "Hey! Mary!" I see her—a woman from Hard-Hatted Women.

"Kathy! How's it going!" I shout.

"They hired on a new woman today!" She pointed to the woman flagging traffic further up the street.

By this time, the traffic is jamming up behind me and people are laying on their horns. I have to move on, but I shout hurriedly, "Great! Call me sometime!"

Something like this makes my day. I'm such a loner at the phone company. By now we're down to just a handful of women in outside jobs, and we're spread all over the city. It's nice to see expansion in other areas and to get that little boost that says, "You *aren't* the only woman!"

Pulling into the garage, I see Daniel walking over to me. He tells me a story about the woman from a job I had early this morning. I had to refer the job to cable repair (Daniel's crew) due to major trouble underground. When Daniel arrived to let her know he'd be working on it, she told him, "The other lady was here this morning." Daniel said, "Ma'am, I may be funny looking, but I'm no lady!" They laughed and then he asked her, "Was she a short little white woman?" Surprised, she replied, "Yes—how'd you know which one?" "Ma'am, she's the only one we have!" The obvious answer.

I told Daniel I thought he handled that very well—I get told about the "other *guy* who was here" quite a bit myself.

I go into the meeting room to fill out my timesheet—they're real picky about how we code and account for our time. Sometimes we have to do weird tricks with the pencil to make our productivity goals and get the desired result on paper.

Everyone's yelling, telling stories and acting pretty rowdy—after all, it's Friday and most of the guys don't have to work tomorrow. The big joke for the day is the meeting the boss called this morning to tell us about a customer complaint. Seems this woman spends lots of time watching the cable box situated in the bushes in front of her house on Washington Boulevard. She's complaining that the phone people are urinating on/in the box—not a bad place actually, since it's so enclosed by bushes. The boss had a rough time keeping a straight face. Then Bob yelled out, "It must be Mary—Mary's doing it boss!" Everyone cracked up pretty royally—me being the only one who most probably was *not* doing it. Now everyone's asking me whether I made it through the day without stopping to pee at the box on Washington.

While Bob's flashing the centerfold in his new Playboy at a "respectful" distance from me (looking to make sure I notice, of course), Carver takes me aside to tell me discreetly that Bill, one of the installers, "likes" me. It feels like junior high school in here sometimes! I say that I "like" Bill, too.

This doesn't suffice. "No, Mary... I mean, Bill *likes* you!"

Brother... "Oh," I say. "Hey, Carver—why don't you just casually tell Bill that Mary's pretty busy *liking* someone else. A whole lot. That way nobody puts out much effort and everything stays cool."

"Oh yeah. Good idea—I'll take care of it."

"Hey, Carver. Thanks for the warning."

"No problem. I thought I'd better tell you."

Most of the guys are quite a bit younger than I am—especially here in our garage where the seniority is lower than elsewhere. So I get tickled when they treat me like a younger sister or when someone throws a few hints around. One guy asked me to go to coffee and came right to the point, saying he'd like to "have an affair" with me. We didn't and we're still friendly, having had a long conversation that day about the hazards of open marriages, the pros and cons of monogamy, etc. I have to say that, aside from scattered sexist and off-color jokes here and there, I've experienced very little direct harassment of a sexual nature from co-workers. We play a lot with sexual content when we banter around the garage, and everyone pretends shock and dismay when a loaded comment or four-letter word occasionally issues from my mouth!

We all say good-bye and take off in our cars and trucks. I decide to drive my pick-up down the street to the car wash. I think back on how obsessed I used to be with being accepted or fitting in—how I'd let every little negative nuance get to me. Funny. Now all that doesn't matter so much and I've learned just to roll with it from day to day. I'm beginning to feel comfortable, relaxed. And, come to think of it, I've heard myself referred to as "one of the guys" on more than one occasion....

I pull into the Circle Car Wash, a great all-by-hand place where they scrub your whitewalls, vacuum out the inside for no extra charge, and suds and rinse your car while you wait around an old pot-bellied stove by the office. A couple of workers are taking their warm-up break there, chatting with customers. One guy asks me about the wire-slitter hanging from my belt. I explain, "I use it on my job to cut phone drop wire."

"You work for the phone company?"

"Yes. I repair lines."

"*No!* Don't tell me you climb them poles!"

Mentally sighing, I give him my usual: "Yep, it's part of the job."

"*Man!* I didn't know they had ladies!"

And so it goes...

Sue Doro • Machinist
Interview by Karen Matthews

I was born in 1937 into a working-class Milwaukee family. My father worked in a factory and sometimes as a child I'd go with him to his job. Milwaukee used to be the machine tool center of the country, which meant that there were more machine shops and heavy-equipment metal-cutting jobs there than there are now. When I was growing up a lot of people I knew were machinists or were working where machining was done. They were mostly men, though I knew some women who did assembly-line work. But not until the last three years I was working as a machinist did I come across another woman machinist apprentice who was working at another factory. We weren't very common.

I went to school to become a machinist under the Manpower Training Development Act, MTDA. This was before they had CETA, which was the predecessor to the one they have now, JTPA—they keep changing the names. The good thing about the MTDA program was that you got paid for going to school. This was in 1972–73. They gave you six months of training, and your schooling, books and transportation were paid for. You received wages for the entire six months. Then there were two weeks of job development. This was a joke because all you did was go to a job counselor, who handed you the morning paper. You looked at the paper to decide if there were any jobs for you.

I was the first woman in the machine shop training class, so the teacher didn't like me. The men in the class were very helpful. The one guy I had trouble with was the teacher. He was a horrible person with an alcohol problem. I mean, he just drank while he was talking to us. It was amazing how he could get away with that. He wouldn't let me train on the turret lathe or on the automatic screw machine. Both of those machines are high money-makers if you know how to run them, because they are high production-rate machines. An automatic screw machine makes thousands of parts in a very short time, so companies love people who know how to run them. But I wasn't trained on one. The only reason I learned how to operate a turret lathe was because the teacher would go to sleep for a couple of hours at a time and then the guys would show me. Most of the guys there knew how to run the machines because they learned in high school shop classes or the military. They all knew what they were doing much more than I did. Because of them I feel I got a good, solid training from the class in spite of the teacher!

After that, I got a job at Hellwig Corp., a small carbon brush factory, in the engine lathe department—where I was the first woman they'd ever hired. There were other women working in that factory, mostly doing bench assembly work. They sat at long tables putting little tiny parts together, going crazy. It was a non-union shop and I stayed there for a year and a half. Several of us tried to organize a union, and lo and behold, I got laid off. The point was that nobody had ever been laid off there. They prided themselves on never having layoffs. They cut people's hours, but they would never lay you off. So everyone just assumed it was because of the union activity. But I also wanted to move on because I wasn't making much money, and the reason I had become a machinist was to have enough money to raise the five kids I had to care for when my ex-husband took off. Being a machinist was one of the highest-paying jobs in Milwaukee at that time because it was a skilled trade.

After Hellwig, I heard they were hiring at Allis Chalmers, a large tractor plant. It had 10,000 workers in it, as opposed to a couple of hundred in the carbon brush factory. They had no female machinists and no women working in the maintenance department where I ended up. This was a union shop. UAW. I had heard that they were hiring so I went down to apply and they told me they didn't have any work. I figured that something was screwy. I knew people that worked there, so I had them report to me about who they were hiring, and what jobs they were hiring for. It turned out they were hiring all men and they were hiring them for everything from sweeping the floor to working as a machinist. Certainly, I knew how to sweep a floor. I went back and told them that I knew they were hiring and I wanted a job, but they still wouldn't give me one.

At that point, one of the people at the shop told me to call his union representative, who was a woman. I called her and she said, yes indeed, they're hiring and she sent me the hiring list which told me who was hired and for what jobs. I marched myself down to the EEO (Equal Employment Opportunity) office and told them what had happened, and I filed a complaint. Within a week's time, I was called in for an interview at Allis Chalmers. At the end of the interview, the guy said, "Well, we'll probably hire you, you have enough experience. We want to put you in the maintenance department. And, by the way, we have this paper from the EEO." He brought out a letter that I was supposed to sign saying that I was hired and therefore was signing away the suit. I said I'd have to think about it.

The next thing was the physical, which, I was told later, was unlike any physical that anybody had ever had. They took so many X-rays of my back and my front that I felt like I was going to glow. They were trying to find something wrong with me so that I wouldn't pass the physical—then they could say that they *were* going to hire me, only I didn't pass the physical. But I did pass the physical! I didn't have anything wrong. Their next tactic was to put me in a department where not only had a woman never worked before, but where all the guys were older, very conservative white men who didn't want a woman there. They wanted to just go to work and smoke their cigars and every once in a while do a little work. At the maintenance department, our job was to fix a part that had something wrong with it—for example, maybe a transmission part had a hole that was drilled too big or too small. Besides being very highly skilled work, it was very complicated for me to learn after going to school for only six months and spending only a year and a half on the engine lathe. But I learned how to do it and slowly won over all the guys except one, whose name (appropriately) was Dick.

Dick had a thing for pornographic literature. When he realized that I really was staying, he always harassed me by leaving dirty pictures wherever I was going to be working. He also tried to sabotage my work. He was on first shift and I was on second shift, on the same machine. When you're working in a specialized place and you set up a machine with a certain part in it, nobody messes with it; they just leave it for you to come in the next day and finish what you have to finish. Well, I had to start checking all the parts on my machine because Dick would loosen stuff on it, which could kill you. Like, he would loosen a big drill, a huge part. If it's not tight, and it hits, it will shatter in your face. Safety glasses wouldn't help; you'd be real cut up. He did stuff like that.

Eventually I went to my union and made a complaint. They said they'd talk to him, but they didn't. So I went back and said, either you talk to him or I'm going to file a suit against you, against the union because this is dangerous, it's harassment. I just threatened them, I never did file anything. Now the union president and vice-president in a big factory like that didn't work in the shop, they are in an office someplace else. They wear suits. So the next morning I see five or six guys in suits come down the aisle and go over to Dick with this piece of paper—I don't know what the heck it is—and they were yelling and shaking their fingers at him. He looked real scared. After that he stopped doing everything. But I had to really fight to get him to stop.

I was at the tractor plant nearly four years and was even elected steward. Then came the massive layoffs. I got hired at the Milwaukee Road railroad, where I worked for eight and a half years. I was hired on as a machinist there, the first woman machinist ever hired. The railroad was under a federal order to hire women and minorities, so after I got hired, they hired some more women in the welding department and a couple of women machinist's helpers. They kind of came and went. They were harassed a lot and didn't feel like putting up with it.

It was pretty good work at the railroad. We would make train wheels. You'd get a raw casting from the foundry, that sort of looked like the shape of a train wheel. Then you'd have to bore out the middle of it, where the axle's going to fit in, to the right dimension, using a boring mill machine. I also ran a fifteen-foot engine lathe. You'd lift both wheels and the axle with a crane and put that in the machine. All this work had to be very precise, like plus or minus one-thousandth of an inch. I also worked in the bearing room, rebuilding the bearings that go on the ends of the axles. When you see a train moving along, that great big round thing on the end of the wheel, that's a bearing; that's what keeps the wheel rolling. It's got grease inside of it so it doesn't freeze up and cause a train wreck.

For awhile I worked in the diesel house, which was not a good job. Nobody really wanted it because it meant crawling underneath the trains. They'd park the train over a big pit and then you'd go inside the pit and work under the bottom part of the diesel engine, regreasing. It was really dirty work; you had to scrape off all kinds of filth before you could even get to the part that you had to work on. I didn't like it at all. But after awhile, when a lot of layoffs began happening there too, your seniority didn't keep you in the job that you liked. If you were low on the seniority, you'd get bumped. Bump, bump, bump. And you'd end up with stuff like the diesel house.

Machining is a process that has a lot of stages to it. It's very dialectical. If you do the wrong thing in the beginning, the end product isn't going to be right. So every step of the way, you have to analyze what you're doing. And when you do everything the right way, it's going to be perfect. That's a very powerful, good feeling. The work requires brains to figure out what you can use besides physical strength. So in other words, if you had to tighten up something, there'd be ways of putting a hollow bar on the end of your tool for leverage. You'd learn how to get little wooden pallets to stand on so you'd be taller, so you could get more leverage. You usually had cranes to pick up the heavy stuff, but you still needed upper body strength—I didn't have enough, which is why I got hurt a couple of times. When I counsel women now, I encourage them to do exercises and train with weights, under proper guidance, to develop their strength. I didn't have that kind of training; I developed my strength on the job, which is not a good way to do it.

The railroad was eventually sold. There's nothing there now except rubble from the buildings, and apparently one or two buildings that they don't know what to do with. All the machine tooling inside has been sold or destroyed. I could list you twenty-five big companies that are no longer in Milwaukee. I have been writing a lot of poetry recently about plant closures. Milwaukee is probably going to end up like Minneapolis, with insurance companies and stuff like that replacing heavier industries. It's hit me in the face that heavy industry is shifting to robotics, with one person in the shop pressing buttons, and no other people around, just a bunch of shiny robots. I could see that the people I was working with were the end of their kind, and we should be celebrating what they know how to do. But the fact is, women who want to be machinists now had better learn how to work with computerized machinery.

I miss the work a lot. I miss the machining itself—that feeling of creating a part out of a piece of raw steel. When you're done with it, you've got this really pretty, shiny part. You put in your eight hours of work and you have something to show for it. I liked that. And I miss the people. We had a real comradely bonding because we were working in a dangerous job. At the railroad we all watched out for each other, because there were axles going over our heads on conveyor belts—anything could go wrong. People got killed doing their jobs while I was there. I almost got hit in the head with an axle. It missed me by about two inches. I was real shook up; I sat down on the floor for awhile and didn't move.

Another thing that I found out in all my jobs was that the people who would be the friendliest and the people that I could bond with right away were mostly Third World men. I mean, Third World women, too, but I'm talking about the men in this situation, because it was mostly men I was working with. They knew. They could see what I was going through. They had gone through the same thing themselves. Earl was the first black machinist, and Doc, another friend, was the first black laborer ever hired, back in 1943. These were people who knew what was going on. They didn't have a feminist consciousness, but they were fair. And they could tell unfairness.

When I look back on it, I have to be very careful, because Larry, my second husband, says that sometimes I gloss over a lot of the hard stuff now, I just like to talk about the good stuff. You know, you look back and think oh, I had these wonderful friends and it was good work. The truth is that it was also very, very hard work and very, very dirty and very, very dangerous. I'd be extremely tired when I'd come home. I mean, now I can stay up until eleven o'clock at night, just like the big kids! But when I was working, I would go to bed some time between eight and nine o'clock. I was so tired I couldn't keep awake any later than that.

My menopause began the last two years of my machinist life. I didn't realize what was happening. I'd had a partial hysterectomy years before and didn't even have the menstrual cycle changes to signal that menopause was ensuing. I thought I was just getting really hot because the shop windows were being nailed shut with plastic sheeting. (Being Wisconsin, it was extremely cold in the winter and they put plastic over the windows to keep the wind out.) Of course, this didn't explain why I was hot walking through the snow drifts in the morning, before I even got to the shop!

When I went to work in this trade, my youngest child was five and the oldest was thirteen. It was very hard on the kids and it was very hard on me. Not just the physical stuff, but the emotional stuff—feeling guilty that you weren't home. Because the mother, in my mind, was supposed to be home taking care of the kids. The main reason I decided to become a machinist was that I could make enough money to support my family. I never got any child support from my ex-husband. None. So the big thing was the money—I didn't have a "pioneer" idea about the job until after I got into it more.

I didn't identify with feminist politics at that time. I thought that the feminist movement was a really good thing, but that I didn't necessarily need it. Because I could take care of myself. I always had this survival thing—I don't need anybody to take care of me. After my husband left, and the divorce was so terrible, I quickly changed my mind. The feminist movement did have something to do with me. And even though I didn't know many women from my class, from the working class, that were active in feminist politics, we talked about it a little bit, and eventually I got involved myself.

Being in the trades taught me to be stronger. I think it taught me to stick up for myself. That and the feminist politics helped to tell me that I was an important person and that I wasn't just a housewife—and that even if I were to be a housewife someday, that was important, too. So it gave me a sense of self-worth. Working with machinery also gave me a feeling of power that I had never experienced before.

Ninety-nine percent of my co-workers were men, so I had to join women's organizations to find the support I needed. I was a member of the Feminist Writers' Guild in Milwaukee for maybe nine years, right from the first year it started. I also joined Tradeswomen, Inc., when I was back in Milwaukee, and Women of the Americas, which was a women's support group for anti-intervention in Central America. So at least once or twice a week I would get together with all women. I really needed that—especially having four sons and one daughter, there was a lot of maleness in my life! And I'm glad that I discovered that being with women was good for me. Another really important aspect of getting involved in the Feminist Writers' Guild was that it helped me develop my poetry. I write a lot of poetry today, mostly about the lives of working people.

I'm now the executive director of Tradeswomen, Inc., which is a national non-profit membership organization for peer support, advocacy and networking for women in non-traditional, blue-collar jobs. I've been in this position since 1986. I help women who come to the office for job counseling and other advice and information, such as how to deal with sexual harassment. We try to act as a resource for women, to keep the women in the trades from leaving when they feel discouraged. If a woman doesn't have any support at her job, if she's working with a bunch of guys who are all just assholes, and there's nobody she can relate to, then at least she can come to a Tradeswomen potluck or support group and find other women to talk to. It feels good to be doing this work, and I'm proud to be part of it. Woman power can change the world!

Notes on the interviewers

Joanne Carlson completed the apprenticeship program in San Francisco's International Brotherhood of Electrical Workers (IBEW) Local 6. She turned out as a journeywoman electrician in 1982.

Shelley D. Coleman is a journeywoman carpenter who has worked eight years in the trade. She has been a co-editor of *Tradeswomen Magazine,* and is originally from Northern Ontario, Canada.

Molly Martin works as a maintenance electrician for the San Francisco Water Department, and is active in grassroots tradeswomen organizations.

Karen Matthews is a journalist who lives in Berkeley, California.

Lisa Parnell has worked in mines in Alabama for ten years. She is an activist in the United Mine Workers.

Nancy Powell turned out as a journeywoman carpenter in 1983. She now divides her time between construction management and body work.

Elizabeth Ross is a visual artist who built her own house in rural Mendocino County, California.

Resource List

Tradeswomen, Inc.
P.O. Box 40664
San Francisco, CA 94140

Hard-Hatted Women
P.O. Box 93384
Cleveland, OH 44101

Tradeswomen of Philadelphia
P.O. Box 5904
Philadelphia, PA 19137

Chicago Women in Trades
37 S. Ashland
Chicago, Ill. 60607

Women in Fire Suppression
411 Marathon Ave.
Dayton, OH 45406-4846

Step-Up for Women
Northern New England Tradeswomen
1 Prospect Ave.
St. Johnsbury, VT. 05819

Apprenticeship and Nontraditional Employment for Women
3000 NE 4th
Renton, WA 99055

Nontraditional Employment for Women
105 E. 22nd St., Room 710
New York, NY 10010

Wider Opportunities for Women
1325 G St. NW
Washington, DC 20005

Women Empowering Women
P.O. Box 6506
Albany, CA 94706

Southeast Women's Employment Coalition
382 Longview
Lexington, KY 40503

PREP/Women in Apprenticeship
1095 Market St., Suite 712
San Francisco, CA 94103

Women in the Building Trades
c/o Roxbury Community College
1234 Columbus Ave.
Boston, MA 02120

PREP Ohio, Inc.
2261 Francis Lane
P.O. Box 68018
Cincinnati, OH 45206

This is only a partial list of organizations which provide support and training for women in non-traditional, blue-collar work. If none is listed for your state, try calling:

State Department of Labor and Industry or Department of Vocational Education;
State Division of Apprenticeship Standards;
State Sex Equity Coordinator for the Department of Education, Division of Vocational Education; or
Women's Bureau, U.S. Department of Labor in your region.

About the Editor

Molly Martin is a journey-level electrician (her mother claimed her first word was "light"), and for many years a worker-activist. She was one of the founders of Tradeswomen, Inc., a national grassroots organization of women in the trades. Now on the board, she has also been editor of their quarterly magazine, *Tradeswomen*. Martin is also on the boards of Equal Rights Advocates and Women in Apprenticeship Program. She lives in San Francisco.

Selected Titles from Seal Press

Women's Studies

The Obsidian Mirror: *An Adult Healing from Incest* by Louise M. Wisechild. $10.95, 0-931188-63-6

Lesbian Couples by D. Merilee Clunis and G. Dorsey Green. $10.95, 0-931188-59-8

Mothers on Trial: *The Battle for Children and Custody* by Phyllis Chesler. $11.95, 0-931188-46-6

Getting Free: *A Handbook for Women in Abusive Relationships* by Ginny NiCarthy. $10.95, 0-931188-37-7

The Ones Who Got Away: *Women Who Left Abusive Partners* by Ginny NiCarthy. $11.95, 0-931188-49-0

Chain Chain Change: *For Black Women Dealing with Physical and Emotional Abuse* by Evelyn C. White. $4.95, 0-931188-25-3

Mejor Sola Que Mal Acompañada: *For the Latina in an Abusive Relationship* by Myrna M. Zambrano. $7.95, 0-931188-26-1

Fiction

Angel by Merle Collins. $8.95, 0-931188-64-4
Bird-Eyes by Madelyn Arnold. $8.95, 0-931188-62-8
Miss Venezuela by Barbara Wilson. $9.95, 0-931188-58-X
Lovers' Choice by Becky Birtha. $8.95, 0-931188-56-3

Mysteries

Ladies' Night by Elisabeth Bowers. $8.95, 0-931188-65-2
The Last Draw by Elisabet Peterzen. $8.95, 0-931188-67-9
Study in Lilac by Maria-Antònia Oliver. $8.95, 0-931188-52-0
Fieldwork by Maureen Moore. $8.95, 0-931188-54-7
Murder in the Collective by Barbara Wilson. $8.95, 0-931188-23-7
Sisters of the Road by Barbara Wilson. $8.95, 0-931188-45-8

Available from your favorite bookseller or from
Seal Press, 3131 Western, Suite 410, Seattle, WA 98121.
Include $1.50 for the first book and .50 for each additional book.